HINDU MYSTICISM PHILOSOPHY & RELIGION

(According to the Upaniṣads)

(Revised and Enlarged Edition)

By

M.N. Sircar

Introduction by

M.L. Wadekar

BKP

Bharatiya Kala Prakashan

DELHI • INDIA

First Published in 1934, London
Revised and Enlarged Edition, Delhi : 2001

Published by **C.P. Gautam**
BHARATIYA KALA PRAKASHAN
3421-A, IInd Floor, Narang Colony, Tri Nagar,
Delhi-110035. Phone : 7153083

ISBN : 81-86050-71-X

Laser Typesetting by :
SHRI BALAJI COMPUTERS
Phone : 7108270

Printed at :
B.D. PRINTERS, DELHI

Contents

Foreword

Our ancient seers were possessing great intuitive intellect and were endowed with uncommon farsight, foresight and insight. The greatest treatises like the *Vedas*, the *Upaniṣads* etc. are repository of perfect wisdom, which they have seen, experienced and handed down through tradition. These are replete with invaluable thoughts regarding the most inscrutable mysteries of life. The *Upaniṣads,* the *Bhagavadgītā* and the *Brahmasūtras*-otherwise known as the *Prasthānatrayī* are the most authentic and authoritative texts for understanding the Hindu doctrines and theories regarding mysticism, philosophy and Religion. Every *Ācārya* has tried to explain his own vision and system as arising from and based upon these treatises.

Among these three prominent philosophical and mystical treatises, the class of literature known as *Upaniṣads*, represent the culmination of knowlege, reached by seers. The esoteric teaching is presented in these small and voluminuous, prose and metrical, simple yet mysterious texts of great antiquity. Prof.N.N. Sircar, the Professor of Sanskrit, Sanskrit College, Calcutta, an outstanding scholar of both Indian and Western philosophy has elucidated in several separate chapters, the Hindu Mysticism, Philosophy and Religion as reflected in these ancient Upaniṣadic texts in a very lucid and clear language and flowing style. He has not only crystal clear understanding of the basic doctrines and principles of Hindu view of life as reflected in the *Upaniṣads* but also has deep insight into the subject of exposition. He has very often referred to & compared the philosophical standpoints held by Western philosophers.

Like his other books, this book-namely-"*Hindu Mysticism, Philosophy and Religion*" was long out of print and was in great demand from the scholars of Indian philosophy and also from general seekers of truth. In view of this growing demand for this book in Indian and Western scholarly world, the re-publication of the book was a necessity. The book incorporates the cream of the Upaniṣadic knowledge, expounded in small but enlightening twentysix chapters.

We, hope, this revised and enlarged edition of the book will well be received by the scholarly world. The publisher Shri C.P. Gautam of Bharatiya Kala Prakashan deserves our hearty congratulations for bringing out this book, so promptly and neatly.

Vadodara **M.L. Wadekar**

Introduction

The Vedic Literature is generally subdivided into four main heads i.e. the *Saṁhitās,* the *Brāhmaṇas*, the *Āraṇyakas* and the *Upaniṣads*. The *Upaniṣads* are the most outstanding philosophical treatises. The word *Upaniṣad* is derived from *Upa+ni+sad* i.e. knowledge derived by sitting near the preceptor. The secret and esoteric teaching obtained from the preceptor is incorporated in these treatises. The *Muṇḍaka Upaniṣad* (1.2.12) says "*Tadvijñānārtham sa gurumevābhigacchet samitpāṇiḥ Śrotriyam Brahmaniṣṭham* (For knowing that secret he should approach politely, with *samidhas* in hands, the preceptor only who is *śrotriya* (well-versed in *Vedas*) and is *Brahmaniṣṭha* (intent on the *Brahman*). The *Upaniṣads* are also known as *Vedānta* which means not only the last portion of the Vedic literature but also as "Supreme or Ultimate Wisdom". The word *Veda* derived from the root-*vid* can be understood in many different shades of meaning like *sattā* (existence), *jñāna* (knowledge), *vicāraṇa* (deliberation), *prāpti* (acquisition), *cetanā* (consciousness), *ākhyāna* (exposition), *nivāsa* (abode). To quote-*Sattāyām vidyate Jñāne vetti vinte vicāraṇe Vindante Vindati Prāptau Vedayate* (*cetanākhyāna-nivāseṣu*).

The word *Vedānta* can be interpreted in the sense of "end of consciousness" - the *Upaniṣads* expound such a supreme wisdom by realizing which there remains no separate identity. One becomes identical with the *Brahman*. Hence there is none to have separate consciousness, awareness of oneself. The *Bṛhadāraṇyaka Upaniṣad* (3.3.22) says, "(*Yatra*) *vedā avedā bhavanti*", (where there is no separate consciousness). As these *Upaniṣads* expound such a supermost knowledge, they are also called *Vedānta* or *Vedāntic* treatises.

Īśa-kena-kaṭha-praśna-muṇḍa-māṇḍūkya-Tittiriḥ
Iaitareyam ca chāndogyam Bṛhadāraṇyakam tathā

Though there are hundreds of small and big, ancient and later, prose and metrical *Upaniṣads*, the ten principal *Upaniṣads* namely, *Īśa, Kena, Kaṭha, Praśna, Muṇḍaka, Māṇḍūkya, Taittirīya, Aitareya, Chāndogya* and *Bṛhadāraṇyaka* are mainly exphasised and resorted for their exposition by the Ācaryas. Hundreds of other later *Upaniṣads*, are considered to be minor *Upaniṣads*.

These *Upaniṣads* explain in a very lucid but forceful language the secret philosophy regarding the Ultimate Reality- the *Brahman*, the *Ātman* (the Individual Soul), the world and relation between each of them and the practical mode of action to realize the Reality and to obtain the *summum bonum* of life- obtaining the Infinite Bliss. This is traditionally known as *adhyātmavidyā* or *adhyātmaśāstra*. Among the two *parā* & *Aparā vidyās*, this *adhyātmavidyā* is *Aparāvidyā*. The *Bhagavatagītā* extols it as the superior to all *vidyās* (*adhyātmavidyā vidyānām*). Yajñavalkya (*Smṛ*. i-106) has laid emphasis on having this spiritual knowledge for the perfection of the *Japayajña* (the sacrifice in the form of repeating of a *mantra*) (*Japayajñaprasidhyartham vidyām cādhyātmikīm japet*). He also declares that among other religious activities, it is the supreme *dharma* (duty) of a person to obtain knowledge of *Ātman* through the practice of *yoga*. (*Yajñavalkya Smṛ*. I.8). This *vidyā* alone can relieve one from worldly afflictions & discontent and bring forth real happiness, satisfaction, mental peace and tranquility.

The *Bhagavadgītā* (8.3) explains *adhyātma* as *svabhāva* (*svabhāvo'dhyātmamucyate*). The Ultimate Reality is all-pervading (*sarvam khalu idam brahma* (*Chāndogya Up*.

3.14.1). The *Brahman* is not only immanent but is also transcendent. The experience of the enlightened that there is existence of the *Brahman* everywhere and in everything is the *adhyātma*. The *Upaniṣads* emphatically assert the existence of *Ātman* as different from body, mind, intellect etc. and that the *Ātman* is superior to them all. To the modern world of science and technology, this basic concept of the *Ātman* or the *Brahman* would appear to be mystic exposition. The *Upaniṣads* presuppose such a kind of mysticism. The mysticism implies something miraculous, mysterious, uncommon, unbelievable to the ordinary mind but is expounded with great conviction by the seers who have actually said to have visualized the truth. These mystics have tried to solve the mysteries of life and existence by internal illumination or special revelation. They expound the nature of Reality through inward spiritual perception. The *Upaniṣads* are the most authoritative and authentic ancient treatises, that envisages such mystical experiences and transcendental knowledge of the enlightened seers. Even when the concept of *Ātman* itself appears mystical to ordinary mind, what to speak of the transcendental experience of the mystic sage declaring-"*Aham Manurabhavaṁ Sūryaśca*" (*Bṛhadāraṇyaka Upaniṣad* I.4.10) (I have become sage Manu and also the Sun).

The *Upaniṣads* are replete with the philosophical speculations. The word 'philosophy' means (*philos*=loving; *sophia*=wisdom) "Love for Wisdom". It in fact tries to understand the basic principles underlying life and reality. The Sanskrit word '*Tattvajñāna*' means "knowledge of the *tattva*-the basic underlying principle". It is always true to its object and is always objective (*vastutantra*) and never subjective (*puruṣatantra*). The word "*Darśana*", when used from the point of view of the enlightened seers is actual experience of the Reality. But the ordinary visual experience through eyes if understood as "*Darśana*" may not be true in real sense. The staff in the water appears to be crooked, but is not so in reality, it is just appearance, due to transformation of light through water. Thus appearance may prove misleading as it is not true to its object. The *Tattvajñāna* is always true to the nature of its object and never to be sublated.

From the philosophical point of view, the *Upaniṣads* expound that there is only one Reality i.e. the *Brahman* alone everywhere. The Individual soul is the *Brahman* only (*ayamātmā Brahma*). The *Brahman* is by nature, *sat* (existence), *cit* (consciousness), *ānanda* (bliss) and one without second (*Ekamevādvitīyam*). The *Brahman* is also omniscient, Omnipresent and all-powerful. As there is no other entity in the world, there is no question of fear, danger, grief or sorrow. The *Brahman* is explained to be the Supreme Reality from which the created beings have come out, due which they are sustained; to which they return and ultimately into which they enter or dissolve. It should be known as the *Brahman*.

Yato vā Imāni bhūtāni Jāyante,
Yena Jātāni Jīvanti, Yatprayanti-
Abhisaṁviśanti, tadvijijñāsasva,
tadbrahmeti- (*Taittirīya Upaniṣad* 3.1)

But still the question arises regarding the non-sentient elements. How can the non-sentient entities come out of the sentient principle. To explain this, the arguments from the worldly experience are presented. Just as the spider prepares the web out of himself and dissolves it or just as the earth creates the trees etc. or just as from body of a living person the hair on the head and body appear. Similarly from that imperishable comes out all this.

Yatho'rṇanābhiḥ Srjate gṛhṇate ca
Yathā pṛthivyām Oṣadhayaḥ sambhavanti/
Yathā Sataḥ puruṣāt Keśalomāni
Tathākṣarāt Sambhavatīha Viśvam (*Muṇḍaka Upa.* I.1.7)

To prove the existence of the *Ātman* as different from the body, mind etc., the *Upaniṣads* have explained the various psychological states like the *Jāgrat* (waking state), *Svapna* (dream) and *Suṣupti* (deep sleep). How can one understand that the Impreshable *Ātman* exists in this perishable body. To explain, the above states would be quite useful. The simple comparison between the body of the living and the body of the dead can point out the existence of the *Ātman*. Though all bodily organs are present in both, the organs of the dead can not work. The eyes, the ears, the nose, the tongue & the skin, these sense organs, though present in both, the dead can not experience any thing. In the waking state, the eyes can see only because there is presence of the *Ātman* in the living body. The *Ātman* present in the body, pervading the eyes, makes them perceive the external object. In the absence of the *Ātman* in the dead body, it cannot see. The eyes, unassociated with any living body, also can not see. The *Upaniṣads* declare that due to which the eyes can perceive the object, which resides in the eyes, but yet is not the eyes and is different from the eyes, that principle is the *Ātman*. This is true in case of all the organs. This proves the existence (*Sattā*) of the *Ātman*. In the state of dream (*svapna*), all external organs get merged into the mind and the mind alone is working. No chariots, horses or anything that we see in dream actually exist at that time, still we visualize them in dream and go from one place to another and experience happiness and unhappiness. In this case, the Self residing in the mind, makes the mind work and conceive all such ideas, events etc. but still the Self is not the mind. Only due to the existence of the Self, the mind is able to work and conceive ideas. This shows that the Self is not only existent but is *cit*-conscious being. But in the State of deep sleep (*suṣupti*), All organs and even mind stop working and they all merge into the *Ātman*. One does not experience anything outside. Still after his awakening, he experiences that he had a very sound sleep, giving him some measure of happiness (*ānanda-sya mātrā*). The Self itself is of the nature of Bliss. Due to unconscious merging into the *Ātman* – Infinite Abode of Happiness, One gets little amount of happiness. Thus the Self is by nature *sat*, *cit* and *ānanda*. The *Upaniṣads* expound the four great truths –

(1) I am *Brahman* (*Aham Brahmāsmi*) (2) Thou art That (*Brahman*) (*Tattvamasi*) (3) This *Ātman* is *Brahman* (*Ayamātmā Brahma*) (4) The intelligence is *Brahman* (Prajñā*nam Brahma*).

The practical way to realize this Utimate Reality and to obtain Unity with the *Brahman* is the *Dharma*. The word 'Religion' is used in the sense of "a sense of duty or reverence towards superior power." The Sanskrit word *Dharma* is derived from the root *dhṛ* "to maintain" or "to sustain". It is the entity that sustains or maintains everything and is opposite of destruction. From the cosmic standpoint, it is that natural order that sustains or maintains everything. From the practical point of view, it is that path of *Śreyas*, that not only leads one utimately to *Niḥśreyasa* but also is a spiritual, rational, psychological, moral, and physical order or set of rules and regulations for maintaining world-order, resulting in individual and social upliftment and good. But this path is most difficult to tread. It is *asidhārāvrata*-walking on the sharp edge of a razor. But still one should get up, wake up and resorting to the Great, try to realize It. A virtuous aspirant should try to obtain knowledge of the Self, should listened to, think about, and meditate upon It. The boat of *Jñāna* can carry one to the other end of this ocean of *Saṁsāra*. In this world, there is no other alternative but to work. Īśa exhorts one only for action, which does not bind him.

Thus the *Upaniṣads* have incorporated not only mysticism but philosophy and practical path of Religion that can lead to personal and social good.

15th Jan., 2001
Vadodara

M.L.Wadekar
Offg. Director,
Oriental Institute,
M.S. Univ. of Baroda,
Vadodara.

Chapter I

Hindu Mysticism

The Upaniṣads are a perennial source of philosophical wisdom and mystical inspiration. The Brahma-Sūtras are garlands of flowers culled from the Upaniṣads. Systems of philosophy have been built upon them. Teachers have received inspiration from them. Vedāntic teachers combine in them the spirit of receptivity with the power of dialectic. But to most of them truth is rather to be received than to be thought about. Thinking can give intellectual satisfaction, but it cripples receptivity by launching us into endless formalism. Conviction gives us faith, power and freedom, and what is finally wanted in this search is truth and not system. Buddha shows the right spirit when he condemns the doctrinaire attitude and admonishes us "to question not, and answer not". When the inner being becomes free from the spirit of questioning or answering, the wonders of the deep begin to reveal themselves. Truth cannot be won by intellect.

The mystic is a great adventurer. He discards the conventional way of thinking about truth, and, emptying himself thoroughly of notions and ideas, waits for the kindly light. He makes himself free from the intimations of the senses, the ideas of reason, to receive the wonders of life in silence.

There may be such a thing as the logic of mysticism, but the mystic soul is not consciously aware of it. The logic of mysticism is not mysticism; it is thinking about mystical affirmations. It traces the possible grounds on which mystical conclusions can be rationally accepted. But the mystic adventures of the soul import a total change in the method and matter of thinking and build up a new organon.

Kant comes near to laying down the logic of mysticism. He discerns the creative nature of the self. He points out the creative freedom of the spirit as distinguished from phenomenal determinism. Fichte removes the realistic element from Kant's philosophy. He affirms the existence of the creative ego and its free spontaneity. The creative ego is not the final vision of truth. In the Vedānta the ego has been supposed to be seemingly creative, but truly transcendent. Creativeness is ideal, transcendence is real. Creative freedom is the great ideal in Kant and Fichte. They suppose it to be the true nature of spirit. Self-expression was the watchword of the German transcendentalists. Self-transcendence is the watchword of the Upaniṣads and the Vedānta.

The creativeness of spirit is a stimulating conception, but the transcendence of a spirit is a comforting and consoling ideal. The former gives the freedom of creativeness and power, the latter the freedom of transcendence and wisdom.

Kant and Fichte are aware of the limitation of the theoretical reason—the inherent limitation of a subject-object relation from which reason can never free itself. They discover in practical reason the freedom of the self to rise above the limitations of theoretical reason. The will, therefore, occupies a prominent place in both Kant's and Fichte's philosophy. And it was not difficult for Schopenhauer after them to install it as the transcendental reality.

The Upaniṣads and following them the Vedānta recognize this freedom of creative spontaneity as something higher than the speculative (logical) reason which introduces us to the world of determination. But they do not stop with the creative freedom of the ego. Creativeness imposes a limitation—it implies a division, a projection. But the Absolute must be above this.

Creative spontaneity can exhibit the pure ego as free act; it cannot exhibit the pure ego as free being. Free act is not entirely free. It requires a field in which to exhibit and display itself. It has a space-time reference. Free being is independent of such reference. Free act is not quite independent of relativity. Free being is. The Upaniṣads find the true secret of life, not in creative freedom, but in transcendent being. They reveal to us the transcendent reality, of which Kant seems to have no intimation; but this ultimately is a revelation not of faith but of reason in its intuitive aspect. Truth lies beyond phenomena, beyond values. It is the highest beatitude. It is the beatitude of the soul. It is beyond all finite ends, itself being the *summum bonum*, for it frees us from the limitations and solicitations of personality. In personality there lies charm, but in truth lies security. Indeed, the highest charm lies in what attracts by its completeness and fullness. The limitation of personality can be removed in impersonal life. And when the soul feels its impersonal nature it experiences unique joy – the joy of freedom. The order of value may exhibit the creative freedom of spirit which the world of phenomena does not possess. It has its delight of creative spontaneity. Kant seems to have been influenced by the freedom of spontaneity as a contrast to the rigidity of the world of phenomena, but his vision is confined thereto. He did not see that the soul can be spontaneously creative and at the same time transcendent. Its creativeness is apparent, transcendence is its being.

The Upaniṣads do not really give us any logical system, but rather intuitions and revelations received in the high flights of inspiration. They are therefore not systematic and methodical. They are really suggestive of the different kinds of thought, but they do more to awaken spiritual inspiration than to encourage logical thinking. They are rich and definite in conclusions. The seers speak in the language of inspiration, and when they wish to convey their visions to their disciples they speak in analogies. They scarcely use the language of dialectic. They freely make use of symbols. Intuition cannot be conveyed directly. The sublimity of the teachings of the Upaniṣads, and above all their perennial freshness, witness to their proceeding from the very core of being. Hence, they make a wide appeal and exert a telling force. If they are approached with the receptiveness of the mystic soul, they will reveal more than meets the senses. Many texts will throw a flood of light, while others minister the grace of life to the soul.

The Upaniṣads do not seem to lay emphasis upon the doctrine of grace and intermediation as a means to final release. Knowledge, not grace, gives freedom. They acknowledge the services of teachers in helping initiates. They accept the guidance of invisible forces which lead the soul (after death) to the path of light and glory, but the final consummation comes through transcendent wisdom. This is not the common opinion among mystics. Swedenborg conceives of a hierarchy of spirits in which there "is an immense chain of intermediation, extending from centre of extremes, which bereaves every agency of all freedom and character. ... Every thought comes into each mind by influence from a society of spirits that surround it, and into these from a higher society, and so on".[1] In Indian mysticism this sense of intermediation is present, but intermediation is not final. It is only to give temporary help and to carry the soul to effulgence and glory. A picture of this is also given in the Upaniṣads. The story is told how the seeking soul is carried from plane to plane amidst diverse scenes of beauty, until it reaches the realm of light. Visibly formless and shapeless agencies scatter influence and help the seeker successfully across the danger zones. They attract the soul to the valley of pleasures. The soul must cross the valley of tears and smiles before it can aspire to reach the realm of light.

But finally it enjoys direct fellowship and communion with the centre of life. The intermediaries assist earnest souls to the direct enjoyment to the life of consummation and fulfillment. And fulfillment lies is an expansive consciousness and direct fellowship.

The Upaniṣads accept a sort of spiritual federation which, directly or indirectly, helps initiates in their attempt to awaken spirituality. But spirituality is not freedom. Spiritual intuition is generally thought possible through a finer nature which gives us wide knowledge, great ease, and transparent being, and can manifest to us the cosmic order as a federation in spiritual fellowship and dispel the ignorance that divides man from man, and man from Brahman. The Upaniṣads do not recognize the least difference between man and God, but this wisdom is vouchsafed only of the few. For those that cannot reach the height, the path of evolution in spiritual fellowship is laid down as the true path. The Upaniṣads do not emphasize the doctrine of special grace and election. The doctrine of grace calls for the spontaneity of love and choice. But there seems to be no solid foundation for such a theory in the Upaniṣads. They seem rather to emphasize election through fitness. The fit can feel the spiritual attraction of the spiritual federation, for the initiate must be pure enough to feel it, strong enough to retain it. This fitness is concomitant with spiritual growth. In the spiritual life, it is indeed a truism, that the more we grow the better we understand, the clearer the understanding the easier becomes the growth. Spiritual radiance is cast equally upon all humanity. The essence of man is spirit, which radiates from within. But this radiation cannot make a lasting impression unless it can be retained, and only a few souls are able to retain it, thanks to their earnest seeking and transparent purity. Life has to pay a price for all possessions, therefore, it has to pay for spirituality. But the final release from the sense of individuality is due to transcendent wisdom – the wisdom of the Upaniṣads themselves. And for this release nothing else is necessary. No grace can give it, for grace is an attraction, a centripetence which can give us a fellowship with Divinity, but cannot give us the wisdom which can make us indifferent even to the divine fellowship, since, it is not the highest spiritual truth. Fellowship is certainly inferior to identity. Grace gives us fellowship, wisdom identity.

The Upaniṣads do not recognize the least difference between man and God, the human and the divine, and therefore, if at times they affirm the doctrine of grace it is simply as the saving power of the Ātman. There is no such thing as "mere man" or "mere God". The Upaniṣads affirm that man is essentially at one with God in the heart of his being. And at an opportune moment, when the initiate is anxious to get rid of the shackles of bondage, he feels the inward power and strength of the soul and its subtle spiritual attraction. This attraction proceeds from the hidden nature of the soul. There is a constant tension felt in the soul because of its apparent finitude. The soul is anxious to break this tension, which implies its apparent divergence from its original nature. The tension indicates the soul's infinite nature, which it cannot for the moment realize. Had there been no intimation, however distant, of this infinite life, there would have been no tension in our being. Grace is really in this sense spiritual knowledge. It is the genial attraction which the self feels for itself. It is the light that self casts upon itself. It implies no external influence. It is the kind of subtle attraction which the self, in its most auspicious moments, feels for itself, and being led by which it can successfully resist all other attractions and tendencies and be absorbed in itself. The blessed peace that lies in the deep of the soul be felt and realized when there is this centripetal movement of itself. This self-centripetence is a kind of blessing, for it gives us the light. The Kaṭha truly says : "the glory of the Ātman can be seen through the grace of the Antaḥ-karaṇa," i.e. if the mind is pure, it can reflect the light.

The real tension is in the soul. It is due to its apparent dual nature, its inherent infinitude and its apparent finitude. If the soul were merely finite, the tension would be caused by the operation and influence of outward forces. The soul can easily free itself from the influence of outward active forces – for these forces are no part of its being. Isolation is enough to give it freedom from such tension. But when the tension is deep-laid in us, because of the contradiction in our being, we cannot be free from it unless we can silence the forces of contradiction and self-alienation in us.

"Our little life is rounded with a sleep." When a man's heart has been made sufficiently pure, and his being highly sensitive to spiritual influences, only then the natural attraction to the self is felt, and life becomes free from the "sleep and the forgetting". This grace and attraction save us from the apparent contradiction of our nature. Few can rise to this level of accepting with kindness and living in fullness the life of silence beyond oscillations.

Religious life is based on direct experiences. All forms of religion bear witness to this truth. Whether the experiences are received through election or through fitness is a matter of opinion, but there is no denying the fact that the inner chamber of our being is suddenly flushed with unexpected and unexperienced light. None can deny it when it comes. Religious life is no matter of speculation. Its possibility can be judged that way. But its actualities is a fact, and any system of thought must be poor if it denies and rejects the felicitous experiences received in the soul. The mystic does not need to see how this experience fits in with the other experiences of life. It fills him with peace and plenitude, and no demand rises in his being to evaluate these experiences or work out a synthesis of all the experiences of life. The mystic is the man of the spiritual heights, all other experiences vanish before the direct experiences of the soul. And since, he becomes free from all the tension that is associated with other forms of life, life appears to him in a different colour, with nobler melody, rhythm, joy, and peace, and he feels no necessity to stand aloof from this, and to adopt the attitude of critical reflection and systematization.

Spirituality is the finest flower of life and its highest fruits are vouchsafed to those who are ready to sacrifice a limited or partial reward for the blessed promise of fullness. Brave indeed is the soul that can welcome it and choose it. The struggle indeed is keen, the fight stern, but the fruit compensates for the struggle. Patience is bitter, its fruit is sweet. Nowhere is this so true as in the spiritual life. The keener the fight, the sweeter the victory. The sun is refreshingly beautiful after the rains.

In the mystical writings of to-day the mystical experience is defined as "a direct awareness of reality conceived as value."

This trend of thought looks upon mystical insight as an effort fruitful of an experience carrying with it enjoyment of the highest value. Mysticism has its origin in the ever-searching effort of the human mind to free itself from the conflicts of life, and mystical exaltation gives the soul and intensive joy which makes a deep impress upon the psychic being. Hence, the mystical consciousness is conceived as a value. But, properly speaking, the mystical consciousness presents reality rather as truth, than as value or an agreeable feeling. In Hindu thought mysticism has its importance as the method of apprehending truth. Thus its end is not different from philosophy, though its method of approach may not be the same. Mysticism is to be defined as the direct awareness of reality conceived as truth. With the perception of truth value may be naturally associated, the value of freedom from the limitations of life and knowledge and the sense of a release from the vicissitudes of life and from the fear of death; but these are only the consequences that follow inevitably from the perception of truth. Mysticism discloses the truth which it has been the proud privilege of science as well as of philosophy to seek. The goal of the search has always been the same, though the methods have been different.

If philosophy and science seek truth through the analysis of experience and facts, mysticism seeks it through the inward flight of the soul. It is the directness of its awareness which constitutes its superior claim. But the search is for truth, the end its freedom.

From Plato downwards all idealistic philosophers in the West have emphasized a suprasensible world, the realm of reality, and however, they differ amongst themselves they do not doubt that there is a supreme suprasensible existence beyond the phantasmagoria of the senses. Plotinus, Eckhart, Dante all speak of the beauty and charm of mystical insight and experience. Spinoza and Boehme bear witness to it. The whole exalted company of teachers in the East—Janaka, Yājñavalkya, Kṛṣṇa, Buddha, Christ, Chaitanya, Rāmkṛṣṇa—are the torch-bearers of the mystic light and truth. Thereby is life made radiant and rich with blessing that will attract and reward the utmost intensity of living.

Mystical experience requires no proof. It is self-evident and self-sufficient. It does not look to anything beyond itself for its verification.

It carries its credentials with it. It is self-luminous. Since, it is direct, it stands in no need of inference or argumentation. Patañjali says : "There the Prajñā is filled with Truth. Its validity is self-validity. It proceeds from the source that is beyond ordinary logical affirmation or denial. It is entire insight and full comprehension."

The philosophy, through the wisdom in the silence of the soul, lifts the veil and discloses the mystery of life. The science of the day has the distant vision of the promised land and declares that the hand that has made us is divine. This union of science and philosophy has given new, refreshing hope and radiant faith to the soul in its attempt directly to visualize truth. The truth given by philosophy and science is directly envisaged by mysticism. Herein lies the beauty and dignity of the mystic life. The richness of scientific and philosophic imagination gives an intimation of the land from where no traveller returns, the kindly light of mysticism installs him in the realm of peace.

Science and philosophy appraise truth in the outer court. They see from a distance the hues and the colours of the realm of light. Mysticism goes straight into the inner court. It carries the struggling soul on its bright wings to the ether of bliss (*ananda maya akasa*).

The mystic thought in the Upaniṣads does not centre round a single person or a single teacher. In Buddhism and Christianity mysticism has centered round teachers who have inspired by their superior character and transcendent personality (*lokottara charitra*). Later Hinduism has been influenced by the divine personality of Kṛṣṇa, but Kṛṣṇa is looked upon (expect in the School of Bengal Vaiṣṇavas) as an incarnation but not God in flesh. Hindus generally have not accepted the sayings of a particular teacher, however great, as final. Such sayings have been affiliated to the general body of knowledge coming down from time immemorial. In this Hindus have exhibited a wide vision of life and shown due regard to its elasticity. The Upaniṣadic thought originates from various teachers. Though the texts show wonderful unanimity of opinion regarding reality, yet every one of them has to be appraised on its own merits. Truths felt and intuited are given out. They are accepted as the sayings of ṛṣis (sages). But riṣis do not claim these truths as their own. They are accepted as revealed. Even the cosmic person of Hiraṇyagarbha, the first originate, has to receive truth in revelation.[2]

The divine inspiration is possible everywhere and to every soul. The realm of truth is no man's monopoly, however fit and fine he may be. Hindus, therefore, believe in a race of teachers, inspired by the greatest one of all, God. God is the centre of all truths, of all existences, cosmical and hypercosmical. True revelation proceeds from Him; but Hindus are catholic enough to believe that God can elect anyone (where the soul is fit) and reveal the higher truth to him. The federation of teachers is a great claim of Hinduism. Its field, therefore, is not limited. Hinduism can even accept the race of teachers of every clime and religion and winnow out the undistorted truth in them. This has been the distinctive feature of Hinduism, showing that the heart of Hinduism is in inner sympathy with cosmic humanity. It believes in humanity as one inspired by the great God who is "one without a second."

The charm of the Upaniṣads lies in their appeal to this cosmic spirit (Puruṣa) as the teacher of teachers who inspires everybody from within and from without. The Upaniṣads hold up nature and the soul as the sacred books of revelation, and the spirit of God is to be traced therein. God is the poet, the world is the divine comedy. Those who have eyes to see can see the living God through it. The teachers of the Upaniṣads have never claimed for them divine origin nor have they claimed divinity for themselves. "I am the path", "I am the light", is never their claim. They seem to have approached truth more in the ordinary humanistic spirit and given out what they felt in their own inward being. They speak with the voice of a man; they attract, therefore, more sympathy than those teachers who claim divinity. One can feel fellowship and akinness in their company. Even if they speak of the transcendental truths, they show that, in a certain attitude of mind, they are properties of every man and woman, for which man does not require a special grace or the intervention of a divine personality.

This humanistic touch, together with the profoundest truth, has made the Upaniṣads in all ages a source of philosophical inspiration. The book of life that has been opened to the teachers of the Upaniṣads is open to every man and he can welcome the message of truth in his heart of hearts just as the teachers welcomed and received it in their being.

A spiritual hierarchy constituting a spiritual federation is conceived in some Upaniṣads, and the influence of teachers in moulding the spiritual life is recognized in others. But this has been the path of those that have not strength enough to follow the path of wisdom directly. It is a kind of spiritual stopgap. For every soul has not the spiritual strength to welcome the silence in spiritual life : they take more delight in spiritual fellowship. The Upaniṣads are alive to this, and consider it the path of the spiritual ascent, but not the path of spiritual emancipation.

The path of ascent has been the favourite and popular one amongst mystics, not the path of final release (release even from the beatitude of the so-called spiritual life). This life, though bright and delightful, should be shunned. Spirit is free, fruition of life high or low implies bondage, and must be done away with. The Upaniṣads are more the gospels of freedom than of radiant spirituality in love and fellowship, which they look upon as inferior to the highest wisdom.

The whole range of existence, cosmical and hypercosmical, including the inferno, purgatory and paradise, are orders in the immanental life, and evolution through them has rich reward in cherubic dignity, seraphic beauty, and enjoyment in the celestial choir. Life there enjoys the sempiternal spring but cannot enjoy the freedom of transcendence. That freedom is not flying away from life. It is to go deep within where, in life's silence, life's most and life's essence are found.

References

1. Emerson : *Representative Men.*
2. Śvetāśvetara Upaniṣad.

Chapter II

Phases of Immediate Experience

The Upaniṣads appeal at once to imagination and the philosophic instinct by the problem they set forth and the promise they offer. Mankind is restive over its little existence and is anxious to get a light that can break through the phenomenal real and can satisfy all questioning. Truth is the summit of existence. Truth is the proper object of search. And so long as the heart is not upon the enduring, the heart cannot have rest, nor the soul be at peace. The search for the enduring becomes the sole motive in life when life's quest in other directions stands baffled at the little they can yield into it. The quest for the Eternal in most persons cannot seriously begin before the conventions set up in the priestcraft and in the popular theological course have had due trial. The sacrificial rites with the promises of subtle sense-delights in the subtler planes of existence cannot satisfy the seeker, for he is still burdened with the anxieties of divided existence; and, however much privileges increase in volume and quantity, life labours in the mire of ignorance. But the failure of the sacrificial rites to give full satisfaction has its effect and use. It established the futility of a life in nature accumulating and enjoying no more than nature's possibilities and privileges.

The sacrificial mysticism cannot give lasting satisfaction, for the gaze is still towards the external and the transient. And the merit which the seeker acquires is ephemeral. It is a temporary benefit which is exhausted with its fruition.

Progress, however high, is attended with a fall, and naturally the earnest seeker has to revise his method of search and manner of approach. The dawn of philosophic instinct is possible when the other courses and methods of approach are found inefficient. Philosophic reflection becomes possible when the smooth and almost blind adaptation, due to the incessant activities of nature's forces in us, meets with a check, and the forces act inwardly in generating thought and reflection without exhausting themselves upon ill-conceived and mistaken attempts at satisfaction in an outward conception of life. Man is an instinctive being by birth. He is a thinking being by experience. He is an illuminated being by intuition. The first impulses are natural. They have hasty expressions and gratifications, based as they are upon the unilluminated instincts of survival. The instinct of survival breeds a semi-mystical attitude towards the forces of nature. The confined vision of man's utter dependence upon nature, his instinct of self-preservation, and the gratification of desires soon evolve in him a mystic understanding of nature as the sole source of power. The primitive insight does not go beyond that, and sacrifices are symbols of what the primitive mind feels towards nature's forces. These forces are soon deified, and this deification reads Devas in the beneficent powers of nature and Asuras in the malevolent forces of nature. With the dawn of philosophic vision the Vedic pantheon is reduced to a unity of Godhead and a cosmic vision of life displaces the least sense of difference between the presiding forces of nature and the immanent Divine Life.

The animated vision of nature's forces give a fine penetration and understanding of nature, and exalts it into the conception of a living and vibrative existence endowed with an oversoul, to which all the forces are subordinate and of which they are inadequate and partial expressions. The vision of such an animated being of nature is immediate. It is a form of mystic exaltation. This form of exaltation takes delight in the wonders that nature has revealed before man.

The first dawn of mystic life begins with the sublimation of nature, where the forces are felt as if living and powerful with the capacity not only of offering us privileges but also of shedding upon us genial light to lead us aright. In this way the mystic sense beings to feel the Divine light through the orb of the dawn, through the silvery rays of the moon, through the shining rays of the stars, and Divine life through the winds and thunders. The mystic soul is bold enough to withstand the kindly and the fierce expressions of the forces of nature, and keen enough to catch the animation which throbs in them. The seeker stands radiant with the mystic sense that nature, however fierce and violent, carries to the soul the message of a new life, though occasionally it may overpower us with the sense of our littleness and utter helplessness before it. Religious consciousness is stirred by the majesty of nature. It excites wonder and admiration. Both these continue to foster a religious feeling and a reverent attitude towards nature. But this attitude can grow only when the intellect has overcome the primitive tendency to regard gods as the carries of privileges and the recipients of oblations. This primitive religious feeling of surrender comes out of the feeling of self-preservation, which is a biological instinct, and religious consciousness originally has a reference to this instinct. The will-to-live abides in the soul and the gods and shining deities are worshipped to satisfy this original instinct.

But soon this attitude is transcended, and the seeker begins to feel more than what meets the senses in nature's forces. This mystic attitude gives the sublimated perception of nature animated and installed in the philosophic conception of a supersensuous reality, and the conception of an all-pervasive spirit soon arises to displace the individuated conceptions of earth-spirits, sky-spirits, etc. This is a distinct advance in the philosophic and religious consciousness and indicates the beginning of true wisdom; for the religious consciousness keeps the soul at rest, not so much by hope of reward here of hereafter as by silencing all expectations by the inward light of the soul. Before the inward light can attain its fullness, however, the outward vision has a finer reading of an identity between spirit and nature. But this identity cannot be complete unless man has a direct vision of spirit in his inward being. The tendency of installing nature's God in place of nature is a definite tendency, and so far as religious consciousness is concerned, it marks a definite advance in spirituality. The pan-psychic idea of nature is a favourite theme in some texts, but if leaves an impression of a life and consciousness as yet not developed into a clear and definite knowledge. But so vast is the experience which almost overpowers the seeker, that definite consciousness becomes impossible. We have, therefore, an indefinable feeling for which there is no adequate expression.

The necessity of feeling this existence in the inward soul is still there, and led by this necessity the external gaze and outward appeal are displaced by inner search and inward vision. However lofty, the inspiration and subtle the vision may be, the mental effort to grasp the meaning and realize the import of the influence received from without, still speaks of an external reference of knowledge and feeling. The mental effort is still objective.

This objectivity makes the apprehension of the spirit-self still mediate and external, and the quickening touch can at best make the experience deep and the expression definite and clear, but cannot change mediacy into immediacy. The apparent immediacy is still an immediacy of the senses outer or inner; it is the immediacy of feeling but not of transcendence.

This form of heightened feeling, however, implies an elasticity not met with in neophytes at the outsets, and is regarded as the acme of spiritual consciousness, inasmuch as the new experience has vivifying and vitalizing force; and nature seems to be vibrating with new light and life. Such a vision has been a fruitful source of a pan-psychic conception which appeals by the immanence of spirit in nature and man. Such a vision proves fruitful in conceiving a super-existence embracing the conscious centres in men and the living centres in nature.

But this vision is still regarded as insufficient. It does not satisfy fully the intellectual and spiritual needs. The animistic vision is a heaven of exalted feeling. But it is not wisdom, though it touches the fringe of transcendental consciousness. The culture of feeling has an importance in waking up esoteric wisdom, but exalted feelings are to be distinguished from transcendental wisdom.

The exalted feeling and animated being are values. They are originally ideal but become actually real in heightened religious being. These feelings are supremely delightful and usher in an ideal existence – the archetypal consciousness which permeates the actualities and facts of life. Such consciousness of ideal forms is to be distinguished from the basic being. It gives a penetration into the causal aspect of basic reality.

It is necessary to distinguish the actual, the ideal, and the transcendent aspects of existence. The exalted feeling aroused by a fellowship with society and nature is a form of consciousness which has its enjoyment of the ideal in the actual but is not strictly transcendental. It is an elevated feeling, a superior consciousness in which serene delight finds its adequate expression, but which cannot pass for the knowledge of the basic reality.

Such an animated vision of nature touches upon mystic consciousness – it differs from logical consciousness. It can fitly be called nature mysticism and is akin to poetic intuition of beauty and sweetness. The adept feels living nature as the mirror of reality. Nature does not replace spirit, nature becomes infused with spirit.

Nature is raised from its inhertness to a medium of expression, and the concrete is felt and enjoyed, but the mind cannot rise above the delight of the rhythm and harmony and embrace the transcendent.

Consciousness cannot approach that height so long as the feeling attitude has not been displaced by a deeper penetration.

This penetration is what really differentiates the teaching of the Upaniṣads from that of the Vedas (the Saṁhitās and the Brāhmaṇas). The vision and the appraisement of living nature have no doubt reduced the Vedic pantheon to the conception of an all-permeating being; still the mind needs greater penetration to touch the basic being.

In the Upaniṣads the search has been into the basic reality. In this sense the mysticism which they represent is transcendental. The search is no longer external, it becomes inward.

The Upaniṣads in this sense are more appealing to the philosophic instinct, for the search for reality must begin necessarily in the inward soul. Philosophy cannot convince if it cannot give the immediate knowledge of reality. The immediate consciousness is the highest revealer of truth when this immediacy is not of the senses, nor of the mind, but of intuition. The Upaniṣadic approach is, therefore, to be distinguished from the Vedic approach of apprehending Truth.[1] The one is inward, the other is outward. The one searches the truth through the intuition of the soul, the other through the revelation through nature.

Forms of Intuition

The sublimated consciousness of nature has to be distinguished from the philosophic or transcendent intuition. The word "intuition" is often loosely used and has a wide application. It has the commom connotation of immediacy of apprehension. The forms of immediacy are to be distinguished, and because they are not clearly distinguished they become the veritable source of error and confusion. The exact appreciation of a phase of truth is always relative to the faculty which receives it, and unless a clear discrimination is exercised, the seeker is apt to confound exaltation of feeling with appreciation of truth.

Intuition may be empiric and transcendental. An empiric intuitioin is the immediate consciousness of reception through the affections of the senses and the mental being. It includes the intuitions of the sensibility, the instinctive Intuitions. It embraces even the intuitions of supersensuous consciousness. These intuitions differ amongst themselves, but there is no difference is kind, for they are phenomenal expressions. The affection of sensibility might have an outward touch of reference, the instinctive intuitions might help unerringly in biological adaptation.The supersensuous intuitions are really not non-sensuous, they differ from the sensuous only in affecting the finer impulses and the more delicate fibres of our being. But still they are forms of affections and cannot be strictly different from empiric intuitions. In this sense the psychic (*yogic*) penetration and the modern spiritistic revelations are, however subtle and fine, still empire so long as they touch the fringe of reality. It may sound strange, but it is so, since such perceptions are of finer sensibility. They must differ from the apprehension through transcendental or philosophic intuition. They affect the finer senses and being but cannot touch the underlying essence or reality. It has been said truly : "Metaphysical truths can be conceived only by a faculty which because its operation is on the immediate, we may call intuitive, if it be thoroughly understood that it has absolutely nothing in common with what certain contemporary philosophers can intuition, a merely sensitive and vital faculty properly inferior to discursive intelligence and not superior to it" (a quotation from Renē Guēnon in George Santayana's *Realm of Essence*). Even religious consciousness, when it confies itself to a fine feeling, is still empire; though such feelings or experiences are far removed from the ordinary sense-consciousness. Of course religious consciousness as grasping reality should be distinguished from religious consciousness as a fine feeling and an urge.

Intuition is not to be identified with sub-intellectual, vitalistic, or instinctive immediacy. It is not even the immediacy of feeling. It emerges as the finest fruition of intellectual culture. It may be supra-logical but not necessarily supra-intellectual. Spinoza's intellectual love, Bergson's intellectual intuition point to its intellectual character. Kant's intuitions of sense, Croce's aesthetic intuition, are not to be confunded with the intellectual intuition of Spinóza or Bergson. Even Bradley's feeling in which the "though, feeling and volition are blended into a whole" is a form of supra-logical consciousness, but not necessarily non-intellectual. Plato's intuition of the supra-sensible ideas comes in the third order of knowledge. Śaṅkara's immediate intuition is the basis of all knowledge, though it cannot be made an object of knowledge. Philosophers are agreed amongst themselves that intuition is the best and the highest kind of knowledge and comes to our help when discursive reasoning fails to achieve the end, viz. Truth. A finer exaltation in feeling may be a pleasing state of consciousness but it leaves us uninformed and unlightened. Poetic intuition even has some truth to deliver to us; it does not attract us simply as yielding delight. Even when Shelley invokes the spirit of beauty ("Hymn to Intellectual Beauty") he does not simply feel its rapture. He invokes it as grace and truth. He feels it as spirit that does "consecrate" with its hues "all it does shine upon".

"The ıight alone – like mist o'er mountains driven
Or music by the night-wind sent
Through strings of some still instrument
Or moonlight on a midnight stream
Gives *Grace* and *Truth* to life's unquiet dream."

Art, poetry, music have their value because they are informant of the deeps of the soul. They give us joy. They present to us aspects of reality. In this latter regard, they are more welcome.

Human reason cannot accept anything which has no bearing upon truth. Romantic aspects of life have truth to teach, they are valuable that way. As mere play they have no value. Our being is put to supreme effort in intuition; and whatever the romantic aspects may be—aesthetic, moral and numinous—it is resorted to as the final attempt to get a glimpse into De Profundis. And where intuition passes into exquisite feeling it loses its special claim as the oracle of truth. Against such kind of intuition Hegal enters his emphatic protest.

Human consciousness is elastic enough to embrace infinite shades and phases. The seeker confuses the glorious feelings experienced on the path with reality. The absence of a discriminating sense has been the fruitful source of false religions that creep up on the finer phases of our empiric intuition. The Upaniṣadic seers emphasize the caution not to make the mistake of identifying an exalted feeling with the apprehension of reality. When the inner consciousness has a sudden elasticity and swift flow of fine ideas and fine feelings, it naturally clings to them and is liable to mistake shadow for substance. And this accounts for the tendency in the later history of mystic thought to install an object of adoration in place of reality. No doubt it is possible that such religious mysticism can stir the depth of consciousness, still one should not identify such feelings with transcendent intuition. Such experiences are flights into supersnesuous consciousness, but bear no comparison with the religious consciousness reared up in philosophic reflection and finally passing into transcendent intuition. Popular religious consciousness perchance hits upon an exalted sublime feeling and is carried on by such feelings, and reason follows to give it a basic. Such emotional enthusiasm is to be distinguished from philosophic or transcendent intuition. The latter dominates more in the truth aspect of reality than in its pleasing aspect. It convinces where conviction is the demand, and in the life of search conviction of truth is the end of the search. If the transcendent intuition delights, it delights because it convinces; and the highest delight is the delight of conviction. Such delight is not shared in the heightening of feeling. Feeling delights but does not convince. Truth convinces as well as delights. Such conviction cannot come unless the intellectual intuition is touched and exercised. It penetrates the depth of being : religious feeling only touches the emotional being.

Forms of Mysticism

At this stage we should make clear the difference between the forms of mysticism, for mysticism is so vague a term with so wide a range of application, that a discriminating knowledge of its different shades is a necessary pre-supposition to a clear understanding of the kind of mysticism we have in the Upaniṣads.

Mysticism is an intuitive approach to truth rather than rational and discursive. It arises from an anxiety to have a face to face vision of truth, and, in this anxious search and deviation from rational pursuit, it has not been infrequently identified with the different tendencies lying deep down in the soul. Though the search has been directed to the appreciation of truth, and all forms of mysticism lay claim to that, still different forms can be distinguished by the manner and method of approach and also by the different conclusions and realizations they set up.

Though the conclusionsn in mystic search is generally supposed to be the same – the vision of truth and the life of expanse – still minor differences arise amongst the mystics. The "life of expanse" is the common promise, but a clear definition makes the vision of truth different in different forms. A tendency prevails amongst thinkers to regard mysticism as a form of intuition, which leaves aside all differences from spiritual life and delights in identity, and limits mysticism exclusively to this form of transcendent consciousness. And they base their contention on the ground that the least difference left between the finite and infinite consciousness does not give a new conclusion nor does it present a new phase of life and consciousness. It gives nothing which is not embraced in popular consciousness and as such cannot pass for mysticism.

The contention has force; mysticism, if it really claims to vouchsafe unto humanity anything, must not only give a fine instinct and appreciation but the appreciation must pass into adoration and finally into the quiet of transcendence. This may be the consummation devoutly to be wished, but this cannot make us ignore the revelations of superconsciousness, which bring in newer forms of experience. No doubt these sublimated experiences are experiences in finite expansion; still their values cannot be completely ignored as showing advances in the mystic life, though not a complete approximation to the mystic ideal. Mysticism in its widest sense is the delightful experience of a wider existence which may in its came reach its utmost expansion and complete transcendence. Such forms of exalted consciousness are far removed from ordinary experiences. But there are forms of consciousness intervening between this expansion and the present limitations, and they cannot be ignored in the life of search since they are pregnant with elevated feelings and illumined consciousness. They also are mystic consciousness, but if mysticism is confined to the transcendent oneness, the term pseudo-mysticism will suit them better.

But in India the term mysticism is not so restricted in meaning. It is used in the wide sense to denote the immediate consciousness of truth and reality; and, though differences of opinion are possible and actually exist about truth, still every form of serious philosophy and thinking which counts, claims this immediate and expansive vision of truth. And this seems to be fortunate in view of the fact that each form of mysticism claims a direct apprehension of truth, though the definition of truth and its presentation may vary, a variation which is sought to be fixed and established by logic.

Such a conception naturally is open to the charge that if the mystics differ amongst themselves in their definition of truth they cannot lay claim to infallibility, and if they do so their position becomes dogmatic. Curiously enough, none are so positive about their assertions as the mystics, none so eloquently expressive. This ideas to a dilemma : the mystics either have or have not realized the truth; if they have, there should be no contradiction in their professions and their beliefs, but actual agreement; if they have not, they should not make the claim to absolute truth. In either case their position is untenable, their mission undesirable.

Mysticism is not a definite philosophy of life. It is the heightening of life and consciousness. It is a process of infinite expansion. It realizes new correspondences, infinite harmonies, new sympathies and affinities. It is life in its unfathomable depth and wide expansion. It differs from ordinary empiric consciousness in that it is freed from its limitations.

As such it has the widest stretch of meaning and embraces the expression of spirit in the indefinite and the definite; and any serious mysticism can hardly ignore the search of the indefinite, since the indefinite, because of its unapproachableness, has always a fascination for the intellect; and, if we mistake not the reading of the inner stirring, we can hardly fail to cognize the eternal quest of the indefinite in man. The definite delights us only when it exhibits from within the shadow and reflection of the indefinite, and in the ever widening mystic consciousness the definite also appeals when it opens on new and untested vistas. The definite has a place in the mystic consciousness only because the definite presents the indefinite in immanence before the mystic, or the definite is seen in the indefinite which adds to its life, beauty, and meaning. The definite itself is never an attraction. And even when the indefinite is not full presented, the definite can attract only because it presents unseen and unexplored phases of life. The mystic is always for the charm of novelty which is the promise of an ever widening and ever quickening life, and this yearning for novelty is increased with the presentation of the newer phases of the definite; but, however deep and fluctuating the experiences may be; the search for the indefinite remains fixed. The mystic sees more in the definite than the laity, for the indefinite is his delight and the uncommon is his search. But even here, in the enjoyment of the indefinite in the definite, his soul has not reached its fullness of delight, for it still feels the stirring of life, the blooming of an unrealized self, and has not the quietude of the deep. Life is enjoyed and lived the most when life and consciousness are felt beyond its expression and stirring. The mystic has the rare privilege of seeing and enjoying life in its expression and in its silence, and he passes from the subtler enjoyment of the expression into the deep of the quiet.

The determinate has its delight. The indeterminate has its quietude. The mystic enjoys both. The transcendence delights him more. The definite delights only as the shadow of the transcendence, just as music delights the more as it dies away. The mystic rejoices in the definite passing off into the indefinite. He is the rare soul awakened unto the subtle beauties and delights of life; and subtler they become as they soar more and more into the indefinite.

This elevation of the determinate in the mystical consciousness and its fine expression therein have made many forms and branches of mysticism possible. Mysticism is sympathetic understanding of the concrete tendencies of the soul in synthetic intuition, in love-ecstasies, and in selfless service. These forms may be fifty called devotional and practical mysticism. Devotional mysticism enjoys the touch of love-consciousness, practical mysticism the delight of active service. Both claim to be mystic forms of consciousness, both have a fine being and expression. Love breathes purity under mystic inspiration. Sympathy becomes cosmic under mystic touch. Both transcend the limit of finite urge and pass into the limitless. They have in them the secret of mystic urge, the look to the beyond. They are anxious to cross the barrier. Synthetic intuition and sympathetic vision enjoy the touch and embrace of the infinite life in poetic intuition and philosophic insight. All these are forms of mystic consciousness inasmuch as they are approaches to the unknown adn the indefinite, and that in a way that does not engage the services of the normal faculty. Mystic love and cosmic sympathy are the hidden treasure of the soul, which cannot be discovered by surface-mentality. Each soars into the unseen. Each breathes in the infinite expanse. Though each has a separate faculty and a special method of approach, still each is anxious to go beyond the fringe of experience and breathe in the free, holy, and rarefied atmosphere of the subtle, the beyond, and the deep. In this sense mysticism is a term that has wide application, and will cover every urge of the soul pressing beyond. The reception and this gift in mystic life require the quickening of the faculties, active, affective, and receptive. The quickened activity of the normal faculties is the promise in mysticism, which touches every function of the soul and makes it highly vibrative and cosmically active. The novice even can feel this, and herein lies the greatest attraction, value, and reality of life.

Mysticism touches every chord of our being, but its great promise lies in quickening the understanding and building up the intuitive faculty to see and feel truth, the essence of being. It is in this fruition that lies the importance of mysticism, for humanity is insearch of the truth and meaning of existence, and no method can be refused in this baffling task. And what is most puzzling to unilluminated understanding is evidently clear to illuminated vision. Science has its use, illumination its value. When the former fails, the latter inspires.

Vision and Intuition

Mystical experiences are of different orders. Some are experiences of the finer appearances, some of reality. The former are forms of psychism, the latter is knowledge.

We shall use the words "vision" and "intuition" to connote the difference. Intuitions may spring from the different chords of our complex being, and they carry with them different forms of experiences, all are equally impressive, but not equally true. Their value and truth cannot be the same. Some are true because they appear, some are true because they endure.

To avoid confusion, a distinction has to be drawn between intuitions giving the final illumination and intuitions yielding the secrets of the finer realms of appearances. Vision proceeds from the fine and causal mental being when it is highly strung up. Inspiration, psychism, thought-transference, etc., are included under visions; it would be wrong to call them intuitions. They are forms of psychism, and cannot touch reality. They are indications of a fine mentality which can work in the different layers of psychic being, but they are not indications of spirituality or wisdom; not of spirituality, because they cannot produce the sense of intrinsic value, nor of wisdom, because they cannot break the sense of division, the spell of divided existence. They are the effects of a highly electrified mental being, waking up his latent powers and exercising them to its psychical profit and advantage. Nature unveils herself, and the secret powers thus attained can be misused unless the initiate is held up by high wisdom and spirituality.

Intuition proceeds from our spiritual being and has no connection with our mental being, lower or higher. It is not to be confounded with the psychic revelations, however fine and high. Even visions which proceed from the cosmic dynamism and not from the individual dynamism cannot strictly be called intuition; for they are indicative of the exercise of Māyā in its causal aspect. Intuition is the final term, which is self-consciousness and not other-consciousness. The other-consciousness is the knowledge of not-self. It may cover the revelation of the cosmic mind; but, since, it is confined to the relative order, it cannot strictly be called intuition. Intuition is confined to the final knowledge of the Absolute; it is that stage of knowledge where the division of subject and object does not obtain, and is therefore unique and immediate. The immediacy of vision is either the sense-immediacy or the psychic immediacy; it is not the immediacy of the Absolute or transcendent intuition. The immediacy of the supra-sensuous revelations is to be distinguished from the immediacy of transcendent intuition. The supra-sensuous revelatins are not truth in the sense in which intuition is truth. Revelations have a reference to supra-mind, intuition has none. Revelations proceed from the cosmic dynamism, intuition transcends dynamism.

Hence vision, revelation, and intuition are not truth in the identical sense. Vision and revelation are truth of the mental and super-mental dynamism, intuition is truth in the absolute sense. The one is empirical, the other transcendental. The empirical here connotes that which is received in sensuous, vital or mental and supra-mental planes of relative existence. These may imply supra-mental sublimites, immanental immensites; but they are not to be confounded with the transcendent intuition, which is beyond all experience, however fine and sublime.

Concrete and Transcendent Intuition

Concrete intuition acquaints the soul with a synthetic vision of realities. It gives a harmony and poise of the higher mental being and is a source of serene joy, not because it gives a pleasing sensitization, but because it is a penetrating touch into the soul and a quickening force to make it realize reality on the point of expression. It feels the being in its concrete set-up with the harmony of relations. The vision it gives is the vision of the whole, the delight it yields is the delight of harmony. It gives a unison, a sense of rhythm. It gives the synoptic vision of reality.

It is to be distinguished from psychism. Psychism gives a fine dynamism, concrete intuition gives a synthetic apperception. It gives, moreover, a dynamic symmetry. Psychism wakes up the fine powers, it endows us with distant visions, but it may not give the symmetry and the rhythm implied in concrete intuition. The one gives us fine power and esoteric visions, the other the knowledge of relations and proportions. The one may accompany the other, but the one should not be confounded with the other. In the unfathomable depth of our inner being symmetry goes along with fine possibilities.

They serve two distinct functions, and in the fine economy of life, power, and organization, possibilities and order help each other. The one supplies the matter, the other form. And our being would have been a dead stone without the unity of both. Psychism penetrates into the secrets of our nature, concrete intuition adjust them and finds their meaning in the whole. It harmonizes them in the common thread of life. The one discovers new forces, new perspectives, the other gives them new syntheses and reads in them new harmonies.

Concrete intuition has the rare privilege of setting up visions and ideas in the order of a whole. Sympathetic vision is its life, synthesis its soul. It has no access into the depth of the inexpressible.

Transcendent intuition is superior to concrete intuition; it claims access into the inexpressible. It claims to touch and penetrate the calm. When ordinary faculties and powers are asleep, the soul is awake from within; and awake it is in silence. In it, it has an illumination which is not possible when the faculties are active and the soul is receptive to all influences from within and without. When the soul is blessed with freedom from the exercise of the faculties, it has the rare privilege of knowing the unknown, of touching the intangible, of getting over the expression and activity of ideas, and of passing into complete illumination. It is illumination without expression, for expression is activity, but illumination is self-expression without activity. Expression connotes limitation, and complete illumi-nation is expression without the impelling urge of passing into concrete forms and moods.

Transcendent intuition has the rare privilege of grasping reality without concrete expression. No faculty of the soul can vouchsafe this consummation. No science, no philosphy can have this rare claim. Transcendent illumination is better to be called silence to distinguish it from expression, for the human understanding has a tendency also to pass into the concrete and it cannot understand expression as different from expressive activity. The term "illuminated silence" better expresses the nature of transcendent illumination as different from symbolical expression.

Revelation and Intuition

Revelation transcends the subjectivism of phychism, for it puts us in relation to a super-mind and implies free reception of ideas and knowledge lying deep in the suprasensuous reality. It is indeed an objective knowledge since, it is not an expression of the finite mind. The finite consciousness becomes the recipient of such revelations in a high receptive concentration. Such revealed knowledge is indeed the highest that the finite can gain, highest in value and greatest in accuracy; the latter, because it proceeds from a source which cannot deceive, the former because it is the inmost knowledge of existence received in a state of super-consciousness. Such revelation is to be distinguished from the sensuous intuition produced by the heightening of the lower mind, the sensibility. These are subjective experiences conseuqent on the fine activity of our sensuous nature and, therefore, should not be confounded with more objective receptions of the higher mind in revelation. Revelation is possible and within access when the supra-sensuous mind becomes active in us.

Revelation, unlike empiric intuition, has an objective source. And the knowledge is direct. But it is no directness of sensuous intuition. This directness gives it a superior claim to reason, for reason works out a system, revelation gives illumination.

The reference to an objective source heightens its value; at the same time it does not suffer because of this reference. Revelation has been, therefore, regarded as a source of knowledge superior to reason by its directness and infallibility and to empiric intuition by its objectivity. Directness, infallibility, and objectivity mark out revelation as a sure source of knowledge.

Revelation is to be distinguished from transcendent intuition. Revelation is a possibility in concrete consciousness, intuition in transcendent. In revelation the supermind in active, in intuition the super-mind has no play. Revelation is a process, intuition is no process and denies the conditions of concrete consciousness. Intuition is then no psychological process nor a faculty. It is supra-logical, supra-psychological; it is the summit of being.

Intuition is no process in time, revelation is a process in time. In one sense both of them are timeless, and ardent souls speak of the timelessness of mysticism, because the truths of revelation are eternal and uniform, time has no influence upon them, and as such the mystics claim uniform perceptions which deny the wear and tear of time. But timelessness has two senses :

(1) Uniform durability through time;

(2) Transcendence of time.

The one does not deny an expression through time, the other denies it. The timelessness of revelation is of the first kind. Revelations are always of the same kind since they proceed not from the surface mentality, but from the source of all light and knowledge. Revelation cannot transcend the time element in Īśvara and is uniform because it manifests what obtains in the causal being of Īśvara. The effectual order and the causal order are orders in time, the events in both the orders are temporal events. But the events in the effectual order are events which have a short history, whereas the events in the causal order have an eternal history. Revelation is an event in the effectual order, it is the expression of the causal in the effectual, and as such it is a temporary event but its turth is enduring. The truth of revelation is of the causal order, the event of revelation is of the effectual order. The event dies, the truth is eternal. The time-series in the effectual order has a past, a present, and a future. The time-series in the causal order has no past or future. It is ever-present. The intuition of duration in the finite mind is different from the intuition of time in the infinite; in the finite mind duration has a history, a beginning and an end; and the finite life is a series of such beginnings and ends. Th empiric intuition of time is the intuition of duration, not in its continuous but in its successive flow, and the division of past, future, and present is natural for the empiric intuition. It has not the capacity of receiving duration in its ever-present continuity. The infinite only can perceive time in eternal continuity without the idea of succession. The soul of time is duration, but duration is not necessarily succession; the logical intellect cannot rise above the distinction of the present, the past, and the future, and its understanding of time is necessarily defective; logically time is identified with succession but this is not true. The understanding of time is not possible, as Bergson has truly pointed out, by intellect or symbolic intellectual, and the intuitive apprehension of time is an unceasing and continuous flow of duration without the intellectual grafting of the divisions of past, present, and future. Time is Life.

Indians thinkers draw a distinction between Kaṇḍa and Akhaṇḍa Kāla, divided and undivided time. The former is the understanding of time through succession. The understanding of time as eternal duration is Īśvara, the dynamic divine. Revelation is the impress of the dynamic divine upon the logical intellect, which reveals a timeless intuition as an event in time. Revelation is then strictly the footprint of the eternal upon the sands of time. It is the reflection through the camera of the intellect. Intuition is timeless expression. Revelation is expression in time. The former is static, the latter dynamic.

At this point divergence arises between commentators of Vedānta. Śaṅkara regards intuition as a *fait accompli,* Rāmānuja regards intuition as intuitive. In Śaṅkara intuition transcends all distinctions and concreteness, in Rāmānuja intuition is concrete; intuition intuits.

It appears then that Rāmānuja has drawn no clear distinction between revelation and intuition, and to him the highest intuitions are revelations. And revelation is the highest source of knowledge. It is higher than Yoga, for Yoga is subjective penetration, revelation, objective reception.

But still it has limitation of reference, intuition has no such reference.

The fundamental difference between revelation and intuition as a psychological process and as a transcendent existence is often lost upon us and is the source of a confusion between the function and the fact of intuition.

This phase of intuition is a new element in Śaṅkara's philosophy, which gives it a form or a shape fundamentally different from the logical bent. Śaṅkara accepts the possibility of revelation. It is a theological attitude of consciousness. The theological attitude is possible in concrete consciousness or self-consciousness, but is not possible in the transcendent. The transcendent is unqiue and cannot be compared to anything else.

When Śaṅkara accepts both intuition and revelation, laying at the same time more stress upon the former, he welcomes the theological source and at the same time is anxious to go beyond, for he clearly feels the limitation of revelation as obtaining in immanent consciousness and therefore capable of communicating the truths of the relative order, but incapable of further penetration. The theological revelation is, therefore, the highest source of the deep mysteries of the dynamic divine, but surely can bear no comparison to absolute intuition.

Though revelation is to be distinguished from intuition, still the truth of absolute intuition as the final illumination and the highest existence is a truth of revelation. In the actual realization of the identity of the subject and the object the very ground of revelation is denied. Intuition is, therefore, a kind of knowledge quite unique and is possible in a plane of existence which transcends the plane of revelation.

The absolute intuition as existence and as truth is the same fact appearing in the different levels of consciousness. As existence, it is the final reality. *Tattvamasi* is not a judgment. As truth it is supra-mental revelation indicative of an existence which is real in a different plane of consciousness. The limitation of relativity is still active, and, therefore, the truth of identity can be indicated in the plane of revelation, but cannot be felt. And therefore, even in revelation it remains as a form of knowledge otherwise unobtainable. The absolute intuition is, therefore, the fact-in-itself. Its truth is given by revelation, but it is realized as the undivided intuition.

Tattvamasi is, therefore, the highest philosophic fact given out in revelation. Just as the symbol of Om carries an amount of sacredness with it because of its revelation, similarly the axiom of Identity has in it a touch of holiness as a truth that can be possibly obtained in revelation, for nothing can prove it. In this way the orthodox opinion establishes the truth of intuition (as transcendent existence). *Tattvamasi* is not, therefore, an affirmation of intellect, it stands on the sure footing of the divine knowledge. It brings to the fore the truth of the absolute Identity. Revelation here becomes the source of the knowledge of the highest intuition which transcends it. But the knowledge which revelation can give of the Identity is only indirect, but it is not qualified to grasp it completely. Revelation is possibly direct of the contents of eternal duration as centred in Īśvara, but it is indirect of the absolute Identity. Its truth it can communicate, though in actual realization its very being is denied.

This is the inevitable consequence of Śaṅkara's philosophy, though the theists fight sky of such a conclusion. And naturally so, for revelation is, according to them, the highest source of knowledge. So, it is with the transcendentalists; but the transcendentalists are bold enough to accept the conclusion of Identity even at the cost of the ultimate denial of the revelation of Śruti.

It appears then that they are having an experience unique in that the common sources of knowledge including revelation cannot by the nature of the case be sufficient to cover it, for revelation is possible in concrete consciousness and not in the absolute. The framework of revelation is the same as that of ordinary knowledge, they belong to the same order, notwithstanding the fineness and infallibility of the one and the grossness and fallibility of the other; but the transcendent intuition is fundamentally different from them both in this, that it denies the very basis of concrete knowledge, and as such philosophic boldness cannot hesitate to deny even revelation in this sphere.

Philosophically speaking, absolute intuition introduces an element which is deeply significant because it gives an experience which is otherwise impossible. The ordinary polarity of consciousness is denied and a unique experience is felt, for consciousness cannot in a normal state break the polarity of subject and object. As such it is an intuition which exists severely alone. It completely changes the whole outlook and adaptation of life. And it is, therefore, psychologically a great fact which cannot be minimized.

Intuition in the Upaniṣads has this sense of transcendent existence in which the highest revelation becomes the highest existence. In it psychological penetration becomes identified with metaphysical truth and it is, therefore, the identity of being and consciousness. Realistic logic has no place here, and here the duality of being and knowing, natural to relativistic consciousness, completely fails.

It may, indeed, sound strange that intuition and being are completely one, and it is this knowledge which characterizes the supreme existence. It is called liberation, in the sense that the division of consciousness and reality is cancelled by the identity of them. They are one and the same; theoretically the two do not exist. The same reality appears at one point as being, at another point as consciousness. That is avidyā; vidyā dismisses this original knowledge and native tendency and takes away the distinction of being and knowledge and finally understands their identity.

Nothing on this side of the polarization of subject and object can give an adequate idea of this transcendence of existence. It is, therefore, in a sense unknown, though it is illumination.

Intuition is not then notion or thought in the Hegelian sense, nor even Nous in the sense in which Plotinus uses the term.

The Hegelian notion is in essence logical reason which sees through relations. The Hegelian thought is dynamic and as such Hegel goes beyond the intellectualists who conceive the relative in a static background, but still the Hegelian notion sustains itself through felations. It transcends and synthetizes relations. And the Absolute in Hegal is the synthesis of the infinite relations. It is the universal reason at the bottom of the connective links.

Plotinus does not exalt the discursive reason to the highest place. In itself, an Aristotle says, it moves nothing. For this reason its world is not wholly real. But Nous beholds all things in their true relations without the need of this process.

Nous is then a form of supra-rational faculty akin to synthetic intuition, for it gives the synoptic view of reality.

But this should be distinguished from transcendent intuition, for in the one the relations are apprehended, in the other nothing is apprehended, neither existence nor relations.[2] The synoptic view of things is possible up to the dynamic divine, but not beyond it.

Mystical Sense : Intuition and Reason

Is there a special mystical sense or faculty? Are mystical visions a gift of a special faculty of soul? Is it common to all or the peculiar mark of an esoteric fraternity? The question raises important psychological issues inasmuch as it discusses whether mystics are the elect of humanity or the full fruition of human endeavours and evolution. And again, if there is a mystical sense, in what relation does it stand to the ordinary faculties of human mind?

The Upaniṣads certainly contain suggestive references regarding the mystic sense. Cf. Kaṭha Upaniṣad I, ii, 12, 22, 23; I, iii. 6, 7; II. vi, 10-17; Prasna Upaniṣad III, 6; Muṇḍaka Upaniṣad II, ii, 7; III, i, 5, 8, 9; III, ii, 3; Aitareya Upaniṣad VI, 5, 3.

The above texts teach us that mystical apprehension is not possible in the ordinary way. The Ātman to be recognized requires a special faculty or power, but this special faculty is not different from the ordinary intelligence. It is its full fruition. Intelligence in its ordinary functioning (especially is empiric intuition) works in collaboration with the mind and the senses, and naturally it cannot claim that immediacy which is its special privilege when it works in independence of the senses. Buddhi is the logical as well as the mystical faculty.

The Upaniṣadic teachers do not seem to have lent their support to a special faculty as suggested by the Greek teachers different from the common faculties, intellect, or reason. Miss Underhill, following the great Greeks, suggests that the mystical faculty is different from the normal faculties of the mind, but is in touch with them : "Heart, reason, will are there in full action, drawing their energy, not from the shadow show of sense but from the deeps of true being, where a lamp is lit and a consciousness awoke of which the sleepy crowd remains unconscious."

William James draws a distinction between a non-mystical or rational consciousness and the mystical consciousness which gives a direct perception of the invisible. F. H. Bradley takes a somewhat similar view. The Absolute cannot be known by the abstract categories of a relational kind. These relations involve self-contradiction. The ultimate reality cannot contradict itself, and in one significant passage he says : "We can form a general idea of an absolute intuition in which phenomenal distinctins are merged". "A whole becomes immediate at a higher stage without losing any richness". Again, "Thought can form the idea of apprehension, something like *feeling in directness.*"

Spinoza's distinction of ratiocination and *scientia intuitiva* is well known and "from this the third kind of knowledge arises the highest possible peace of mind". A host of other writer can be quoted in favour of the distinction between reason and intuition. Bradley makes a significant departure from the Neo-Hegelians who make reason the oracle of truth.

This distinction between reason and intuition is made absolute, probably because of the usual identification of reason with logical faculty, the faculty of discrimination and synthesis; and, since the immediacy of perception is a felt necessity, the *scientia intuitiva* is discovered as a distinct faculty of knowledge having a distinct order of its own.

Max Müller conceives a *facultus occulta.* There is, according to him, in men both individually and generally (ontogenetically and phylogenetically) something that develops into perception, conception, and faith, using the last word as meaning the apprehension of the infinite. He defines religion as "the mental faculty or disposition which independent of, nay in spite of sense and reason, enables a man to apprehend the infinite under different names and under varying disguises. Without that faculty no religion, not even the lowest worship of the idols and fatishes would be possible. and if we but listen attentively we can hear in all religions a groaning of the spirit, a struggle to conceive the inconceivable, to utter the unutterable, a longing after the infinite, a love of God.

"If then we openly admit a *third* function of our consciousness for the apprehension of what is infinite, that function need not be more mysterious than those of sense and reason."

Schleiermacher defines religion as "the sense and *test* for the infinite."[3] The sense and the test have in them a directness akin to feeling. The sense of vastness and expanse, the feeling of unrestricted overflow of being are elements of our experience not covered by the normal feeling. They lie deep in psychic being and become active occasionally. The psychological method lays special stress upon a *facultas occulta* as oracle of transcendental truth. This appeal to special faculty helps the writers of the psychological school of mysticism to prove the timelessness of it. It raises mysticism to a plane where life is not affected by history and environment, and which helps to lend to mysticism an objective or transcendental touch that lies deep in human nature and is not affected by the influences of time and civilization. The timelessness of mysticism is the great appeal of the psychological method.

The Upaniṣadic teachers are quite alive to the timelessness of mysticism, thinking as they do that truth is not affected by time. And there must be in man some such penetration, for the doubts and perplexities natural to a ratiocinative mind must be set aside, and the soul thus freed from ordinary logical or metaphysical presuppositions must be able to embrace the truth. Psychological penetration is the method of the mystics, conviction comes when mists of doubt have been cleared off from the mental horizon by the shining light of intuition. The surface mind is overweighted by the short-sightedness and contradictions of reason. The sense of stiffness so natural to the surface mind and the persistent demand for a conclusion, both help to strike the depth of our being, from which the final illumination comes. The intellectual paralysis is soon followed by the higher awakening of spiritual life; the intellect, which is the most powerful organ of the positive mind, must understand its own limitations before the new path can be sought. The King of the Dead, Yama, rightly tells Nachiketāh that the truth cannot be attained by discursive intellect. "The wise can see it in spiritual intuition and seeing it cross death." (Kaṭha Upaniṣad).

But, however impressed the ancient teachers are with the futility of the intellect as the oracle of truth, they do not go to the extreme of supposing that the mystical sense is completely unique and different from the normal faculties of the mind. Yama expresses clearly that Ātman can be seen by the penetrating intelligence. It is seen by the wise with their superior intellect.

The Upaniṣadic teachers referred the logical and mystical faculty to the same organ, intelligence, which has as it were double function. It has been truly pointed out by Hermann : "That there are deeper levels of consciousness of which the man who lives only in his discursive understanding little dreams and that a sudden awakening or the gentle or persisting knocking of the 'dweller in the innermost' may throw open a door into a new and larger world, is a sound mystical doctrine, but that this implies a double consciousness or that the consciousness ceases to be rational when it becomes mystical, is a gratuitous assumption which has done more than any other to invalidate the message of messages."[4] The Indian thinkers are uniform in their opinion on this point. Though they draw a distinction between reason and immediate knowledge, still they refer both of them to the same organ of intelligence which functions differently.

The Muṇḍaka has it : "The wise perceive it by knowledge (gnosis) which gleams forth as blissful immortality." "This Ātman is obtainable by austerity, by proper knowledge, by the constant practice of chastity." "The meditatie, pure in being, sees the partless by the bliss of knowledge."

We have been told that the Ātman can be realized in Adhyātma Yoga and by Jñāna-prasāda. The former is spiritual intuition, the latter is the peace of knowledge. Again, it is said that Atman is indicated by Neti, Neti. It is apparent, therefore, that the teachers recognize the faculty of immediate apprehension of truth. This faculty is intelligence. It must be chastened and purified before it can vouchsafe the superior wisdom Parā-vidyā (superior or esoteric wisdom) gives us the knowledge of Akṣara (the indestructible). The Parā-vidyā is a special capacity of intelligence to apprehend truth. Intelligence has wide functions. It is the faculty of mediate as well as of immediate knowledge. Even in normal perception intelligence plays an important part. The senses make report to the intelligence whence the direct perception comes. The mystical perception differs from the sense-perception in this, that in it no reference is necessary to the senses. Intelligence works quite independently of the instrumental media of the senses. The mystical sense, therefore, is nothing uncommon, though it can be present in those that possess the faculty of intuitive apprehension. The reference to the pure being in the Muṇḍaka Upaniṣad is significant, for purity of being can awaken the sleeping faculties of intelligence and can endow it with rare vision and uncommon powers. It kindles the fine psychism and evokes the subtle dynamism of our being and brings with them the knowledge of the unseen and uncommon. Psychism, in Indian philosophy, is not the ordinary function of intelligence (Buddhi), for besides the normal powers, the Buddhi has in it esoteric powers which become evident and manifest when it has been developed by discipline.

The fine psychism develops the cosmic powers inherent is Buddhi; Buddhi in its causal aspect can receive inspiration from the cosmic dynamism working in and through it. The more the intelligence is purified, the more subtle it becomes, the more it moves with expansive vision and cosmic sympathy. Indeed, there is no limit to the potentiality of Buddhi, and if our mental dynamism be freed from the obstructions of the gross elements and unresolved collision implied in them, the cosmic intuitions and powers inherent in Buddhi can be clearly felt. Buddhi is then no longer the logical faculty which discerns the consistency and squares the contradictions of ideas, it is also the mystical faculty which gives intuitions of the subtle motions of life and consciousness.

The fine psychism should not be confounded with the apprehension of birth. The fine psychism can give us lofty vision and fine powers. It may penetrate into the mysteries of immanent life, it can reveal the hidden truths of instinctive and supra-instinctive urges. It is competent to do so, for it is endowed with the luminosity of Sattva. The luminosity of Sattva cannot leave any part of our mental and supra-mental dynamism hidden to us. It is more luminous than the X-rays. It can penetrate into the subtle and casual aspect of our being.

If the Sāttvic intelligence is competent to reveal the hidden mysteries of life, it is no less competent to go deeper and feel the self-luminous Ātman. The luminosity of Buddhi is the luminosity of Sattva, and the luminosity of Self is the luminosity of consciousness. The two differ. Since, the transcendent intuition denies all relations, it certainly cannot be intuited by the luminosity of Buddhi. On the other hand, the luminosity of Buddhi is clearly felt to be the borrowed light of the self-luminous Self. This luminous Buddhi feels the transcendence of Ātman for the final illumination comes with the unique experience of the immediacy where the psychic dynamism can have no play. And, therefore, this experience is quite new and clearly unanalysable. The immediacy of revelation in psychic dynamism is different from this kind of immediacy in which psychism plays no part. The former is the immediacy of knowledge imparted by the highly strung Buddhi, the latter is the immediacy of Ātman. The one is super-sensuous but still empire, the other is quite transcendental.

The latter is, therefore, a change in the mode of apprehension. It is quite different from normal apprehension. The moment intelligence has a foreshadow of this apprehension it dies a natural death, and the whole outlook of the mystic life changes from *via contemplativa* to *via negativa*. The subtle joys of life are lost in the timeless focus of existence. The truths of relative existence and supra-mental revelations vanish. The *via contemplativa* gives positive delight of an elastic psyche with its new promises and vistas of refined delights. The *via negativa* silence the dynamism gross or refined, and gives the unique feeling of an intuition which denies the framework of experience. The knower vanishes here with the known, and the supposed timelessness of the mystic life in transcending the gross and the physical is replaced by the real timelessness of absolute silence. The previous experience completely changes here and a new realm is presented demanding a novel mental adaptation to receive and welcome it. Just as a line cannot be perpendicular to intersecting lines on the same plane – it being possible on a different plane of existence – similarly, however far-reaching and penetrating the psychic vision may be, in the dynamic spiritual life it can throw no light upon the absolute point were the subject-object experiences completely die away and a new form of immediacy is presented. Hence, the Yogic psychism cannot appreciate the Absolute which denies all dimensions of existence. The finest intelligence can indicate this existence by *via negativa* – not this, not this.

The denial of empiric intuitions, sensuous or super-sensuous, incuding the fine experiences of dynamic psychism, is the sure indication of the fixation in the Absolute. The cosmic drama with its hopes and illusions must have its scenes closed before the awakening in transcendence can take place. Intelligence with its illumination must cease to function before the liberation can be reached. The finer illumination of intelligence takes away all the promises of life, the meanings of values, and prepares the mental being for a new outlook filling it with the new meaning of emancipation from the divided outlook of life, from the personal hold of consciousness, from the beauteous experiences of the endless perspectives of life and for the installation of "naked" consciousness in its silent dignity and sublimity. The final illumination of intelligence, therefore, sounds its death knell for good; but even in this, intelligence yields a self-offering allegiance, not that the final end appears to it as destruction, but that it appears to it as the consummation.

The *via negativa* and the *via contemplativa* are strictly speaking two forms of the functioning of psychic intelligence. The *via contemplativa* gives an access into subtler forces and powers. The *via negativa* gives an access into transcendence. The fine psychism of Buddhi in *via negativa* recoils from the reception of forces and powers, for it works in a quite different way. A new light shines before it, a new form of thinking takes place in it. It becomes the faculty of transcendental appreciation. Buddhi becomes free from the natural and spiritual urges, however fine and however graceful. It becomes active in its discriminative function. The discrimination presents before it the timelessness of being as distinguished from the expression in time. And the more the timelessness of being becomes clear to it, the more it surrenders its functions. Buddhi is informative of every form of existence, and the moment it becomes informative of the timeless being it has the natural withdrawal from its normal functioning, and the drama of life is brought to a close. The timeless Absolute is so marked a contrast to the sensuous and super-sensuous experiences that intelligence can see no longer any value in holding to their professions and charms. It has a natural recoil from their activities.

The transcendent philosophic intuition fosters a kind of consciousness different from the empiric or psychic intuition. It sets up a new psychosis, which breaks the spell of life, its stir and stress. The transcendental apperception of identity has strictly the unqiue psychosis about it, but the psychosis of identity is to be distinguished from the being of identity. The psychosis sets up a new vision which has the immediate effect of removing the crude or fine mental complexes; this identity psychosis ultimately comes to the breaking or melting point of all inherited or acquired convictions. The distinctions of space, time, and space-time events completely die out, and it may be said that identity psychosis is the last space-time event denying the order of space-time events. The sense of an "I" is the hold of the space-time order, and the more the cosmic sense of Buddhi is established, the more the space-time events lose their distinctions and histories; the whole existence becomes one totla space-time event. This is the experience of the Cosmic Puruṣa (or Iśvara). But this expereince is in space-time order and beyond it. But the particular psychosis of identity is different from the experience of the total space-time event in this, that it denies the total space-time event or at least its reflection in a particular centre. It is, therefore, the denial of common experience in space-time and may be called the intimation of transcendent identity. Indeed, it is so rare an experience that it cannot bear comparison to ordinary experiences however subtle. *Via negativa* is, therefore, the final illumination of Buddhi, the exercise of its transcendent functioning. This transcendental apperception is, then, in the beginning a space-time event, but in the end, it is the denial of itself as well as the manifold of experience. The identity psychosis brings to the fore the truth of the Absolute, and, after its informative function, it dies away completely. *Via negativa* in the Vedānta has this significance and meaning. The Upaniṣad presents both the contemplative and the negative method, since it presents two forms of immediate knowledge of the Cosmic Puruṣa and of the Absolute.

References

1. This is a general statement. There are passages in the Ṛg-Veda, which indicate that the truth of the Upaniṣads is implicit in the Vedas, *Vide* Ṛg-Veda, 10th Maṇḍala; Sūkta 80, Mantra 2; Sūkta 81, Sūkta 82, Mantras 3 and 7; Sūkta 114, Mantra 5,381; Sūkta 121, Mantra 1.
2 This is conveyed by Plotinus in his conception of '*Ev.*
3. Oman's translation quoted in Watt's *Intuition of God*.
4. Hermann's *The Meaning and Value of Mysticism,* p. 272.

Chapter III

The Upaniṣadic View of Truth

The Upaniṣads deal with and describe the nature of the ultimatie reality, the Absolute, not evidently so much by reasoning or dialectics, as by inner experience and realization. Dialectical passages are few in the pages of the Upaniṣads. They are full, however, of the records of the intuitions and experiences of seers, and these have enriched their value as inspiring texts. Logic may convince us, but intuitions and experiences inspire us. Interest in Upaniṣadic study in intensified because of the finer vistas of intuition and feeling they open in the seeker. The corret research of the seers, their definite answers to intensive queries about the ultimate reality, exhibit the deep and varied spiritual expe-iences which cannot fail to strike the imagination, excite wonder and admiration, and silently inspire the realization of Truth.

The Upaniṣads lose their meaning and significance to those who are anxious to find a developed philosophy in them, but when the search changes from a rational inquiry to a mystical penetration, their import and depth are felt and realized. They exhibit the highest intuitions and experiences of spiritual life.

Brahman

A treatise on mysticism would naturally refuse a categorical setting of conception about being, and would rather prefer to read the development of the conception through life's experiences and intuitions, not becuase it is demand of the mystic spirit to shut out the intellectual measurement of truth and reality, but because this has been specially the method of pursuing truth in the Upaniṣads. The Upaniṣads appeal more by spiritual intuitions and psychological revelations than be a set form of philosophy; and, though they have been the basis of the later philosophies, still it cannot be doubted that in them life and spirit have been of greater concern than the systematization which has been thrust upon them. The texts read like gospels of revelations and intuitions, and in many places it has been shown how life is felt in its subtle delicacies of movement, and spirit in fine intuitions. And, since the inspiration has been direct, logic has hardly a place in the Upaniṣads, though no doubt they are richly suggestive to logicians.

That this is the natural conclusion can hardly admit of any doubt; and when this has been lost sight of and the life's quest has at last his refuge in the intellectual understanding, the Upaniṣads have been the fruitful ground of combatants, eager to raise side-issues and concentrate their efforts and energies upon them. This demand of logic has risen when it has not been able to follow life's movement and intuition in all its phases, and their demand has the invariable effect of confining the spiritual quest to a definite phase of expression. But spiritual life denies in its soaring such confinement most eloquently, for its constant tendency is to feel life and spirit in their fullness and glory and not in partition. The Īśa Upaniṣad has rightly characterized the spirit to be complete and full. And therefore it has been beautifully laid down :

"This is full, that is full, the full originates from the full. When the full is taken away from the full, the full remains."

This couplet expresses the mystic promise in the most effective way. Life is actively energizing for fullness. Spirit cannot bear division, it cannot tolerate incompleteness. Fullness is its being, and since it is the only bing, it cannot conceive the world of spirit either in being or in expression as incomplete and fragmentary. Hence, spirit is the fullness of being both in transcendence and in immanence. It is inexhaustible.

The fullness is perceived in the younder and in the beyond, in the widest expansion and commonalty of spirit, it is perceived in itself beyond expression in transcendence. Life's motion is in spirit, its stay is in spirit. Spirit is all, spirit is in all. Spirit is beyond all.

Though the effort has been the presentation of spirit in its fullness, still it has been necessary to conceive the spirit in transcendence, and the spirit in immanence, in reference to the expression or concentration. Spirit-in-itself is transcendent, spirit is immanent in reference to the order of expression.

This has led us to conceive Brahman-in-itself and Brahman-in-relation. The former can be called the Absolute, the latter Īśa.

This fullness of transcendence goes beyond the fullness of immanence. Thought and language both fail to understand it and express it. So, unique a presentation is this height of existence that there is no means of indicating it save by a negative method and process. The positive intuition of it is impossible. Whatever meets the senses or the intellect, is not Brahman.

Our approach to the study of the Upaniṣads will be mainly analytical of the spiritual expereinces revealed therein. This analytical study can alone discover the most sacred spiritual convictions about the nature of reality.

We can at once see that the conception of the Viśvadeva in the Vedas could not satisfy the Upaniṣadic seers. The reception of the finer vibrations of supra-mundane life in its wide diffusion in supramental visions, cannot silence the quest of the teachers, for it is supposed to be still external. It can set up fine vital and mental currents, but cannot touch the inmost being in us. The search in the Upaniṣads is the search of the inmost being, the being above and beyond the world of revelation, internal and external.

The Upaniṣads transcend the limits of expression and realize truth in transcendence of the cosmic stirrings, the vital and mental urges.

Their importance and appeal are enhanced by reference to the Absolute. The relative world with its vast experiences and possibilities cannot make a lasting claim on our attention, for they are bounded and passing. The relative has value in so far as it draws our attention to the Absolute by drawing up a sense of contrast. It calls for the unlimited, the permanent, as its background. When the fullest promises of the relative existence have been exhausted, the real search for the Absolute begins; when the delights and joys of the relative order have had their fullest trial, then alone the worth, the value, and the meaning of the Absolute as the only enduring can be apparent to us. In this sense the inquiry into the Absolute and the quest of its security of being can seriously begin, only when the satisfactions of the values in the relative order, gross or fine, have had their fullest trial. This is not often clearly understood and the intellectual synthesis of the relative and the Absolute is often attempted. The relative joys and values are given an absolutistic meaning and impress, and the fountain of our experience has established a claim upon us, and life clings to it so keenly that it often refuses to accept the breaking of the continuity between the natural and the supernatural, between the relative and the Absolute.

But this attitude is rudely shaken if penetration is made into the recesses of our being, where a sense of freedom at once convinces us of the twofold character of the relative and the absolute existence. This freedom is unique : it is not the freedom of eased mentality and highly strung vitality, it is not the freedom of an embracing synthesis; it is the freedom from the mutations of life, freedom from the reciprocities of intellectual life, freedom from insistent vital and mental demands. It is the freedom of transcendence.

The Upaniṣadic search is after the real and the enduring beyond the temporal; this real is Brahman in the Upaniṣadic terminology. The freedom which awaits the realization of Brahman is freedom from the relative values and concepts.

The chief attraction of the Upaniṣads lies in adducing the conception of Brahman as the Absolute. The seers are penetrative enugh to go beyond the veil of relative existence to the One Absolute, which denies division and completely transcends the relative existence.

The Upaniṣadic method has been chiefly mystical penetration, and the penetration has been keen enough to reach complete transcendence. The text conceives the Vast as the state of existence, from which the relative order of the senses and mentality drops completely.

The Chāndogya has it : "The manifold has been in the beginning as 'Sat' (existent) and the Sat has been one without the second." No doubt the texts are rich in references about the emergence should not be referred to the Absolute which transcends everything, including the desire and act of creation. The Absolute is, (Kaṭha, II, vi, 12, 13). Nothing more can be said of it, no definition is possible of it, for it is beyond knowledge (Kena, II, 3), beyond any categorical thinking.

"It moves, it moves not, it is far and near, it is in, it is out." The intellectual attempt to define it positively completely fails.

What, Then, is Brahman?

The word "Brahman" has been used to indicate the vast, the unbounded, i.e. the Absolute. In the texts the word has been used in many places identifying it with the forces of nature, the inner psychoses, the vital principle, etc., and this has been perplexing to the accurate study of the Upaniṣads.

Hence, a clear analysis of the passages in which the word occurs is necessary for clarified understanding. The texts use the word in diffeent senses in diverse contexts, and if the context is forgotten, confusion is inevitable.

The understanding is helped at the outset if we remember the doctrine of transcendence and immanence of Brahman as taught in the Upaniṣads. Brahman is the soul of the appearance, it denies the appearance. It is in it, it is out of it. Such contrarieties are only possible if Brahman is viewed in and without relation to the world of phenomena in the same sense. Immanence of Brahman is relative to the cosmos. Transcendence is not. And, therefore, the passages covering immanence are of less importance than the passages covering transcendence. This distinction is to be borne in mind to help a clear understanding.

Significance of this Distinction in Spiritual Life

The conception of Brahman is and out of relation to the immanent life has an important significance in spiritual life. It accepts the possibilities of spiritual life and expression in the relative and absolutistic consciousness. The experiences may differ, they may be of different character, they may have different values, but still it cannot be denied that they are potent in life. And intellectual considerations may persuade us to accept the one and deny the other; but such considerations seem to be a categorical determination which has no value in spiritual life. The Upaniṣads recount the spiritual experiences in life with and withc ut expression; and if finality is fixed upon any one of them it is because the gratification and the blessedness which are the promise of spiritual urges are more complete in the one than in the other. But this distinction does not take away the full value from the life in its partial expression and incomplete fruition.

The Upaniṣads are careful to unfold an evolution of spirit

in its immanent expression, and since this expression is due to self-alientation of spirit, it can offer only partial satisfaction even in its fullest development.

The spiritual fruition in the Upaniṣads, therefore, has a twofold meaning. It may mean a self-opening and reception of the cosmic spiritual life through nature and society and in its development in the soul.

But this unfolding of spiritual consciousness is evolution in spirituality, but should not be confounded with emancipation in transcendence. The spiritual consciousness at the outset is the acceptance of the cosmic life through the fine and the finer planes of existence. It is the stage of the ever expansive dynamism, and so long as the spirutual life energizes in the concrete, it enjoys the finer revelations of spirit through nature and soul and yet transcends them in the world of the finest expression in itself. The spiritual vision has in it still the concrete outlook, for experiences, however fine, are still confined to the original limitation of consciousness in expression and immanence. Spiritual life is, therefore, essentially dynamic, and howsoever expansive and rich it may be, it cannot transcend the original restriction. And, therefore, the highest philosophic truth which such experiences can indicate and imply will be naturally an all-inclusive existence. It lies in everything. It transcends everything, for nothing can exhaust its being. Its being extends far beyond the ethereal expanse, far beyond the highest heavens.

The Śvetāśvatara eloquently describes the vision of the all-inclusive spirit in its widest commonalty. The all pervading spirit is represented as the Cosmic Person, encompassing endless existence in its embrace : –

"The person with its thousand heads, thousand eyes, thousand feet, surrounds the earth on all sides and stands ten fingers' breadth beyond.

"The person, in truth, this wide world is, whatever has

been, and whatever will be; also ruler of immortality, and whatever grows up by food."

"It has a hand and foot on every side, on every side an eye, and head and face, it has an ear everywhere in the world. It stands encompassing all." (Hume's translation of the Śvetāśvatara. iii, 14, 15, 16.)

"The God who is in fire, who is in water, who was entered into the whole world, who is in plants, who is in trees – to that God be adoration, yea, be adoration!" (Śvetāśvatara Upaniṣad, ii. 17.)

Again we have in the Ṛg-Veda (Wilson's Ṛg-Veda Saṁhitā, Maṇḍala 10, Eighth Aṣṭaka, Fourth Adhyāya, Sūkta, vi) : –

1. "Puruṣa, who has a thousand heads, a thousand eyes, a thousand feet, investing the earth in all directions, exceeds (it by a space) measuring ten fingers."
2. "Puruṣa is verily all this (visible world), all that is, and all that is to be, he is also the Lord of immortality, for he mounts beyond (his own condition) for the food (of living beings)."
3. "Such is his greatness, and Puruṣa is greater even than this, all beings are one-fourth of him, his other three-fourths (being) immortal, (abide) in heaven."
4. "Three-fourths of Puruṣa ascended; the other fourth that remained in this world proceeds repeatedly, and diversified in various forms, went into all animate and inanimate creation."

Though these texts eloquently describe the all-permeating nature of the Absolute, in the gross and the finer forms of existence, still they do not give us the conception of transcendence. Hence, these texts have value for the spiritual life in initiating the cosmic sense of the cosmic being. They are, in short, the vision of the Reality in forms, or the vision of the formed reality (Mūrta), they do not indicate the understanding or the vision of the formless.

The Bṛhadāraṇyaka has it : "There are assuredly two forms of Brahman : the formed and the formless, the mortal and the immortal, the stationary and the moving, the actual and the yon." (Hume's translation, iii. 1.)

The texts bring out clearly the conception of the formless, which is, therefore, as a conception more advanced and subtle than the presentation of Brahman as Mūrta. This makes way for the perception of the finest essence of existence immanent in all existence.

But even this is not enough as the true indication of the Upaniṣadic teaching. For as a source of spiritual inspiration the Upaniṣads see far beyond such poetic inspiration which feels the animation of nature by spirit, and go deeper in declaring the identity of existence in nature and man.

The spiritual life, therefore, is not merely the reception of spirit in wise passiveness through the finer forces active in nature and man; it is not the sense of the vastness and overpoweringness of existence; it is, as the Bṛhadāraṇyaka points out, the feeling of the exact identity of spirit beyond the dynamic of nature and spirit. The text reads : "As an identity is to be looked upon, this indemonstrable, enduring being; motionless beyond space, the birthless soul, Ātman, the great and the enduring."

This perception of the enduring as seated in the soul (*Yo eṣa antaḥhṛdaya*) is the promise of the Upaniṣads. The self-opening does not only move the fine dynamism of our being, making it receptive and responsive to the finer forces active in us and in nature and to their correspondence and unity in the Godhead, but it finally helps that penetration which feels the identity of existence in Ātman. The self-opening in succeeded and displaced here by self-realization, and the finer expressions of life by silence of wisdom. The wisdom which the spiritual dynamism carries with it, is the revelation of the finer oscillation of life and spirit in the deep of our being, the subtle joys and music in the life of nature, the rhythm and having of the cosmic life in and beyond the formed (Mūrtta) existence. But it is to be distinguished from the wisdom which is discoverable in the deep abyss of our being, the knowledge of identity. Transcendent wisdom then presents a unique experience which cannot otherwise be obtained. It is the wisdom of the formless, the shapeless.

In the life of realization the Upaniṣads lay more stress upon the truth of transcendence than upon the immanent spiritual life. It is not because the Upaniṣadic seers do not see and feel the finer delights and truths of supra-mental existence in the dynamic divine, it is because they feel the truth of all truths, the truth beyond the immanental immensities. The supramental truths hold true in the order of expression, and as such are truths which lie beyond the surface existence. They reveal realms of harmonies, beauties, and sublimities; but they can have no access into the silence of the Deep. It is beyond the reach of the sensuous or the super-sensuous mind.

The word "truth" is confined to this aspect of transcendence in the Upaniṣads, both in the ontological and the spiritual sense. Not that it is the fixity of existence amidst the diversities of change. The dynamic divine is no less fixed an existence, for no one seriously conceives it to be vanishing. It may have occasional withdrawal of its expression, but the occasional withdrawal of its play in the cosmic drama does not reduce it to nothing. It is the source and fountain of all life, all streams of thought, wisdom, and power, and therefore, it is idle to deny its truth out-right and to refuse its spiritual influence and potency. But when the emphasis is laid upon the transcendent aspect of truth, it is done in the clear conviction that the transcendent is Truth without the least limitation, it is the sole truth, truth unadorned and naked. The transcendent is truth-in-itself. The dynamic divine is truth in relation to the order of revelation in the supra-physical and physical planes of existence. The truth implied in both cannot be the same. The dynamic divine is truth in relation to the orders of revelation and creation, it cannot be truth in the sense in which the transcendent is truth. But this should not for a moment be construed as meaning that there are two forms of truth, actually different, if not conflicting. The transcendent alone is truth, the dynamic divine is the transcendent presented in the aspect of relation. The same thing is seen, but interpreted differently. The intellectual necessity of thinking in the terms of a first cause presents the transcendent as the dynamic divine manifested in the mental and the supramental universe, in the physical and the vital planes of existence. But when intellectual curiosity is displaced by truth-vision, the distinctness, native to conceptual thinking, dies away, and transcendence is presented in its undivided oneness.

The supra-intellectual perception of truth gives us the consciousness of the divided oneness of being at every point of existence, and hence presents the essence of truth which cannot be apprehended if the mind allows itself to be governed by the concepts it has developed in the course of evolution. The truth out of all reference to the order of expression is, therefore, truth in the metaphysical sense. It is the highest truth in the spiritual sense also, in so far as its value is greatest because of its nature as the essence of being, and because of its being ever present and most intimate. The highest truth in the spiritual sense is never distant, is never far; it is ever present, ever inmost. The least difference, the least mediacy makes truth foreign to us, and makes reconcilement between the seeker and the sought impossible. And when, therefore, truth is sought in ever-growing experience, mental or supramental, the face of truth can never shine before us, for it is not there in its prestine purity and undiminished radiance. The sense of distance still troubles us, the sense of reception bespeaks the difference; but truth denies difference and can neither by sought nor received, for in the unbounded expanse of its being it exist in its transcendent purity for ever. It can never be received, nor be sought.

Truth, then, in its highest sense is that which is, which can neither be presented nor received. It is the presentation of the absolute fact, and in this presentation it goes beyond the sense of the fullness of life, the completeness of power, and the highest security of our finite being. It is the overshadowing of the concrete life and consciousness. The stretches of the finer vision into the immensities of life and the occasional depths of feeling which so often pass for the highest religious beatitude should not be confounded with the intuition of the Absolute.

Hence, the spiritual truth of the Absolute is to be distinguished from the spiritual truth of the dynamic divine. The one is true because of its being the highest fact, the maximum existence beyond limitation; the other is true because of its influence and power. But they are not to be distinguished as two forms of truth – the highest fact in self-alienation appears as the highest unity of existence pregnant with knowledge and power.

In view of the above distinction, it is natural to characterize the highest truth in two ways : truth in its transcendence and truth in its self-expression. Truth in its transcendence is truth absolute, free from the limitation of expression. Expression implies concreteness and concentration. It is the spiritual life and expression in time, but it cannot present the aspect of spiritual life which transcends time and expression in time.

To distinguish the truth in transcendence as different from truth in self-expression, it is natural to indicate as *Neti, Neti,* not this, not this. The highest spiritual experience seeks to describe the greatest spiritual truth in negative terms, in terms of denial of all that meets us in the sensuous and the supersensuous realization. *Neti, Neti* indicates the impossibility of knowing the unknowable. Positive knowledge is in a sense a limitation, for it implies the duality of the seer and the seen, the experientalist and the experience. *Neti, Neti* denies this possibility of knowledge, it denies the possibility of indicating the truth by clear characterization. All characterization is thought-description, and truth evades the grasp of thought.

The Absolute : Neti Neti

Neti denotes that Brahman is not what meets the senses, inner and outer. It is not even the object of thought. Even the highest stretch of imagination and the finest sensibility can neither feel nor touch it, not the finest vital urge can reach it. It is beyond, far beyond, the grasp of human faculty.

When intuition and existence are identified, the problem of knowing Being cannot arise; for, in the height of being, the ordinary conditions of knowledge do not prevail. But the denial of knowledge in concrete sense does not commit it to agnosticism. Knowledge is not denied of reality, though knowledge is denied in the sense of discursive and mediate reasoning.

But it is not nothing. It is the acme of existence, the essence of reality. *Neti, Neti* does not deny the reality of existence, it denies all the empirical characterization of reality. The supreme fact cannot be grasped by the ordinary process of knowledge. It escapes the effort to grasp by all the faculties that men are endowed with. Hence, the highest spiritual experience and the greatest spiritual fact are beyond the pale of our knowledge.

This truth finds most emphatic expression in the Bṛhadāraṇyaka Upaniṣad : –

"The Ātman is not this, it is not this. It is unseizable, for it cannot be seized. It is indestructible, for it cannot be destroyed. It is unattached, for it does not attach itself. It is unbound, it does not tremble. It is not injured." (iii, 9, 26; iv, 4, 22).

The same truth was taught by Bādhva when he was questioned about the nature of Brahman. "Teach me the nature of Brahman, Reverend Sir," Bāskali besought Bādhva. The latter remained silent. The question was again put. The sage was still silent. The inquirer still persisted. The answer came : "I teach, but you do not understand. Silent is Ātman." (Śaṅkara-Bhāṣya, iii, 2, 17).

The denial of attributes and qualifications to Brahman does not reduce it to a void. The Upaniṣads are definite about that. The primal reality is the essence of being—our pragmatic and conceptual limitation of thinking creates such an apprehension. So long as the pragmatic instincts are active, the mind cannot rise to the height of accepting the truth of the non-relational planes of existence, for the pragmatic instincts are fed upon the consciousness of value and reality of the relativities of existence. When, therefore, at the height of existence and possibilities of pragmatic satisfactions are belied, the pragmatic mind refuses the highest truth and is anxious to designate it as a void. And naturally so, for the pragmatic mind has not the power to deny its inherent limitations attendant on the divided outlook on life with which it is naturally associated, and to welcome a truth which can sound its death-knell. And because religious seeking is falsely identified with pragmatic satisfaction, the higher approaches to truth which cannot appeal to the pragmatic instincts are rejected by the surface mind as quests in the wilderness. The persistent demand of our vital and pragmatic instincts has, therefore, the baneful effect of confining the mind to the satisfactions of the divided life and withholding from it the superior vision of truth which denies pragmatic values. The Upaniṣadic conception of the spiritual truth cannot be understood, far less appreciated, if life seeks merely the satisfaction of pragmatic instincts.

The realistic or pragmatic consciousness is guided by its narrow vision and it cannot accept the truth which is revealed when the mind has been able to forgo its limitations. And, therefore, the intuitions and revelations coming from the height of existence, transcending the pragmatic, cannot be understood and accepted by the lower mind. And because of this, the Śruti says that "neither the learned nor the intelligent among men welcome this truth." And verily so, for the appreciation of truth and its final illumination require the quelling of the lower and pragmatic demands of the soul and the waking up of the finest intuitive intelligence which sees but does not understand. And so long as the requirement is not fulfilled, the highest intuitions will be lightly passed over, not that they have no realities, but that the mind has not the fine susceptibilities to feel them and correctly appraise their values. And so long as the vital and pragmatic demands are insistent with the empiric intuitions in life, the transcendent truth cannot make its impression, and perchance, even if it does, it cannot make the impression enduring.

It is better for the correct estimate of the Upaniṣadic truths to indicate that its highest truth can be apprehended not so much by the process of reflection or the intuitions of the empiric and pragmatic mind, as by the supramental revelation and transcendent intuition. The thinking mind may not find much food for it in the pages of the Upaniṣads, save in the form of fine hints pregnant with constructive suggestions, but the inquiring and the truly mystic soul will find in it sufficient food for itself, for its advance and realization.

The mystic demand and the mystic understanding are different from the pragmatic and conceptualistic demand and understanding. Mysticism has its own claim; if the pragmatic vision could have satisfied the soul, the mystic demand and inquiry would have no value and the mystic approach no meaning. The mystic sees and reads life in a way different from the rational or pragmatic method of approach, and, therefore, the truths and the conclusions which the theoretic and pragmatic mind are slow to receive and accept, the mystic consciousness unhesitatingly appropriates. But for this immediate acceptance of a truth that cannot otherwise be seen, felt, and appreciated, the mystic claim and approach would be regarded as groundless and unconvincing. The real attraction of mysticism lies in offering a new venue of realization and a novel method of apprehension. And this explains why the simple truths felt by the mystic require so long and circuitious an effort to commend them to the theoretic reason, Nay, often reason stands baffled in its attempt.

And this becomes evident when the mystic claims the identity of fact and knowledge, the identity of reality and consciousness, for it is more an experience in the transcendent heights of knowledge than a demonstration of logic. Logic may follow, but in the acme of consciousness the truth is felt.

This is why we see that the Upaniṣads have not drawn the distinction between fact and knowledge; on the other hand, they have characterized the reality to be knowledge and consciousness. The Aitareya Upaniṣad has it in the conclusion : "All this is based on intelligence. The basis is intelligence. Brahman is intelligence."

Brahman denotes the highest existence. The highest existence is intelligence, or, more properly, consciousness. Though the Absolute is intuition, it cannot be intuited. The texts are positive about this. The Kena has : "He who knows not, knows; he who knows, knows not." (i, 2, 3.) Again, the Bṛhadāraṇyaka (iv, 5, 15) has it : "Who has ever known the knower?" Evidently the hint is that intuition cannot be intuited. "The knower of all cannot be known."

This suggests that intuition excludes all relativity, all reference to the process and the object of knowledge. The text has also : "Brahman is immediacy of intuition. It transcends all knowledge, though it is knowledge. It is the essence of cognition, without being the cognitive process. Brahman is illumination." (Bṛhadāraṇyaka, iii, 4, 1; iii, 5, 1.)

This conclusion puts into clear relief the character of the Absolute. It is one. It is intuition. It is luminosity.

But this denial of knowledge in pragmatic and concrete sense does not make the highest affirmation of the Upaniṣads open to agnosticism. Such a charge can only arise when knowledge is defined in empiric terms or in terms of relativity. The pragmatic mind is accustomed to think in terms of relative verity, and therefore, it fails to appreciate truth when it is presented in terms which do not represent the actualities of relative existence. The finest imagination cannot picture so sublime a truth, so dignified an existence. The Kena Upaniṣad is perfectly justified in saying that "it is different from the known, it is different from the unknown". The inmost truth, "the truth which cannot be perceived by the Manas, and felt by the senses," the truth which is different from the object of adoration, is the finest existence which, by its integrity and simplicity, passes comprehension. And yet it is not far, it is intimate, it is too near to be fully apprehended. The highest truth is the greatest dilemma in knowledge. All knowledge presupposes it. All existence is supported in it. It is the consciousness of consciousness. It is the fact of facts. It is far and near. It is in and out. It is the whole and the parts. Still it cannot be seen, it cannot be felt. The texts are positive about it. Who was ever known the knower of all things? None can experience the revealer of experiences. It is, as the Kena points out, inherent in individual psychoses but can scarcely be felt by itself. The sun and the stars illuminate by its light, but none can express it. The world within and the world without are illumined by its light, but the brilliant orbs of the heavens cannot cast in it "their purest ray serene". The stars twinkle with its reflected light, the soul illumines with its borrowed splendour.

The mellowed brilliance of the twilight and the dawn, the dazzling brilliance of the sun, are but its shadows. It illumines the intelligence. "The sun shines not there, neither moon, nor the stars. These lightnings shine not, much less the fire. This shining, all others shine. All this is illumined with His light." (Kaṭha, v, 15).

Intuition cannot be intuited. The Māṇḍūkya (verse 7) has it : "It is not an object that can either be seen or used, it defies definition and reflection, it is incomprehensible, it is essentially the knowledge of the oneness of self."

Where the object has been identified with the subject of knowledge, the history of experience has been closed there; the Prapañca, the cosmic manifold, is withdrawn completely from this height of existence. It is, therefore, not the seed of the creation in which the world sleeps, but it is the integral existence, beyond space, beyond time, beyond the creative urges. It is the silence which is not disturbed by the gush of life, it is the great beyond from which no traveller returns, it is beyond the joys of life and the fear of death. It is the greatest wonder of existence. It is rare in its widest commonalty, it is simple in its highest dignity.

The Chāndogya is more appropriate when it says that "the Sun does not truly rise and set for him who perpetually lives in the knowledge of Brahman of the Upaniṣads." (iii, 11, 3.)

In a more significant passage in the Bṛhadāraṇyaka Upaniṣad we are told by Yājñavalkya, in reply to a question from King Janaka, that "when the Sun has set, the Moon has set, the fire has gone out, and speech is hushed, the soul (Ātman) still shines, for the soul is his light, for with the soul, indeed, as his light, one sits, moves around, does his work and returns." (iv, 3, 6). The Śvetāśvatara Upaniṣad also characterizes the highest truth as the consciousness of consciousness, the superconscience (vi, 13). It calls the supreme soul Jña, conscience. It is Gnosis (vi, 17). The *Brahma* Upaniṣad characterizes it as Sākṣi Chetā. It is the percipience, the conscience.

This conscience is the summit of knowledge, free as it is

from the mental or supramental limitations. It is, therefore, to be distinguished from the wisdom of Hiraṇyagarbha or of Īśvara, for it can reflect only the sum total of experience in the fine or casual dynamism. These are still relative verities and cannot cover the absolute intuition. The supramental revelations may give out the hidden mysteries laid deep in the root of existence, but cannot present the timeless intuition before us. The suprasensuous revelations do not transcend the operation of the causal law, they are events in time, impressed upon the Sāttvic, luminous, mind freed from the limitatins of its working through the senses, but the invariable implication of a reception and a gift in knowledge is there. This reception may be very swift in psychological process, but it cannot forgo the implication of reciprocity in knowledge. Revelation may open a direct access into the mysteries of the divine life in Īśvara, but it cannot transcend the implication that knowledge is relative. The conscience is, therefore, unique in the sense that it transcends the implications of relations. It is self-luminous, it is luminosity of intuition as distinguished from the luminosity of Sattva. The luminosity in intuition is self-luminosity, the luminosity of Sattva is reflected luminosity. The one is luminosity of intuition, the other is the luminosity of intelligence (Buddhi). Conscience is intuition. Intuition is being.

This conscience is to be distinguished from the super-mind (Īśvara) not only in the knowledge aspect, but also in the existence aspect. It is the supreme existence, and it is indestructible : supreme because it is the ultimate reality beyond which nothing can exist. Īśvara is the Absolute in reference to the creative order, and this reference makes it distinct from the Absolute, since it always implies a reference to the totality. So long as our knowledge implies reference, Īśvara's being is supposed to be supreme, as it is all-embracive totality; but the moment the reference to the subjective locus is lost, the idea of the eternity, of totality also drops from the mind. Eternity, therefore, has two senses : (1) eternity in the sense of the transcendence of time; and (2) eternity in the sense of existing through time. Avyaya in the former sense is true of the Absolute, i.e. Brahman transcending all relations. Avyaya in the second sense is true of Īśvara, for it is an existence which is identified with time, the history of the Absolute expressing itself and subsisting through time : Īśvara is then the Absolute seen in reference to self-expression through time. The time order is an order in Īśvara, it is not an order in the Absolute.

Self-expression is, therefore, strictly true of Īśvara, but not of the Absolute. The Absolute in reality transcends self-expression : the limitation of self-expression is in Īśvara, but not in the Absolute. The dynamism of expression does not play any part in Being and the Absolute is a plenum beyond the ripples of dynamic expression. The Upaniṣads emphasize this aspect of absolute existence, and a clear realization of such an existence is supposed to give that undisturbed calm which is the promise of unrestricted vision and undivided life.

In this affirmation the Upaniṣads draw sharp line of distinction between the conscience and the spiritual dynamism : they do not completely negate the dynamic aspect of spiritual life – they recognize its spiritual values; but they consider them to be a partial expression of spiritual life which does not represent its complete nature and full depth. Spiritual life is, to the Upaniṣadic teachers, neither evolution nor emergence, either of which means an upward motion and fine expression of our inward being. The common notion of spirituality as the fine blossoming of the inward nature implies the movement of life from its gross to its fine nature. Nay, it has implicit reference to the truth of spontaneous generation of spirituality. Just as the biologist thinks of the evolution of life out of the lifeless, similarly it is thought that fine spirituality emerges out of gross vitalism – that spirituality is an offshoot of vitalism in the course of its emergence into finer expression. The Upaniṣads cannot in the least favour so neo-realistic or neo-vitalistic a conception of spiritual life, for in such a conception but only the spiritual sense and life in man is supposed to leap into a fresh stage of evolution, but also the very centre and object of spiritual life, viz. God, is conceived as coming into being in the course of emergent evolution.

The greatest shortcoming of this theory is that it makes the fine come out of the gross, the highest values out of the coarsest existence. It does not explain how mass and quantity can pass into the specimens of finest life and spirituality.

The Upaniṣads steer clear of such a conception. They do not generally believe in spiritual evolution, and, when they do, they do not necessarily accept the emergence of the lower into the higher, of the grosser into the finer. The fine, to them, is a higher and truer reality and is immanent in the gross; the fine, therefore, is the essence, the gross is the appearance. In spiritual life there is no room for spontaneous generation, the spirit can be a spark of spirit, life of life. The highest reality is spiritual, the only existence in spirit. The non-spiritual is not exactly non-spiritual, it is the shadow and the restriction of the spiritual. Spiritual life is them more a close understanding and appreciation of the essence of our being than an evolution or emergence. Spiritual evolution can be true of the divided self, which, from the self-imposed conception of a division, sees in it the possibility of degeneration and evolution. When the perfect balance and equilibrium of the spiritual life in transcendence is lost, the spiritual life can either be active for a higher evolution, or can degenerate into death. Life, when divided from the source, can work ceaselessly for the evolution of finer instincts and powers, or degenerate into lower forms of existence which check the free flow of vitality, the quickened sense of morality, and the fine intellectual and spiritual receptivity. The Upaniṣads recognize the path of evolution and the gradual regeneration of the spirit and illumination through successive planes of finer existence; but this has not been recognized as the right spiritual quest, for this cannot emancipate the soul from the sense of a false individuality; and, however fine it grows, however delicate becomes its being and penetrative its powers, they still suffer from the original limitation and cannot rise above the perfection of powers to the right understanding of the integral being. Spiritual life is them more the installing in the silence than the search of fine being and receptivity.

Being and Bliss

Delight is the soul of Being. "Brahman is Ānandaṁ," the text says (Taittirīya, ii, 7). Spirit is delight, and delight is spirit. There is no difference between the two, nor is a difference conceivable. And corresponding to spiritual transcendence and spiritual expression, delight has two forms : the delight of silence and the delight of expression.

The delight of silence is delight-in-itself, not enjoyable, nor ever enjoyed. Still it is delight, for delight is being, and where being is the essence, delight is *in excelsis*.

Such delight in transcendence is accepted as calm and refused as delight. This is a common mistake. Delight is not seldom identified with a psychological state, and even in spiritual life the psychological sense or feeling is sought to be multiplied and intensified. Delight, in spiritual life, is therefore supposed to be the heightening of feeling. Such, however, is not the delight felt in transcendence. Still it is delight, and though it has not the warmth of feeling, it has the joy of an unbounded expanse. It is not the delight of a free flow of spiritual dynamism, the ease of a fluid and elastic being, it is the delight of a luminous consciousness and transparent being which is beyond the touch of spatial expansion. It is not the delight of spiritual experiences, it is the delight of spiritual being. Though it has not the vibrative blessedness of love, it has the blissful repose in itself. It is not the joy of life, it is the joy of freedom.

Ānandaṁ has the highest spiritual value and is the index of value in spiritual consciousness and is not infrequently set as the value-concept. Felicity is sought. Felicity is realized. Such is the case in spiritual life. But the Upaniṣads say : "Felicity is Being" (Taittirīya, iii, 6). Felicity is the essence of the soul. It is not a value-concept, it is the concept of existence. Where being is complete, felicity is full. It is not to be realized, it is there. It is not in fruition. It is not to be, but eternally is. Ānandaṁ is then not the value of being, it is being. This delight does not delight itself. It is delight, but not self-delight. It is delight without rise or fall, it is bliss without ebb and flow.

As such it differs from the delight of expression or concentration, either analytic or synthetic, though no doubt the spiritual life in immanence feeds upon such delight. This is the plane where delight meets delight – the joy of enjoying delight, and not the joy of being delight. When the self moves in the world of becoming and relativity, it sees not the delight in the self, it seeks the delight in the other, the other in the self. This reciprocity meets us in the order of expression, and such delight of reciprocity is to be distinguished from the delight of being. The former is essentially an elevation in psychological consciousness, the latter a fixity in being. The Taittiriya lays special stress on the transcendence of bliss. "Speech turns back from it, mind cannot attain it. He fears not at any time, who knows the bliss of Brahman."

The former is well indicated in Taittirīya, Śruti, i.e. it is the wine of life, the nectar of the soul, and he becomes suffused with gladness who is filled with it (ii, 7). The psychological consciousness, no doubt, awaits a consummation, but this consummation is still an opening in the fine sensibility and fine shades of being, and not the delight which waits on the transcendental awakening. But this distinction is thin, for bliss or delight is initial expression : being is bliss, and the first contradiction must be the multiplication of bliss. And, therefore, the text reads after two lines : "Who could have breathed, but for this ether of bliss?"

The delight of expression is delight in the widest commonalty in ever fibre of being, manifested and unmanifested. But, even in this wide distribution of bliss, the Upaniṣad conceives higher and lower stages in proportion to the assimilation of wide or restricted bliss in life. Life moves in bliss; and the movement of life is merely rhythmical where bliss is more profound and expansive. Men, nature's gods, the creative deities, cannot enjoy the life of bliss in its completeness. They live by its touch. Their being is confined, naturally they cannot enjoy the rarest privilege of unbounded delight.

The hierarchy of beings is determined by the possibility of more elastic life in bliss. Bliss is life; the more the bliss, the more the life and the greater the privilege. This scheme pervades from the smallest to the highest existence. The Taittirīya and the Bṛhadāraṇyaka bear testimony to the scheme of distribution of bliss in the different grade of being. The higher assimilates the bliss of the lower and contains still more. In this way we reach the highest.

The text runs thus : –

"A hundred human blisses are one bliss of the human Gandharvas (genii) –

also of a man who is versed in the scriptures (śrotiya) and who is not smitten with desire."

"A hundred blisses of the human Gandharvas are one bliss of the divine Gandharvas –

also of a man who is versed in the scriptures and who is not smitten with desire."

"A hundred blisses of the divine Gandharvas are one bliss of the fathers (Pitṛs) in the their long-enduring world –

also of a man who is versed in the scriptures and who is not smitten with desire."

"A hundred blisses of the fathers in their long-enduring world are one bliss of the gods who are born so (ājānaja) –

also of a man who is versed in the scriptures and who is not smitten with desire."

"A hundred blisses of the gods who are born so are one bliss of the gods who are gods by merit (karmadeva) who go to the gods by merit –

also of a man who is versed in the scriptures and who is not smitten with desire."

"A hundred blisses of the gods who are gods by merit are one bliss of the gods –

also of a man who is versed in the scriptures and who is not smitten with desire."

"A hundred blisses of the gods are one bliss of Indra –

also of a man who is versed in the scriptures and who is not smitten with desire."

"A hundred blisses of Indra are one bliss of Bṛhaspati –

also of a man who is versed in the scriptures and who is not smitten with desire."

"A hundred blisses of the Bṛhaspati are one bliss of Prajāpati –

also of a man who is versed in the scriptures and who is not smitten with desire."

"A hundred blisses of Prajāpati are one bliss of Brahmā –

also of a man who is versed in the scriptures and who is not smitten with desire."

In Bṛhadāraṇyaka we have a great teacher's exposition of the hierarchy of bliss : –

" 'If one is forutnte among men and wealthy, lord over others, best provided with all human enjoyments, that is the highest bliss of men. Now, a hundredfold the bliss of men is one bliss of those who have won the fathers' world. Now, a hundredfold the bliss of those who have won the fathers' world is one bliss in the Gandharva-world. A hundredfold the bliss in the Gandharva-world is one bliss of the gods who gain their divinity by meritorious works. A hundredfold the bliss of the gods by works is one bliss of the gods by birth and of him who is learned in the Vedas, who is without crookedness, and who is free from desire. A hundredfold the bliss of the gods by birth is one bliss in the Prajāpati-world and of him who is learned in the Vedas, who is without crookedness, and who is free from desire. A hundredfold the bliss in the Prajāpati-world is one bliss in the Brahmā-world and of him who is learned in the Vedas, who is without crookedness, and who is free from desire. This truly is the highest world. This is the Brahmā-world, O King!' Thus, spoke Yājñavalkya."

Delight of rhythm is to be distinguished from the delight of transcendence. The delight of rhythm is the delight of life, and the whole creation enjoys this kind of delight, it is inherent in its constitution, and none can live without it. Life is delight, for life is rhythm; the more the harmony, the easier the flow of life, and this rhythm does not exist in even proportion everywhere. Where the rhythm is the highest, the delight is the greatest. Life and more life is the prayer that goes out from men and gods, for life is rhythm, and rhythmic existence is felicitous existence. The rhythm of life is cosmic and the cosmic rhythm is distributed amongst individuals according to their capacity and power. Cosmic joy in individual life is, therefore, the reflection of the cosmic rhythm. Where the life's dance is the most intensive and extensive, there the joy is the greatest, and the Taittirīya and the Bṛhadāraṇyaka most probably mean this apportionment of the cosmic rhythm to the gods and men, when they are representing a hierarchy of the beings, men, creative and preservative gods. The delight of the collective men is focussed in the gods, for they feel the greater rhythm of life. The greater the rhythm, the finer and the wider the delight, and the rhythm may be intensive enough to feel the cosmic life in the inward and outward urges.

But the delight of rhythm is essentially the delight of life, it cannot be the delight of expanse; for, however intensive and exclusive the urge may be, it is still limited in its being. It may be life and eternal life, but it is feeling the pulse of life in expression. It has then the limitation of expression. It is lived and enjoyed, it is the delight of life. The delight of being (Ātman) is the delight of an awakening from the urge and rhythm of life. Urge is the index of limitation, it is the sing of concentration. However vast and expansive be its influence, it cannot be the plenum of existence, and as such the Chāndogya truly says that in the expanse of being, no experience is possible of it, no urge is felt in it. This expanse has been called delight by Sanatkumāra. It is an expanse without the oscillation of life, it is an expanse which can be lived but not felt. It is the expanse whence disappear the waves of life, the urges of cosmic consciousness and feeling. It is the expanse of undivided bliss, the bliss of calm and not the bliss of life. The bliss of life is the joy or rhythmic dance which widens our sympathies and enlarges our visions, and can give expression to the finest currents of the soul. And few can stand indifferent to the intoxication of life and welcome the silence beyond. Religious attraction is often the attraction for the subtle delight of life, and the more life is freed from grossness and its restrictions, the more it becomes the source of pure delight. The joys become almost overwhelming when life reveals its unfathomable depths and its finest currents. The more it is enjoyed, the more constant becomes the attraction.

But this intensive attraction of life ceases to be effective in the transcendent calm, when the soul becomes completely freed from its intoxication. The joy of life cannot compare with the dignity of silence. Life has ebb and flow. Calm is life without ripple, without ebb and flow. It is the plenitude of existence.

Spiritual life in academy and parlous is so often identified with the finest dynamism of our being that the calm in spiritual life as distinguished from its rhythm is not seriously taken into consideration, and this probably has been the cause of confounding the silence of spiritual life with emptiness. It is not emptiness, it is the *Pleroma of Eternal Light,* as the Gnostics call it. The urge of life is so insistent and so attractive that the seeker experiences difficulty in passing beyond the urges and appreciating the illumined silence. This pleroma of eternal light is to be distinguished from the radiating effulgence which the seeker feels in the dynamic being when the rhythmic oscillation of life is at its highest. The rhythmic oscillation produces an apparent calmness in the dynamic being and is very often accompanied by an all-pervading transparent orb of light. This orb of light is perpetual in Īśvara, but transient in man; for in the one case the finest dynamism exist in the state of an apparent equilibrium and in the other it is in a state of unstable and disturbed equilibrium. The undisturbed rhythm of life is always associated with the finest transparence of dynamic being and the widest form of expression. A stage, it will be made clear later, is reached where the light shines eternally, undimmed by the veil of ignorance prevalent in man. The former is the genial light of the dynamic divinity, but not the light of silence. The divine light is the orb of light in unbounded space, the light of silence is the light beyond space, limitless space. This is the light of Ātman.

Present-day mysticism seems to be so much appreciative of life and rhythm, probably as the inevitable after-effect of the devitalizing World War, that it cannot rise above the melody and the music of life and welcome the silence beyond the profounder urges and meanings of life. Count Keyserling appraises the value of the basic tones of the melody of life in its eternal process of change. "It is the eternal truth which ensouls all temporal sense-formations just as it is eternal life which animates every life." "The ultimate terminus, undefinable as such, the Logos-side of which I call 'adjustment', is nothing else than Life itself. For it is life which gives its content a meaning." Keyserling has shown sympathetic appreciation of the Indian spirit of rising above "name" and "form" as necessary to the apprehension of truth (p. 194, *Creative Understanding*), and he says (p. 196) : "The East recognizes as a self-evident fact that spiritual light—as is true, ultimately of all life—can only come from a Beyond of the plane of formations," This "Beyond" is the life above all concrete formations.

So, deep is the conviction in life that it is indeed very difficult to raise our vision from the fluidity it promises to the appreciation of the affirmation of the ancients that the Beyond transcends life, transcends formations and expressions. The mystic urge is generally the urge of finer life. The finer the rhythm felt in the dance of life, the greater the attraction felt to life, and the mystic vision has the possibility of being clouded by and fixed upon the dance of life : in fact, it may not get over the conception of life as the basic reality. So great may be the hold of life, that in our aspiration to rise above its concrete expressions in the details of existence, we may read finer values and deeper appreciations into them in reference to their cosmic setting, in their profounder sense-consciousness. We may thus live in the Beyond while holding on still to the immediate.

Almost akin to the appreciation of life, mysticism by another writer has been identified with *the contemplation of value.* "One day life will emerge, and warmed by the Sun of Pure Being, will come to rest in the contemplation of value which the mystics have called the vision of God. ... There are the mystics who achieve in sudden flashes of illumination the vision of the world of value which will one day, if evolution goes aright, be the privilege of all things that are living." "This intimation logically involves, and in practice includes, the conviction that life is purposive, in the sense that it is trying to develop a clearer and fuller apprehension of what is now but imperfectly felt and, for some of us, a recognition of the fact that in the mystic this clearer and fuller apprehension has intermittently been achieved." (C.E.M. Joad, *The Present and Future of Religion,* p. 193.) Joad conceives a spiritual world in addition to the everyday material world : "The latter is the world of struggle, change and imperfection, the former is the world of permanence, perfection and changelessness." Life evolves to a fuller and more continuous knowledge of this world. The mystic world, to Joad, is the world of absolute and permanent values which can be apprehended but cannot be created by us.

Keyserling's vision of the Life Beyond and Joad's vision of the Order of Values as the end of the quest do not fall in with the Upaniṣadic ideal. Neither of them has been able to rise above the basic conception of life, and life in its basic being is associated with permanent values. The vision of a Beyond and a Beyond deep with meaning and expressed in values, is the vision of the causal and the subtle beyond the physical. It is the revelation of the mysteries lying deep behind the division of life on the physical plane, it is continuous with our present experiences which are in effect expressions of them. Joad seems to have been captivated by the fine turns of life in the rarefied consciousness of mystics, and his imagination is struck by the transcendent world of values as offering the blessed contrast, of order, peace, and perfection to the disorder, confusion, and conflict of the divided life.

Be it transcendent life or value, the mystical ideal cannot confine itself to "the identification of the object of mystical experience with the transcendent world of values." The mystic search is after the one, after that beyond which nothing exists, without which nothing exists and that which is the essence of our being, which saves us from the insurgent demands of a restricted itself. The great promise of mysticism is, therefore, this felicity of an emancipation from the inrush of the vital demands of a divided life. The emancipation is certainly different from the values and ideals that lie hidden in life and find expression in the order of finer existence and appreciation in a truer vision. We shall see that the Upaniṣads are alive to the finer order of values and show insight into life beyond, but their finest contribution to mysticism is that they seek to present the ineffable as beyond values, beyond life, the spring of all existence, yet the intangible reality which none can divine, a wonder to gods and men, the bliss of existence.

In the delight of rhythm life enjoys a freedom from the discord inherent in the surge of conflicting impulses. Rhythm gives us delight because it offers a relief and a deliverance from discord and therefore presents the aspect of life which is not usually experienced. No doubt life has in every stage of its expression some degree of rhythm, and discord is possible because we have not life in the fullest. Life is rhythm, and the more we have it the more we enjoy the joy of rhythm.

Be it noted here that the joy of rhythm is more apparent in the cosmic than in the individual life, for in the cosmic being life has its fullest possible expression without the least possible discord. The more rhythmic the dance of life, the more it is freed from the anxieties, hopes, and fears of life. It enjoys the evenness; but this evenness is felt where the oscillation of life is free from the claims of the divided life. It is in a sense a recovery from the battlefield of desires, from the vital and mental urges. It is enjoying the dance inherent in life itself. The freedom from the waves of impulses is a freedom from the desires natural to vital and mental life. This freedom is the enjoyment of the wider life, stimulating and inspiring us in every moment of our existence. Its rhythm is deep, its delight pure, its harmony musical. It is the joy of life which the adept alone can feel.

It appears more delightful only because it secures a relief from the stir and stress of the surface life. It is, as it were, a temporary forgetfulness of the insistent demands connected with our vital existence. The more life converges towards the fulfilment of desire, the more it is restricted to a plane of existence where it cannot feel itself as its highest and enjoy the blessing of a forgetfulness and escape from the limited urges of expression. The higher urge of life has a freedom from this constant tension of a concentrated purpose. Life is enjoyed most in its elasticity, and the more free it is from limited visions, the more is the possibility of enjoying the wider and deeper currents of the soul.

The finer appreciation of life, therefore, always requires the greater freedom from its limited urges. This truth is seen by Joad. He sees in æsthetic experience a freedom and release from the constant urges of life and a momentary forgetfulness of life's claims and interests. Joad says : "We who are part and parcel of the evolutionary stream stand for the time outside and above the stream, and are permitted for a moment to be withdrawn from the thrust and play of impulse and desire ... for so long as we enjoy the vision of the end, life leads us alone. We feel neither need nor want, and losing ourselves in contemplation of the reality beyond us we become for the moment selfless." Joad has almost the true appreciation of the mystic consciousness as chiefly self-forgetfulness. In other words, it implies transcendence over the surface ripple of life, but he seems not to be quite alive to the delight of silence. The finer rhythm may give us release for the persistent claims and counter-claims of desires, life may be tasted with its full cup of delight in its serene melody and absorbing harmony. The riotous claims mav be hushed in the silence where the original music of life may enrapture the soul and flashes of light may overcome it with the rich experience of the sublimities and beauties of the cosmic life. The strength and vigour of the cosmic self may stir our being to its very depth. Still such a mystic consciousness has not the full expression and unique presentation of the transcendent. The forgetfulness of our confined experience and the enjoyment of the dance of cosmic life meet us on the patheway to the realization of the silence of the Beyond, but they should not be confounded with the true appreciation of the mystic consummation. The order of aesthetic beauty and moral value with their possibilities is not to be compared to the delight of silence. A persistent demand there is to rise from the discords into the harmony of life, but this music of life is not the ultimate in the mystic exaltation. The Upaniṣadic seers have the final appreciation of the calm beyond the waves of life, of the great Beyond in which silence reigns supreme. It is, indeed, a terrible experience for those who are anxious to enjoy the dance to life and who have not the boldness to go further. The mystic silence is a unqiue experience beyond all description in the terms of concrete experience. Life here is hushed into silence, experience vanishes into nothing, the dream of life for every dwindles away, the cosmic dance comes to a close, the joy of fellowship in an eternal fraternity evaporates for ever. Life is awakened from the fatal division which for every binds it. Silence reigns supreme. The final delight is this delight of Silence. Gods, archangels, angels, and men do not know it; knowing it, they cannot exist. It is the eternal wonder, the everlasting Yea behind all existence, the either of consciousness, the eternal background, the ever-present. Now, the stay of all, but the ever inaccessible, the ever impenetrable, the eternal mystery that always attracts but always eludes our grasp.

Chapter IV

The Delight Supernal

When the realistic consciousness evaporates in the height of ecstasy the adept begins to feel the all-pervasiveness of delight. Existence is felt to be nothing but delight; delight fills the finner being, delight permeates the outer being; the small and the great present alike delight in full. The sense of gradation and hierarchy of delight no longer persists, for in the inmost being delight is spread in its widest commonalty and utmost expansion. In this height of realizaiton the full is presented in equal magnitude in the tiniest as well as in the largest of objects. In reality it has no magnitude and, therefore, it is possible for it to permeate the essence of all things in its entirety. This appears strange; but this is the fact, this is the truth. Division, magnitude, proportion are terms compatible with finite existence, they cannot be compatible with the Absolute. The Absolute is, therefore, present in its fullness everywhere and in every form of existence, great or small.

If this is true of being, it is equally true of delight. Delight is great or small so long as it is infite delight, so long as it is human delight; but delight as the essence of our being is everywhere the same. To know this is the highest wisdom, to feel this is to rise above the joys of the flesh and the joys of the heart. With proper training and discipline the adept soon learns to feel the joy which knows no bounds and the delight which has neither ebb nor flow. Everywhere it is felt the same, because it is in itself beyond the Ken of distribution and limitation. We have a coprehensive description of the ecstatic vision of delight in the Bṛhadāraṇyaka Upaniṣad (Ch. II, 5th Brāhmaṇa) :

"This earth is honey for all creatures, and all creatures are honey for this earth.

This shining, immortal Person who is in this earth, and, with reference to oneself, thus shining, immortal Person who is in the body –

he, indeed, is just this Soul (Ātman), this Immortal, this Brahma, this All.'

"These waters are honey for all things, and all things are honey for these waters.

This shining, immortal Person who is in these waters, and, with reference to oneself, this shining, immortal Person who is made of semen –

he, is just this Soul, this Immortal, this Brahma, this All."

"This fire is honey for all things, and all things are honey for this fire.

This shining, immortal Person who is in this fire, and, with reference to oneself, this shining, immortal Person who is made of speech –

he, is just this Soul, this Immortal, this Brahma, this All."

"This wind is honey for all things, and all things are honey for this wind.

This shining, immortal Person who is in this wind and, with reference to oneself, this shining, immortal Person who is breath –

he, is just this Soul, this Immortal, this Brahma, this All."

"This sun is honey for all things and all things are honey for this sun.

This shining, immortal Person who is in this sun, and, with reference to oneself, this shining immortal Person who is in the eye –

he, is just this Soul, this Immortal, this Brahma, this All."

"These quarters of heaven are honey for all things, and all things are honey for these quarters of heaven.

This shining, immortal Person who is in these quarters of heaven, and, with reference to oneself, this shining, immortal Person who is in the echo –

he, is just this Soul, this Immortal, this Brahma, this All."

"This moon is honey for all things, and all things are honey for this moon.

This shining, immortal Person who is in this moon, and, with reference to oneself, this shining, immortal Person consiting of mind –

he, is just this Soul, this Immortal, this Brahma, this All."

"This lightning is honey for all things, and all things are honey for this lightning.

This shining, immortal Person who is in this lightning, and, with reference to oneself, this shining, immortal Person who exists as heat –

he, is just this Soul, this Immortal, this Brahma, this All."

"This thunder is honey for all things, and all things are honey for this thunder.

This shining, immortal Person who is in thunder, and, with reference to oneself, this shining, immortal Person who is in sound and in tone –

he is just this Soul, this Immortal, this Brahma, this All."

"This space is honey for all things, and all things are honey for this space.

This shining, immortal Person who is in this space, and, with reference to oneself, this shining, immortal Person who is in the space in the heart –

he is just this Soul, this Immortal, this Brahma, this All."

"This Law (Dharma) is honey for all things, and all things are honey for this Law.

This shining, immortal Person who is in this Law, and, with reference to oneself, this shining, immortal Person who exists as virtuousness –

he is just this Soul, this Immortal, this Brahma, this All."

"This Truth is honey for all things, and all things are honey for this Truth.

This shining, immortal Person who is in this Truth, and, with reference to oneself, this shining, immortal Person who exists as truthfulness –

he is just this Soul, this Immortal, this Brahma, this All."

"This mankind (mānuṣa) is honey for all things, and all things are honey for this mankind.

This shining, immortal Person who is in this mankind, and, with reference to oneself, this shining, immortal Person who exists as a man –

he is just this Soul, this Immortal, this Brahma, this All."

"This Soul (Ātman) is honey for all things, and all things are honey for this Soul.

This shining, immortal Person who is in this Soul, and, with reference to oneself, this shining, immortal Person who exists as Soul –

he is just this Soul, this Immortal, this Brahma, this All."

"Verily, this Soul is the overload of all things, the king of all things.

As all the spokes are held together in the hub and felly of a wheel, just so in this Soul all things, all gods, all worlds, all breathing things, all selves are held together."

(Hume's translation)

This delight cannot be the pragmatic satisfaction on confined vision. It is the subtlest of existence. It is in everything that meets our senses. It is in us, it is out of us. The Bṛhadāraṇyaka goes on to tell that the same which is in the stars, the sun, the moon, the lightning, the air, and the ether is also in us. No difference exists, no difference can exist. The heart of things and beings is filled with the integral being and, because of this, the eternal sympathy is felt everywhere the same, everything brings the message of joy to everything. Beyond the apparent differences which create jarring discord on the surface of existence, lies the unbounded bliss present everywhere in its absoluteness. This joyousness is perceived in self as well as in others. Everything appears as delight to everything, and a serene peace, security, and freshness is felt everywhere. The spirit which is our essence and which we feel in its nakedness with the disappearance of all pseudo-truths of pragmatic consciousness, at once sets up a feeling and a delight untasted before. The freedom from all forms of restriction is decidedly a new and unique experience; and this freedom of unrestricted being gives us a feeling which sees no pain of division of separation anywehre and can embrace everything as the carrier of the delightful intimation of immortal bliss.

The texts apparently draw a distinction between the delight spread out in nature and the delight felt in the soul, but they dispel this distinction when they clearly lay down that the delight felt in the inward being as well as that perceived in outward existence are identical. The one is not the shadow of the other. The one does not originate or stimulate the other. The division dissolves in the height of consciousness, where the highest freedom and the greatest delight are felt. The least sense of difference which can make the one the recipient of the other, which can make them categorically different as the enjoyer and the enjoyed, is set aside. Everything is perceived and the psychical dissolves in the perception of the identity of bliss running through the inward and outward existence.

Such is the perception where the realistic existence becomes etherealized and idealized in ecstatic vision. The apparent division between the inward (adhyātma) and the outward (adhibhūta) existence cannot obtain here, for the same truth is perceived, the same delight is felt in both.

The idealized vision has two stages. In the beginning it is of the commonalty of delight, in the end it is the intuition of Ātman, the essence of delight. The abstraction becomes complete in the second stage where the least distinction between the inner and the outer is displaced by the finer perception of the distinctionless Ātman.

The initial perception of the all-pervasiveness of delight is never dissociated from self, though its reference to it is not present in the earlier texts. A finer vision must be developed before it can see the delight of all existence to be the delight of self. The mystic vision and realization in its inception and birth cannot reach the high level of the intuition of the self. It reaches the acme of realization by stages of refinement. The conscious reference to delight to self and the perception of them are, therefore, a distinct advance in realization and a unique presentation of delight *in excelsis,* for it is the feeling no longer of delight immanent in the outward existence or inward self, but it is the sense of the self being the delight-in-itself. The reference to the self identified with delight makes the vision of the transcendent; it is no longer and finer feeling of blessedness which the soul feels and the heart enjoys. It is the blessedness beyond feeling. It is beyond appreciation. The soul is identified with it. When one has a foretaste of this blessedness, one ventures to proceed beyond the delight felt in the inward being and the outward existence.

But this transcendent bliss of Ātman cannot come at once.

The intimation of Ātman as the lord of all creatures (adhipati), the king of all beings, precedes the transcendent vision; the inner and the outer existence are synthesized in it – "the devas, the men, the prāṇas, all are consecrated to Ātman."

This vision has a necessity inasmuch as it displaces the idea of a confined self by the conception of an all-inclusive one free to project the whole universe out of itself. The restricted vision of the empiric and the pragmatic self has no place here. Though the self has not been realized in transcendence, yet it is felt to be the thread, the support of the whole existence.

This reference of the cosmic existence to self has a deep meaning. It brings out its expansive nature and inspires mystic vision. It elevates our conception of the soul from its mistaken identity with its internal psychoses to the level of a supramental existence, enlivening the finite centres of consciousness as well as the cosmic deities and at the same time feeling within it its own transcendence over them. The delight of such an existence is also transcendent. It has a uniqueness of its own, being different from the delight of the finite centres of existence. It is the delight of the whole reflected in the centre.

But this delight of the whole is to be distinguished from the delight transcendent. The former has a reference and a concentration, the latter has none. The delight of the former is, therefore, the delight of unrestricted movement, life, and freedom. It is the delight of all-comprehensive knowledge and overpowering being. The delight of the latters is the delight of stillness. It is the delight which latter is the delight of stillness. It is the delight which cannot be felt, it cannot be tasted. It can be lived.[1]

Yājñavalkya taught his wife the gospel of Self as delight when he was about to retire into the life of contemplation and absorption. His reason is simple. His appeal is deep. Nothing is dear to us which is external to us. Everything is dear to us by its reference to self. The human relations, the external possessions, the culture in Vedic lore become our joy when they become ours, when they are related to the self. The touch of "I" enlivens all. They are mere existences by themselves. They are sources of delight by this reference to self. This delight is borrowed delight. That which by its touch makes life easy, existence happy, and all things attractive and felicitous is necessarily the highest beatitude. This beatitude is Self. It is the supreme puissance.

Yājñavalkya is above the usual notion and fatal mistake that delight is consequent upon eccentric relations and projections of Self. His vision is precisely the opposite. Delight awaits the penetration into the centre of being. The more centralized becomes our vision, the more beatific becomes our normal experience, since every element of experience is seen in reference to the self. The reference to self grafts upon relations and experiences not only a meaning but also an attraction. This can prove that the self is in essence delight. The more rarefied the consciousness and the more inward the penetration, the more is the experience of delight. This is a sure proof and testimony that the self is delight.

Sanat-kumāra in the Chāndogya Upaniṣad reiterates the same truth. Expanse is delight. The more life rises above the sense of divisoin and the restrictions of relativity, the more it enjoys delight. Delight is, therefore, the invariable accompaniment of free being, and complete freedom is possible only in unbounded existence. The Chāndogya defines Bhumā as installed in and identified with silence where one sees nothing else, hears nothing else, understands nothing else. This silence is the Plenum of Existence. This plenum is established in its own greatness. This plenum is below. It is above. It is to the east. It is to the south. It is to the north. It is all. The Bhumā is self. The Chāndogya tells us further. The soul is below. The soul is above. The soul is to the east, etc. Verily he who sees this, who thinks this, who understands this, who has delight in the soul, who has intercourse with the soul, who has bliss in the soul, he is autonomous, he moves in all the worlds freely.

The Chāndogya makes clear and explicit the reference of the delight to self, and its freedom from all limitations. The autonomy of the self is complete. It is the conquest not over urges, but over life and its limitations. Indeed, Svarāja is a unique experience. It is the complete awakening from the falsity of division and concentration. It is the freedom of aloneness of the self, which nothing can defile. It is the freedom from the instinctive error of pursuing the truth out of self. This freedom gives silence to the quest, for the light of the self removes the darkness and dispels ignorance.

The word *Bhumā* needs a little explanation. The sense and the joy of expanse is the common promise of mysticism. And, whenever life has freedom from limitation, it has the taste of a new delight of expanse, of an oceanic existence. The joy of unrestricted existence with the consciousness of greater elasticity of being is the attraction of mystic life, and all forms of mysticism afford such joy and such elasticity. But, even when enjoying elasticity and freedom, the soul may not have complete freedom. The touch of the little self may still linger, preventing it from the traceless plunge in the deep. The soul may be in tune with the infinite life, it may be life in its endless vistas and perspectives, but still it may not realize the acme of realization in the Calm. The Upaniṣads undoubtedly enhance this aspect of mysticism. They notice the unfailing power and vision that invariably accompany mystic realization, but these are sidelights in comparison with the ideal on which they insist.

Bhumā, then, is not the feeling of expanse which is often the common experience in a mystic life. It is not the synthetic vision of reality comprising within it the details of existence in a dynamical symmetry. Such a vision may be a passing phase on the way to realization, but it is not the finale of it. In the teachings of Sanat-kumāra and Yājñavalkya, Bhumā has the clear sense of transcendent vastness and aloneness. The common idea of a magnitude – and unbounded magnitude – of Bhumā is the idea of an all-inclusive being, but this meaning is rejected in favour of a transcendent oneness in which there is not the least sense of distinction and difference. It is the basic being, beyond perception, beyond understanding. It is the abyss of mystic life, the seeker and the sought vanish alike in the identity of existence. This experience is unique. Certainly it is different from the vision of the synthetic unity of the Infinite. The infinite thread of existence is realized in its finer and finer essence, with greater and deeper penetration. This thread runs through the cosmic existence as the principle of unity, but this form of mystical penetration is surely different from the consciousness whence drops the thread of existence, whence vanish the waves of life in their highest amplitude and greatest magnitude.

This experience is not the experience of vastness as ordinarily understood. It is vast in the sense of the disappearance of the subject-object experience which characterizes all finite knowledge. The empirical sense of vastness is not free from the subject-object reference of knowledge. This super-sensuous consciousness is not always free from this reference, though it may be free from the sense-connection. When knowledge becomes completely free from the subject-object reference, it attains the consummation. Consciousness and being are fully identical here. Their mutual reference and relativity which characterize the mental and supramental activities, are fully absent here. And, therefore, this intuition is unique. Its promise is also unique.

Reference

1. Śaṅkara's interpretation of the texts may appear different, but it is not exactly different. Śaṅkara explains the text in the light of cosmology. Still he seems to be quite alive to the mutual

dependence of the finite existences. This mutual dependence speaks of their unity in the ultimate existence. See Śaṅkara-Bhāṣya, Bṛhadāraṇyaka Upaniṣad : *Madhu* has been used by Śaṅkara in the sense of an effect. But since the effect is one with the cause, the essence of being, therefore, permeates it. Hence, the word *Madhu* would convey a better sense, especially from the mystic standpoint, if it is taken in the sense of delight. Whatever the cosmology may be, there can be no doubt that the mystic vision sees the spirit immanent in the world of appearnace, for the great claim of mysticism is the immediate vision of truth here and now. And, therefore, to the mystic the world of effects has a meaning different from the one presented to the laity. If delight is the essence of being, this delight is in the appearance, and, therefore, it cannot be far from truth if the texts are interpreted as representing the mystic vision of delight immanent in the heart of things.

Chapter V

Truth and Value

An interesting comparison suggests itself. The scientific cosmology of the day has an approach to the Upaniṣadic truth. Professor Alexander has conceived the growth of the world out of space, time, and energy, and has borrowed from science the indissolubility of space and time. Time enfolds space and the primal energy plays in the eternal space-time order generating out of it the finer forces of life and spirit. Evolution begins with the cosmic dance of energy in the silence of illimitable space and the three are the basic elements of reality. It is the space-time-energy entity. The complexity of the fabric of being arises as evolution proceeds. And the higher the ascent in evolution, the more complex is the emergent in evolution. Life is its cosmic dance loses its original simplicity and acquires in the process of emergent evolution a growing complexity and multiplicity. This dance has as it were a periodicity, and the drama is not played all the time with equal intensity. A forward push is succeeded by a temporary inertia. Life appears first on the scene. Matter is ruled out of order. It gives place to energy. When the play of the vital forces becomes too complex, the signal for the next higher emergence is hoisted. A greater integration and a higher unity in the form of mind with its light of intelligence appears in the surrounding gloom. The primal darkness is dispelled and the illumination of consciousness is hailed as the welcome guest. Evolution cannot stop with the mind which can illumine a centre but not all centres. In the corner of this consciousness is felt the jostling of a wider life and, eventually, we reach the next higher stage in the onward march of life, the social mind and the Deity meeting the higher instincts of morality and religion. Professor Alexander conceives a scheme of cosmology from space and time. God is the last element in the evolution. Religious consciousness is its first blossoming in man. The more complex the integration, the higher the unity. God is the highest unity because he is last in the evolution.

Professor Alexander is inspired by the noble instinct of establishing a synthesis between science and religion, between reality and value. And his intuition is correct when he confines himself to the world of concrete realiteis. Science is confined to reality and facts; religion, essentially to values. He, therefore, conceives a scheme of thought in which value has its place and recognition with reality. Behind the order of values lies the bare reality of space, time, and casuality, and the realm of value has a unique quality, not to be found in the basic reality, though it comes in the order of posteriority. But this does not take away from it the truth of the values, for they present an experience not to be found in the basic elements. God may not be the Absolute of philosophy, but still in the sphere of values, which is the province of religion, it is the highest concept.

Professor Alexander has shown much ingenuity in setting up a religious system in empirical metaphysics. But it is difficult to reconcile the order of values with his Absolute, and more so to derive the one from the other. The order of values necessarily is concrete and, therefore, may have full expression where self-consciousness has its full play of creativeness. Value and creativeness go together, and, where the dynamic conception of the self is not at its highest growth and development, art and religion have not their finest expression. The Upaniṣads confine religious values to the realm of the concrete expression of spirit, but even here the emphasis has been laid upon the finer and, subtler play of life and consciousness yielding a wider range of intuition and higher intensity of activity. The values, however fine and sublte, are actualities in the restricted life of creative expression. They have no reality in the realm beyond expression.

This realm of truth is the realm of fact. But whereas to Alexander the realm of absolute fact has no reference to consciousness, but is the province of unilluminating space and its indissoluble companin, unending time, to the teachers of the Upaniṣads the realm of the absolute fact is ever shining in the native light of intelligence. The universe is more illumined in the centre than at the circumference, for the silent light of the centre is not equally reflected at the outskirts of existence. Life in the centre is more serene, free and easy, for it is undivided and integral there and is not agitated by the surface waves. The order of space and time is the structural frame of life in expression, they are the forms of the immanent consciousness, and cannot claim the absoluteness which Alexander ascribes to them. They may be intimately related to the Absolute, but to install them in the place of the Absolute is more than reason and intuition can accept. The Upaniṣads have confined religious life in the concrete sense of the world of appearance, and though they have laid down a course of fine evolution in spirituality and freedom and an introduction into the finer orders of appearances and absorbing values, still they are clear that the finest intuition surpasses these experiences and reveals the transcendent truth beyond space and time.

The supramental vision makes us acquainted with the Absolute of Alexander's philosophy, for its very existence cannot be known unto itself. Alexander makes the dawn of the universe surrounded by an impenetrable gloom, the Upaniṣads see the dawn in the kindly light-rays that tarry not. When, therefore, the concrete religious life is sacrificed for this majesty of Silence, surely the seeker does not pass into the inconvenient and undesirable existence which the gods forsake and men avoid.

On the other hand, those who have once tasted it fervently desire it as a state of unique blessedness inasmuch as it frees us from the pangs of a divided consciousness. Life may grow in complexity in the course of evolution, but this complexity is the sign of finiteness and imperfection, for complexity is invariably associated with other-reference and other-dependence. The highest existence is the simplest. It denies all externality and all reference. And, therefore, the tendency to seek spiritual life in its fullest expression in the ever-growing complexity of life is to lose it. The Upaniṣadic teachers are quite alive to this truth, and, therefore, their quest after the eternal life does not begin with the world affecting the surface life and surface existence, but in the finer currents lying deep beneath and surface. Even the finer order of values cannot be the last in evolution, it must have been working since long from within. The gross cannot give rise to the fine. It is rather the arrested expression of the fine. The sudden emergence of the fine cannot be accepted as a reasonable conclusion. The occasional expression in the order of reality, it only proves that the fine can have rare expression. Evolution of the higher values does not mean that the higher develop out of the lower. It implies that the higher are at the heart of things and can express themselves under fit and proper circumstances. The law of continuity is never broken in expression, and it is easier to believe in the archetypes of existence than to accept the sudden emergence of the higher concepts of existence and value from the lower. The Upaniṣads teach that the deeper we penetrate into existence, the wider and finer it is, and it presents realms of archetypes which are always complete and perfect. The external is shaped according to the internal plan and harmony, –it is always regulated and moulded according to it. The eternal values are always present at the heart of things, shaping things and beings according to the eternal purpose, and they cannot be conceived as coming into being at a period of world's history. The perception of the eternal world of values, therefore, requires a deeper intuition into the finer planes of existence. The order of values is an order in space and time. It is an order in which our ideals are fully realized and we become free from the dualities of the gross life. And the ideal is more real. In the finer intuitions we realize them in their purity and in their transcendence. They are not here mixed with their opposites and their limitations. Life is, therefore, more serene and smooth, intuition more expressive.

The realm of values becomes more evident as we rise above the sense-mentality and dive deep into the silent waters of life. But the values cannot find a place beyond the supramental plane of existence. Their right place is the supermind, they can have no existence in the transcendent reality. They are essentially creative forces, and they can be true on the creative plane. And naturally they suffer the restrictions natural to creativeness. They are dynamic. They mould the initial force. The highest values that we prize and realize in our own creativeness are dim reflections of the eternal values of the ideal world. And, therefore, in the moments of happy visitation of the land of wonders hidden in the bosom of creation, we are overpowered by its symmetry, its orchestral harmony, its creative accuracy, and the vastness of its being. Religious consciousness cannot rise above this form of revelation, and so absorbing is the realization that the seeker who has attained this height does not feel the impulse to see beyond. And it is the common experience of mystic life to be enchanted by the richness and the music of this high level of consciousness and life and to mistake it for the final intuition of religious life. Indeed, it is the final realization in the personal consciousness, and unless the seeker is bold enough to lose the personal hold of life and to forsake its experinces of rapturous delight, access cannot be gained into the sublime calm which resides at the centre. The intuition of the Calm is the final illumination of reality, beyond expression, beyond the space and time of empirical metaphysics.

The religious life is an expression not beyond space and time of the supramental vision, though it is continuous with the supramental life. It has, therefore, the intimation of immortality. It is not limited by the empirical time series. The Upaniṣads perceived the value of the religious ideal, and, therefoe, have laid down a path for the aspirant to this ideal; but this ideal has not been insisted upon as the final pursuit after the transcendental truth. Immortality as immortality in time is the invariable consequence that follows the path of light, the path of Devayāna, which allows access into the realm of light. It is still the personal immortality but it is not the immortality that follows upon the realization of the timeless Absolute. So long as personality clings to the soul, the world of values has a meaning and a deep one, but when it finally dissolves into the absolute background, the importance of value disappears. Value, therefore, is not a higher category of existence than truth. It may appear as presenting an aspect of existence not covered by truth. But it is so covered when the different phases of existence are emphasized in the relative thinking. It cannot be true when the aspects of existence are lost in the Absolute.

The Upaniṣads have prized truth more than value, for value has always a concrete reference, and truth has no such refernce. When, therefore, the Upaniṣads welcome delight as the highest promise, they hail it not as a feeling-consciousness, but as a freedom from limitations and restricted urges of life. It is freedom from concentration. Truth does not imply concentration. Value does. Truth is, therefore, a unique presentation. Nothing of the relative and empriical consciousness can compare to it. The delight of value is essentially personal, the delight of truth is impersonal, – it is the delight of the evenness of existence at the centre of reality and not the delight of the creative order arranged in a hierarchy in order of the fineness and expressiveness of manifested being.

Chapter VI

The Immanent and the Transcendent

Yājñavalkya has emphasized the immanence and the transcendence of Ātman. Ātman is in all things. It is out of everything. Such contrariety occurs in almost all places of the Upaniṣads. The Chāndogya says : "This Ātman of mine within the heart is smaller than the grain of rice, or a barley-corn, or a mustard-seed, or a grain of millet, or the kernel of a grain of millet. The soul of mine within the heart is greater than the earth, greater than the atmosphere, greater than the sky, greater than these worlds." Then again; "His greatness is of such extent; yet Puruṣa is greate. still, all beings are one-fourth of Him, three-fourths, the immortal in the sky." And again attributes are ascribed to the Absolute and also denied of it.

This apparent contrariety is necessary to indicate its true nature. The vision of immanence has a deep meaning. It is helpful to the understanding of the permeation of Ātman throughout the whole existence. It establishes the allness of Ātman. It is in the everything in its fullness, for it allows of no divison in it. The intuition of transcendence is not possible at once. The world of appearance strikes our imagination as the reality scattered in space, and naturally the summary rejection of the appearance would perplex the native wit. A better and natural appeal lies through that which meets in us and out of us, for they carry to us intimations of reality. Yājñavalkya, therefore, seems anxious to point out the eternal presence of Ātman in everything before he can teach its transcendence.

A direct appeal to transcendence might have suggested a form of dualism and a complete division between the world of appearance and reality. To avoid this he appeals to our ordinary experience to read the ultimate reality in everything. Thus in answer to Cākrāyana, he said : "Brahman is your soul, and it is in all things." This was not clear to Cākrayana; he, therefore, again asked : "Which one, O Yājñavalkya, is in all things?" Yājñavalkya answered : "He who breathes in with your breathing, is the soul of yours, which is in all things." Proceeding further Yājñavalkya said : "He is in your soul, which is in all things." Again, in reply to Gārgī, Yājñavalkya said that the ethereal expanse which supports the whole existence is supported in Brahman, the nameless, the formles, the measureless.

Transcendence in the true sense of the term can be clear when nothing can remain outside its reference. The reference of all things to Self or Ātman has an important significance for the aspirant to the highest realization. This becomes apparent when an intellectual understanding is sought to be confirmed by the deeper illumination of the spirit. Spiritual illumination in immanent life has a significance which is not always clearly realized. It gives an elasticity of being and allows the all-pervasive nature of Ātman. This has a meaning for the seeker whose vision at first is naturally narrow and confined. This indeed cannot be the final stage in realization, for the finer the intuition grows, the more the perspective of truth changes. This growth of vision and change of the truth-concept are actualities in the life of realization. The mystic life, therefore, contains in itself infinite shades of realization which are progressively true, though the truth of the higher planes may deny the lower forms of truth. The lower form is necessary to lead to the higher and to prepare us for the reception of the higher presentation of reality; but when the higher is presented, the lower cannot retain its existence, for the higher and the lower are not two realities, – they are the presentation of the same reality in different forms. The reality is an undivided whole, and in its presentation it is always complete, though this completeness has not always the same kind of perception. And, therefore, in the gradual ascent of the soul the conception of Ātman as the allpervading reality has importance is not always recognized, and, therefore, the reference of the whole creation to Ātman and the spiritual intuition of Ātman seems to be a superfluity.

But it is not a superfluity. It is an important advance in the life of the seeker. The seeker realizes the highest stretch of being in the expanded vision of supersensuous consciousness. But this supersensuous consciousness is still a play of consciousness in the relative order. Its perceptions are subtle. Its range is comprehensive. It is free from the limitations of finiteness. It has an all-expansive radiation. It finds the entire existence brimming over with the one life. When the perceptions have grown so subtle, it becomes easier for the adept to overcome the limitations of this consciousness and be fully aware of the truth and value of transcendence.

The supramental sense reveals to us the Ātman in the centre of existence as that in which moves the world of space and time, not as something different from it, but as its manifestation. The timeless Ātman holds its eternal truth of being beyond this manifestation. The vision of a totality of existence is a vision that unfailingly meets the seeker on the path, and it is not often understood by those that see life through the limitations of the realistic logic. The mind trained in the realistic logic cannot appreciate the extreme mobility of spiritual consciousness and the different layers of our mental being. The supramental vision, therefore, overcomes the limitations of realistic bent and assent of the soul, and manifests the Ātman as freed from the burden of sheaths and in its spontaneity as a free creative agent. Nay, the vision may proceed so far as to demonstrate the complete control of it over everything in existence, including the cosmic creative agents, the shining forces of nature. Its existence is not confined to the world of manifestation. It bounds the earth, it embraces the heaven. The realistic mind cannot rise to the height of apprehending the reality beyond the sense of division, and, therefore, the truth of the reality as presented in the Upaniṣads appears as a set of contradictions. With the active functioning of the supra-mental sense the wonders in intellectual and spiritual life begin to happen. That which appears as distant now appears as near, the small as great, the mortal as immortal.

The great advantage of this supramental functioning in man is that it opens an infinite range of perception, and the world of knowledge remains no longer confined to the senses. This freedom from the senses at once reveals a range of perspective too wide to be fully grapsed. The restrictions of space and time no longer hold. The external sense of space is displaced by its internal sense. In fact the division of inner and outer space gives way to the integral and undivided plenum of existence. The soul rises to the unbounded perception of the totality of existence in the one single unit of eternal space. Nothing restricts its vision. This internal sense of space does not in any way establish its subjectivity. The subjectivity and the objectivity of space are distinctions true to the divided consciousness of the finite being and have no real meaning for the undivided and all-embracive perception of the supramental vision. To it the whole existence is an appearance in the spatial and the temporal orders and nothing can remain hidden in yonder space and distant time. The supramental intuition is in a way, therefore, transcendent vision in the sense of a simultaneous perception of the whole existence. The mental vision of things takes place in the physical space. We may also call it the empirical space. The vision of space as a plenum of existence, undivided and integral, is not possible in the finite consciousness. It is possible in the supramental plane. Space-perception is here completely independent of the external reference and appears as a form of the supermind. This perception is the true realization of the ideality of space, and the intuition of the supermind does not suffer the restrictions of the finite sense-perceptions. The supramental vision is necessarily the vision of the totality in the eternal complexity and diversity in the plane of physical expression, but in the finer planes of existence the supramental vision gives the clear sense of the movement of self-expression in the subtler and the finer forms. Nay, in the supramental vision all perceptions are simultaneous, for they are focussed at the point of consciousness. The very ideality of space makes the perception of all things and beings possible. It also raises the conception of the Self from the figment of being to the all-pervasive transcendent being. And a new range of intuitions and freedom is the immediate experience. The supramental space-perception by presenting the integral experience at once elevates the conception of Ātman. It gives the subtler conception of the Self as finer than space. It gives the truth that Ātman is the finest and the greatest of existence. The distinction of the experientalist and the experience is not there. The whole existence is focussed in the dimensionless Ātman. Strictly speaking, knowledge is possible there without the implication of a process. The Chāndogya feels it and says that the Brahma-loka always shines in its own splendour. The dualities of life and the logical intellect cannot obtain there, and, therefore, the text truly says that nothing of this side of existence can be there – this Brahma-loka cannot be infected either with pleasure or pain, merit or demerit, old age, birth or death.

But even in this height of existence there is a difference in intuition or superconscious vision. The intuition at this stage is still all-pervasive. It reveals every point of existence. Though it does not suffer the limitations and the relativity of the subject-object reference, still it is not freed from the content of the self, – the spatial and the temporal. The order is presented as a whole to the supermind, and that in a way not involving the ordinary relativity of knowledge; for, even at this height of intuition, the character of knowledge is changed from outward reference to inward vision. And this vision is, therefore, unique. It is self-expression in the ideal forms of space and time, and, therefore, the immediate intuition of the totality must be a form of knowledge different from the ordinary perception. The superconscious perception attains the final stage when the reference to the ideal forms and contents is transcended in the spaceless Absolute. Here the supramental vision passes into transcendental intuition. The former has still the limitation of a reference to self-expression in the ideal forms of space and time, the latter has no such reference. This transition of knowledge from the all-inclusive experience to complete transcencence is well indicated by Yājñavalkya, when he passes from the positive qualification of Ātman as all-knowing and all-seeing to its indication in negative terms. The final intuition cannot in the least be described, for it is different not only from the ordinary perception, but also from the supramental perception. And, therefore, the real meaning of this height of existence is indicated by Silence.

The Absolute has no reference to a content, real or ideal, and the absolute intuition is, therefore, a form of knowledge quite unique, in so far as it transcends all reference to relativity of the mental or supramental vision. The supramental vision changes the conception of time from a series of succession to a continuous whole. The distinctions of the present, the past, and the future do not obtain there, for the supramental vision allows no gap in the perception of time. The empiric time-sense cannot trace the continuity running through the past, the present, and the future and thus reveals time in continuous succession. Time is, therefore, a bar to its restricted vision. The supramental vision transcends the realistic divisions of time into past, present, and future by an intuition native to it; it rises to the understanding or the perception of time as an undivded continuity. The past is revealed with the present, and the present with the future. When such a consummation is reached, the empiric time sense to whcih the past is for even passed and the future is for ever secured, is felt to be an illusion and a restriction of the realistic consciousness. The illusory division of time really makes its true understanding impossible for us, for whatever time may be, it glides on for ever. Our perception of time is, therefore, defective, and, truly speaking, we do not perceive time, but infer its concept from the series of events in succession. The supramental vision of time reflects the present, the past, and the future at the same moment. The distinctions are for ever removed. They are realized to be the accidental divisions of eternity and conventional measurements of time. This form of time has the virtue of presenting the events simultaneously before the super-conscious vision. The vision presents the totality at a stretch, in fact the past and the future are lost in the ever-present. The past and the future are relative to the finite and empiric consciousness; in the supramental sense the empirical has no significance, and, therefore, there is no distinction between the past and the future.

Time in the sense of eternal duration is apprehended in a single act of intuition. The sense of division is not inherent in it and the flow of events appears uninterrupted and unbroken to it. The sense of division and multiplication of events is the perception of the surface mind. But this supramental perception of time is rare in finite souls. It is impossbile to them unless they can develop in themselves the transcendental time sense. Even the saints and the sages who are credited with the capacity of the triple time sense, cannot claim this rare possession every moment of their lives. In their psychical being they may feel occasional presentation of cosmic events otherwise inaccessible, but they cannot claim that gift which can make them constant percipients of the eternal duration. The sectional presentation of duration is all that is possible to the most highly receptive souls. Even the creative and the protective gods and the presiding deities have limited vision of time – their time sense and vision may be more durable than that in the possession of man, still they have also the sectional presentation of time and beyond this they cannot command the perspective of eternal duration. Their time sense does not differ fundamentally from man's. Though their perception of time may be more extensive. Though their perception of time may be more extensive, fitted as they are with better and more powerful organs of perception, still they can hardly have the intuition of eternal duration. They are active in the causal order where the conception of time has been associated with the causal nexus. The causal order presents the functioning of events in the eternal loom of time, and naturally surface vision may identify time with the succession of events. The eternal time sense cannot, therefore, be present to the intelligence accustomed to this habit of thought, and especially to those whose intellect sees only the sections and cross-sections of experience.

But in the intellectual intuition duration is presented in its unbroken continuity and is not limited by the sectional presentation of becoming. In this height of existence the vision of the becoming is integral and transcends the causal order of the creative and the preservative plane and the divisions natural to it. This intuition, therefore, differentiates this conception of the totality of consciousness from that of the deities, nay, even from that of Īśvara in his triple aspects of the creative, preservative, and destructive being.

This intuitive vision of eternal duration is the vision of becoming in its even flow. But a state conceived previous to this is the state of suspended activity of the becoming. In the dance of life occasions arise when the flow of cosmic life is brought to a standstill before a new cycle of existence can emerge. Between the rise and fall of the cyclic orders becoming exists in a state of equilibrium. This equilibrium cannot be eternally stable as the forces gather up for the expression of life in a new order. But during the period of momentary suspension the sense of duration is also lost, for duration has a meaning only in reference to change. And strictly speaking, when becoming ceases to function concretely, it exists in an indefinite form and state. With the passage of becoming into the state of indefiniteness, the definite consciousness of duration ceases. Even the supramental vision is nothing indefinite, though its range of perception is wide and all-embracive. But the definiteness is relative to the modification of becoming; when the modification of becoming ceases, the supramental vision passes from the intuition of eternal duration to the intuition of the ever-presence. Space and time vanish here. This form of intuition reveals the indeterminate becoming. This is the non-relative experience of becoming, for becoming is strictly a functioning, and when its intuition becomes possible without its functioning, the character of intuition must be different. Be it noted that intuition as such does not differ and cannot differ, for it has the virtue of reflecting things everywhere; but the character of knowledge differs according to the nature of things it reflects. This is especially true of knowledge when it is confined to the relative plane of existence.

The world of space and time falls asleep and the supramental experiences with their infinite range of perspectives and sublimities pass into the Silence. The stirring of life with its infinite harmonies is hushed into the Calm. Life pushes out of the Calm, and, after its dance in space and time, falls back again into the Calm. Calm encircles life. It encircles space and time. Eternally the process of a birth and a forgetting goes on encircled by the perpetual Calm. The moving universe and the endless void appear and disappear "in accord with the endless rhythm of the sleep and awakening of the eternal sense. That eternal exhales; words are born and multiplied; inhales, matter returns to spirit."

This silence of the cosmic stirring is the withdrawal of the space-time-energy world into the basic principle. The relative order is completely removed from the scene and sleeps in the bosom of the Absolute. Whilst the supramental vision is still active, it can enjoy the complete withdrawal of the life and the void into the eternal calm, for here the supramental vision is the final intuition and the greatest reality. It is the transcendental reality. The life of intuition is one continuous thread, be it in immanence or in transcendence; and its designation is relative to the objects it reveals. It is transcendental when it reveals nothing but itself, and in its functioning in the relative order it is better designated as vision, for here it cannot work by itself apart from fine mentality. The supramental vision, therefore, extends up to the transcendental perception of space and time and energy, for they require the activity of the higher mind. But when these ultimates of the relative existence vanish into the Silence, the supramental intuition passes into transcendental intuition. Intuition shines in itself, its true character is revealed.

Chapter VII

That Thou Art

The Upaniṣadic Mysticism does not leave the least distinction between the Cosmic Being without and the vivifying Self within. This is a bold conclusion which may appear repellent to some and which may be denied by many; but the conclusion cannot be ignored. It is there. And in this we can understand the height of thought which the Upaniṣads reached.

The promise of elevating philosophy must lie in the assertion that the human spirit is one with the Divine, for mysticism and philosophy which cannot offer and establish this conclusion do not really meet the incessant demand of spirit for an expansive life. The urge in human life is always an urge to embrace more life, more light. This is the growing demand of our being, and nowhere is this yearning after the expanse so well conceived and described as in the Upaniṣads.

The finite is anxious to overcome its finiteness. It seeks to get over the shortness of its being. It is a great revelation, that the spirit which shines in man is the spirit which illumines the Cosmos. And this revelation gives freedom. Freedom is the possession of the Absolute, and unless man is installed thereto, his freedom is a shadow.

This consciousness is the "Paradise Regained", i.e. the recovery of the "Paradise Lost', through human ignorance, which screens the Being in its transcendent identity and pristine purity. This identity allows no difference. Life is essentially creative and is indicative of an expressive necessity; but the

Absolute has no such necessity, and so long as life in us is expressive, it creates history, and more often this creativeness is thought to be our highest privilege. The Upaniṣads differ. They lift the Soul above creative urges and install it to its identity.

Strange it may sound that the finite can feel its identity with the Infinite. But mysticism is nothing if it does not claim this simple truth, which appears strange because of its intimacy, new because of its familiarity. This truth is realized only when the depth of our being has been stirred and fathomed.

When the self is thus cut off from its finiteness and finite hold, it may not have the wealth of experience, but surely it has the height of being. This being is not mere potentiality, but reality. Potentiality is the mark of finiteness, but not of the Absolute. The Absolute is existence without inexhaustible potentiality and manifest actuality. It is being.

Analogy can be but an imperfect expression of this truth. "The stream lost in the Sea" is an inadequate description, for the finiteness is more an accident than a reality. The immersing can hardly be an expression of the truth of identity. The identity is the supreme fact, it is not to be established. We have no fall from such a beatitude. It has been screened for the moment. This truth is momentarily lost and conseuqently we have to suffer from the sense of an "I" and lose ourselves in the mazes of attractions and distractions, and in the labyrinth of pleasures of a divided life.

Such an existence is a silent awakening. It is the complete destruction of illusion. It should be distinguished from the forms of oscillations often enjoyed in mystic life. The delicate urges felt in love, service, and enjoyment are fine expressions of a heightened and intensified life. The finite life is still active. The thread of division still runs. The risen song of life still deceives. And eloquent becomes the voice, when the approach is nearest the centre. Life entices most when its spell is about to be completely dissolved, and it becomes restive to present all its sweetness and fragrance to mystify the vision that is clearing up.

Such experiences are infinitely sweet and immeasurably subtle, but still they belong to the life of expression and cannot compare to the impenetrable depth of the Calm. It surpasses the joy of creation, the quiet of absorption, the delight of concentration. Complete transcendence it is, full denial it is, of the mystic voices and mystic slumbering in the voiceless void.

Identity and Contradiction

The Upaniṣads seem to lay more stress upon identity than upon contradiction. Spirit denies contradiction. Contradiction is the mark of finiteness and illusoriness, but tradiction may be consistent with immanent urge of growth and development. Growth implies the constant denial of previous stages, but surely this cannot be said of Reality. The mystic enjoys the life of contradiction, in the sense that the mystic life is infinitely elastic and does not bind itself to the rigidity and fixity of moral and intellectual conventions. This elasticity is the great promise of myticism, and, therefore, it is supposed to be the dominating principle in the mystic consciousness. Contradiction can be a law of diffusion in mystic consciousness.

But it must be said that identity is a distinct ideal, for the Upaniṣads have distinctly laid down the superiority of Absolute consciousness. The solitariness of the Absolute is the end of the quest. "Know that to be the great where nothing is seen, nothing known, nothing heard." "The Absolute is the vast, the Absolute is the immortal, the Absolute stands on Its own glory." (Chāndogya Upaniṣad, 7th chap., 24th part.)

The freedom from expansion and contradiction in the stillness of the Absolute is naturally the ideal, for contradiction and diffusion fit in with expression, but not with the Absolute. The Absolute is identity and denies contradiction. The

Upaniṣads certainly do not emphasize the fellowship of spirits, they assert boldly that finality in mystic consciousness is reached in the denial of differences, for difference cannot be true of spirit. Spirit is all sameness, and however rich the life of expression may be, it cannot compare to the sameness of the Absolute. Such sameness is enjoyable by the contrast it offers to the diversity and the richness of mystic life in expression.

This transcendence can be distinguished from the fine urges of becoming only when a discriminating sense of the different forms of intuition is reared up, otherwise the danger of sleep in the joy of life and expression may form almost an insurmountable barrier to realization, and the seeker may have his progress impeded. The Upaniṣads therefore lay down the desirability of transcending the experiences following the realization of Saguṇa (Apara) Brahman and appreciating the transcendent One.

Spirit has its analytic expression in the finite and its synthetic expression in the Infinite : and beyond the expression it enjoys an identity. Contradiction is the shadow of being and is true of expression. Contradiction plays an important part in the expression, but no part in the transcendent. Expression is not possible without self-alienation, and as such contradiction or self-alienation holds true in expression.

The law of contradiction is the key to the understanding of the order of appearance and an appearance is not true in the same sense as reality, for appearance subsists by self-contradiction. It has in it the necessity of denying itself and passing through infinite phases. Such necessity is inherent in self-alienation. Unity runs through them, still this unity is possible because the self-alienating process has not totally cut itself off from the identity immanent in it.

This law is certainly true of mystic life, for life in its immanence has the same law to depend on, be it in gross or fine expression. Mystic life is the constant denial of the finite, since it is a constant aspiration towards the infinite life. The denial may be partial or complete, but there is no doubt that elasticity in life is not possible, if there is not incessant shifting of the immediate and constant receptivity to the successive phases of life and experience. The law of contradiction in mystic life affords the enjoyment of life in different phases.

So long as the spiritual life is a life in expression, contradiction has value and importance; it brings out the full meaning of the concrete expression. Meaning follows upon contradiction, and so long as the spiritual life moves in contradiction we can find a meaning for it. Naturally contradiction is the law of concrete spiritual life. It finds its fullest expression in the life of love.

The Upaniṣads do not confine the spiritual life to expression, they lay more emphasis upon transcendence. And, since contradiction is true of expression, it can be the best law of expression, but it cannot be reconciled to identity. The common tendency to synthetize these aspects is erroneous, since, they are true in two different senses. Contradiction is true of spiritual becoming but the spiritual becoming is appearance, and not reality. Appearance endures in time, Reality transcends time. Hence, the forms of apprehension also differ. And the timeless fact cannot be identical with the eternal duration. Therefore when the Upaniṣads lay down the truth of identity and the truth of contradiction in spiritual life, they do it in two distinct senses. If, therefore, there is a synthesis in spiritual life, it can be only in the life of immanence and not in transcendence. Identity is true of spiritual life in transcendence, synthesis is true of it in expression and immanence. Spiritual life in expression has a fundamental difference from the spiritual life in transcendence. The one always refers to the breaking of the hard crust of the finiteness of the soul, the other refers to its complete denial.

The mystic life is rich in fine fruition and enjoyment,

because it always brings a new vision, a new meaning, a new adjustment in experience : it reaches a fuller life through the constant unfolding of life and its meaning. It promises a fluidity of life.

Contradiction has a great force in the spiritual life. It sets aside the fixed ideas and formed habits of realistic consciousness, and creates in man the aspiration for the infinite life. The greatest drawback of the realistic logic is that it works under the pressure of hide-bound formulas, and does not see the value of elasticity following the constant shifting and denial of the finite references. Spiritual life always means transcendence and in fact is not possible unless the limiting references and restraining influences can be set aside. The finer meaning is conceived, the finer life is realized through the reception of the wider spirit and life by contradiction; and, finally, the reception of the infinite life is possible through the denial of the finite self, and in this self-denial the Truth of Tattvamasi emerges as the great truth in spiritual life.

Faced by the alternative of identity and contradiction, the Upaniṣads seem inclined to the former. The spring certainly is better than the fountain, and if pressed far, they would assert that the spring is the fountain, the difference is imposed by the intellect. The intellectual understanding of Truth necessitates a distinction between appearance and Reality, and between identity and contradiction, but in truth these distinctions do not arise, for Reality is the only fact, the only existence. The problem of appearance is a self-created problem of intellect, since intellect cannot see Reality, it raises the issues, which are no issues forthwith.

Contradiction gives us the flow and mobility of spiritual life and therefore the mystic teacher like Ouspensky (in his *Tertium Organum*) has seen in it the true law of spiritual life, and this has led him to find the ultimate identity of man and God, for it is contradiction that makes God to alienate Himself into man and urges man to deny himself to be a God again. Contradiction, the constant denial of position and negation, presents the spiritual life in its finest elasticity. It is hardly intelligible by the set categories.

Ouspensky sees in this unity of man and God, Tattvamasi, the highest essence of spiritual life, for the spiritual quest through constant denial establishes ultimately a unity between man and God, and unless this elasticity and urge is there, this possibility can hardly take place.

This is true of the concrete spiritual life where there is the constant interfusion in our beings, for the difference between the finite and the Infinite is not fixed and has been possible by contradiction, and a further contradiction due to an elevation in spiritual insight can set aside the distinction and bring unto man the vision of God and his identity with God.

Contradiction illustrates the truth of inversion in spiritual life. The highest concrete spiritual experience is centred in the law of inversion. Man wants to resolve himself into God, God into man. Inversion displaces the fixed difference between the soul and God and establishes the fundamental unity which is the quest and refuge of spiritual life. Spiritual life in its ordinary expression cannot rise above the truth of inversion. But this law holds true of the spirit in life of expression; and those who conceive the spiritual life as essentially dynamic cannot see further beyond inversion in mystic ascent.

The law of inversion is the law of contradiction in its application of spiritual life. Contradiction or inversion cannot be final, it is only an expressin of a deep-seated unity underlying the spiritual life in its expression.

The Upaniṣads (in most cases) have seen far above the truth of contradiction and inversion in spiritual life and are bold enough to sacrifice contradiction to identity in spiritual life. The religious consciousness is moved by the contradiction, for it seeks to go beyond the finiteness of spiritual life to embrace the expansive life, and the religious life is nothing if it is not expansive. And the embracive life of spirit must not allow external or internal difference and must deny the limited experience of the finite. The mystics of all ages affirm the feelings of unbounded vision and being, and this speaks the truth more of identity than of difference. The denial of contradiction in the ascent establishes identity. The identity which Ouspensky speaks of is the identity in the dynamic expression of spirit, or the identity of spirit in its dynamical conception. But the identity which the Upaniṣads establish is the identity of Essence, which is established by denying the contradiction of spiritual expression.

The former gives us the infinite possibilities of spiritual life in expansion, the latter the unique experience of transcendence of spiritual life. This identity is an accomplished fact, the supreme fact of existence.

Poussin said that the Indian teachers did not recognize fully the importance and value of contradiction in life and thought. The Upaniṣadic teachers find the value of contradiction more in immanent consciousness than in the transcendent. Identity is a unique presentation, which is nowhere experienced.

Contradiction has two forms – (1) Contradiction in expression, (2) Contradiction of expression. The former is the incessant denial of the aspects of presentations and constant shifting of them. This is true of the phenomenal changes, for the changes, though they have a history and a duration, are really momentary phases of the flow of becoming. They are constantly denied to create a history, and the constant denial keeps up the flow. Reality is not constant with concentration, far less with constant denials which contradiction implies.

Even this law holds true of religious consciousness. Religious consciousness is not seldom identified with the delight of fellowship with the Divine, but in this fellowship there is the constant denial of the finiteness, for the finite cannot experience far less embrace the Infinite, unless the finiteness is surpassed. And this elasticity of life has been the secret of the drawing power of religion.

But this elasticity only proves that the distinction of the finite and the Infinite is hardly tenable and religious consciousness embraces the identity of spirit and discards false divisions. Rare is the visitation of such experience, and so long as life has it not, it is impelled by the force of contradiction in spiritual life. The finite cannot be large enough to enclose Infinite in its bosom, and the fact that it has the experience of unbounded being and knowledge only proves that the finiteness is only a temporary phase of our life.

When contradiction ceases to impel spiritual life, identity is felt, but it requires a high mental preparation before contradiction can be overcome. It requires a new understanding, a new penetration. The penetration is to find out a freedom from elastic or shrinking consciousness and to secure rest in the waveless Calm. And here begins the contradiction of expression, the contradiction of the original analytic and synthetic concentration. The idea of simultaneity and succession – the space-sense and the time-sense – dies out. The absence of simultaneity and succession is incompatible with the ordinary notions of space and time. "To know in this manner is therefore to free ourselves from extension and duration, to prolong the perception of the present beyond every assignable limit, to enjoy an eternal now, to lose oneself in an immensity without bounds" (*Les Maladis du Sentiment Religieux,* pp.61-62; quoted in Pratt's *Religious Consciousness,* p. 415).

The charge of Poussin is partially true – not that the Indian mind cannot see the value of contradiction in life, but that the Indian mind sees further and feels deeper. Contradiction cannot be final in the life of spiritual realization, contradiction implies self-alienation. In spiritual life self-alienation should be replaced by self-realization, and therefore, the Indian teachers see that if contradiction is involved in self-denial in creation or emanation, it cannot be the law of spiritual realization. Spiritual realization implies a drawing in, an immersing in the centre. In the process of drawing in there is a sort of contradiction, contradiction of our finite history and expression—the life of concentration. But this prepares us for the final realization. Mystics all over the world will testiy to the silence of spiritual life, where the identity is felt and realized.

The Indian mind, therefore, exhibits the correct religious attitude when it emphasizes identity more than contradiction in spiritual seeking. Strictly speaking, contradiction has no place in spiritual life, for spiritual life is essentially an even life. Contradiction is true of appearance, but not of Reality. Reality denies self-contradiction. The play of contradiction in spirit to keep up the richness and variety in spiritual life is only a metaphor. This is explaning Reality in the terms of appearance. Contradiction can play its part in time, but Spirit is above and beyond time, and the law of the temporal cannot be the law of the spiritual. This is the implication of the spiritual life; and mysticism makes this implication very clear. If the spiritual life in its expression has its full charm, value, and attraction, mystics would have not voiced forth the plunge into the Deep and the fixity in the centre. Life, therefore, exhibits the greatest truth in its centre rather than at its surface. Mysticism in its call to return to the centre presses upon us the correct significance of life.

Illusion of Time and Change

Spiritual life, to be of any consequence, must rise above the illusions of time, change, and difference. The three go together. The empirical mind is dominated by these categories, and it is natural for it to read events and relations in the terms either of time or change. The Spirit transcends them all : otherwise it cannot be unique, no difference would be left between the empirical and the spiritual. This is clearly indicated in the Upaniṣads in the axion of identity. To deny difference is the beginning of the spiritual consciousness, to realize identity is its fruition. The distinctions of space and time cannot obtain in the spiritual life, for these distinctions, if ever they are there, cannot establish the identity which is the true objective of spiritual life. Spiritual consciousness differs from the sense of empirical consciousness in this, that it installs identity in the place of the divisions of the latter. Spirit looks beyond space and time.

The mystic consciousness has this superiority to the empirical consciousness, that it is freed from the rigidity of the latter imposed by the conditions of space and time and their distinctions. Science and philosophy labour under the limitations of empiric or rational mind, mysticism breaks the limitation and apprehends the Great Beyond. What, therefore, is to a mystic consciousness an axiomatic truth, takes long to establish itself in science and philosophy. The Kaṭha Upaniṣad says that the wise forsake the name and form and cross the sins and the miseries of the flesh and become freed from the knots of divided existence.

Spiritual life cannot seriously begin if the spirit cannot rise above the idea of development and history in time. A finite being can grow, it has a history. Spirit is eternally perfect, it cannot grow; but this idea is so foreign to us and seems to be so much opposed to our experience that, in spite of its simplicity, it takes long to realize in full its truth and implication. And, therefore, the transition from the realistic attitude to the transcendent consciousness appears so great that sometimes initiates fight shy of such an ideal. Hence, it is often a perplexity and appears as a void because the wealth of life and experience is withdrawn.

The search for the Reality has passed various stages and phases, until it has come to rest in the bold conclusion—Tattvamasi—Thou art That. In the dialogue in Br. Ar., 2,1, and Kauṣitaki, 4, it is accepted that Brahman is the essence of being not only of the cosmic phenomena, but also of the inner vital and psychic functions. The vision of the cosmic person of Ṛg-Veda, v, 10, 90, is displaced by the vision of the Ātman in the Upaniṣads, and therefore the spirit of the latter is quite different from that of the former. The former sees the all-pervading existence in the external forces. This vision of the animated nature is different from the intuition of Self as the finest essence of existence.

The Bṛhadāraṇyaka gives also a picture of such a cosmic person. So also Chāndogya in some places, as 3, 18. Such a vision has importance, for it really disestablishes the realistic viewpoint and stirs our psychic being with animation and inspiration. But still the vision is of the immanent. Being cannot give us that intuitive outlook which sees the identity of being irrespective of all differences. The former inspires a pantheistic conception of life. The mysticism it induces is nature mysticism, which may pass into spiritual mysticism of the theistic type. Rāmānuja and the Vaiṣṇavic teachers are of this persuasion, and to them the nature mysticism of the Vedas is to be synthetised with the spiritual mysticism of the Upaniṣads to indicate their fundamental unity. Nature mysticism gives us the vision of the cosmic person through the powers and the forces of nature; spiritual mysticism is the vision of the cosmic person active in us and holding moral and spiritual fellowship with mankind. The former gives the idea of God in relation to nature, the latter gives the idea of God in relation to soul.

There is a distinction between the intuition of a cosmic person and the intuition of Ātman. The cosmic person and Ātman are not the same kind of reality, and their experiences are not identical. The former is an elevated feeling and inspiration, the latter, intuition. Feeling and intuition differ. Feeling or sentience is a kind of psychism, a finer working and stimulation of our mental being; intuition implies no psychism, it really transcends it. It is illumination without any stir of the inner dynamism. It is unique and unanalysable and no experience can compare to it, for it is an immediacy peculiar to itself in the sense of a non-relational experience. The immediacy of feeling is the immediacy below relations, the immediacy of intuition is the immediacy transcending relations. The former presents a unity, the latter an identity. The former idealizes life and its relations, the latter denies and transcends them. The former gives a fine feeling and exaltation, the latter calm.

There are texts which present side by side the cosmic person and the individual self and their identity. In Chāndogya Upaniṣ ad, chap. (B, ii, 14) vi, 1, 2, 9, 10, 12, 13.

These texts first give us the experience of the cosmic being and the individual being, the immanent principles underlying the cosmos and the psychic processes, and then by a fine perception rise to the conception of the integrity of being. The idea of a unity of being does not inspire, for the texts are clear and positive about the identity of being. In spiritual life the idea of a cosmic person meeting us all round is not thought enough, the texts are careful to add that the vivifying principle which underlies nature is also the vivifying principle which underlies the vitalmental complex. These texts, it should be remembered, present the absolute truth of identity, for the spiritual life aspires to get over the falsity of division, and it is not clear how immortality can be realized if the sense of division still persists. The community of spirits maintains the distinctness of them, but the Upaniṣads plainly tell us that the Ātman is Brahman, not in the sense of community, but in the sense of identity. No doubt, the cosmic being or force can inspire us, can widen our vision, can make our being more elastic, but this elasticity is still confined to the rhythm of the life immanent in spatial and temporal order and cannot rise to that vision which sees the identity behind space and time. If the rigidity of crude realistic consciousness has a rude shock in the rhythmic expansion of being, how can the process of expansion stop unless the finality is reached in the Absolute? The expanse felt in rhythm is the expanse of dynamic being. It is psychic expansion, as distinguished from the expansion beyond space, beyond psychism. The psychic expansion is of the mental-vital self, it can ultimately lead us to feel, enjoy, and live the Cosmic Self. It can give us the comic consciousness—the Immense of the Spiritual Space, still such an existence cannot be said to be the ideal of the Upaniṣads. Though there are indications of such a life here and there in the Upaniṣads, still such a possibility cannot give the promise of identity. The expansion is still confined, though it can widen the range of our experience from pure sensitivity to highly spiritualized mentality. This expansion and elasticity do not offer a quite new experience, though they open new channels of perception and new fields of vision. But they are still empirical, and impress the finer sensibilities and finer feelings. They do not and cannot deny mentation, the new meanings and values they present are implications of the old ones in a new setting of a delicate and refined sensibility. They may give ease and repose of the cosmic life, the fluidity of the higher planes of existence, but still they cannot penetrate the Calm which transcends the dance of life in all-pervading space. The Upaniṣads are quite alive to it, in the emphasis they lay on the identity of being beyond divisions of space and time.

Phases of Spiritual Experience

In religious consciousness the contradiction of finite experience and the affirmation of the identity is the necessary postulate, for it means a transcendence of the spirit functioning through psychic changes and concentration. In every form of religious enthusiasm transcencence is the right instinct and the true objective. Hence, Tattvamasi can have strictly two implications : – (1) the implication of the unity of the self with the Divine : this implication cannot rise above the distinction between the finite and the Infinite : and though the finite comes to feel the inspiration of the Infinite and thus enjoys the spiritual life in its widest commonalty and highest expansion, it cannot give complete transcendence. The self is actuated here by its dynamic fullness and enjoys the infinite life in its manifestation, through the mundane and the supra-mundane world, as the ineffable light that enlightens nature, gods, and men; but it cannot completely enjoy mystic silence, which becomes possible when the soul is released from the relativistic consciousness. The divine orientation of the self has its charm and attraction, it opens up the wide panorama of spiritual life in expression. (2) Tattvamasi signifies further the truth of cosmic intuition in which the vision of the whole is made clear to the seeking soul. The vision comprises within it the details of existence in a cosmic setting : it is the vision of the Oversoul identical with the things gross and subtle. The mystic consciousness in this stage is still determinate, and the Cosmic Self is realized as the existence which vibrates through things, great and small. The sensitization of the Oversoul produces a different feeling in us. It induces inspiration as it touches the different chords of our being. The vision has, therefore, degrees of fineness as it reflects the Oversoul through the gross or the subtle expression. The Upaniṣads are rich in these, and hence to the non-adept the mystic ideal in the Upaniṣads may appear different. And this divergence in attitude and receptivity has been probably the source of the different interpretations set upon the text in latter-day philosophy. But the key to the better understanding of the Upaniṣads is offered to us, if we do not lose sight of the fact that the Upaniṣads represent spiritual realizations and not systematic philosophy. The Upaniṣads present the mystic experiences, and cover all the phases of mystic consciousness.

Mysticism, if it truly reflects the soul's anxious search for Truth, should show a wonderful unanimity; for it is really the adventure of the soul to experience Truth in immanence and transcendence. It is a new approach through life and experience, and therefore, it cannot deny the suprasensuous revelations through nature and the soul and through an experience which transcends such revelations. And the proper valuation of these phases of experience is not possible unless the soul has a direct knowledge of them. Gifted is the soul that can command all the phases of mystic experience and is bold enough to surmount them in the transcendent Calm. Hence, the same fervour of mystical feeling does not meet us in all the texts, and this probably has been the fruitful source of classification of the texts, as theistic, pantheistic, or transcendental. But there can be no doubt that the Upaniṣadic mysticism is not confined to the cosmic intuition of the Oversoul—and this is an experience which can fit well with our personal feelings—but it soars beyond all finer perceptions, and the revelation comes to its highest phase when a change in personal consciousness takes place and the soul has the unique intuitioin of identity.

The Upaniṣads lay more emphasis upon this supramental intuition, and evaluate all other forms of mystic delight and experience as partial visions. They are the temporary visitations of the living soul. The mystic ascent, therefore, must complete the final transcendence before the soul can have its full satisfaction. The sense of limitation cannot be strictly removed even if the cosmic intuition leaves the least distinction between the finite and the Infinite. To the ardent aspirant the finiteness is more than a troublesome disease, for it means not only a spiritual fall but also an eternal limitation. The Upaniṣads truly record the natural aspiration of the soul of transcendent identity, for that alone can remove the sense of restriction and limitation. It sets the soul free. The vision of an Oversoul or a Godhead cannot satisfy for the very sense of division and difference is a wrench, and spirit denies division. Satisfaction in spiritual life cannot be complete in the finer experiences of the soul; these experiences only indicate a delicate psychic being responsive to the subtler vibration and cosmic urges. More often, the subtle delicacies of perception in beauty or holiness pass for true spirituality. Sometimes an ever-growing life is supposed to be spirituality. But true spirituality is the perception of the formless and the nameless Being. Psychism and spirituality are indeed different. The one gives a delightful feeling, the other Truth. The one affords exultation, the other freedom. In such an approach the soul does not feel the *intoxication* of the life of ecstasy, for the approach is not emotional. It does not play upon feeling. It steers clear of it. It is more philosophic and represents intellectual love with its serenity and equableness. But it is not even that. Love-mysticism gives a fine joy and keen attachment. But here feeling even in its highest delicacy has no exhibition. It is a life which becomes more and more conscious, more and more detached from all forms of values, including even the religious joy and the mystic ecstasy. It may look like a "milder form" of mystic consciousness (Pratt), since it lacks richness in content, but it is the highest, for it is the recoil of life back to its source. It is indescribable. It is ineffable.

Tattvamasi can, therefore, posit either (1) the unitive consciousness or (2) the absolutistic consciousness. Both have found favour with the different schools of thought and research : but what seems to be the mystic implication is that both represent the same life and consciousness in immanence and transcendence, for the mystic sees the spirit in its essence as well as in expression.

The Mystic Ideal

It will be hardly true to say that the mystic ideal of the Upaniṣads is the delight of absorption in God which has the appearance of an identity : the Upaniṣads clearly establish an unbroken identity of essence behind the seeming difference between the finite and the Infinite for the Absolute cannot admit of or allow in itself the least difference.

The mysticism of the Upaniṣads differs from all other forms of mysticism in the clear emphasis which they lay upon the dissolution of the finite hold of life and experience. The Infinite is felt and touched in the finite consciousness. It is the normal mystic experience, though this feeling may be at times so deep as to overshadow for the moment the mystic joy in the mystic quiet; but such a quiet is still consciously felt and leaves behind an impression in finite consciousness. But the quiet of transcendence as taught by the Upaniṣads is totally different, it is the quiet in which the finite delight or feeling is completely dislodged with the finite hold. It is not felt, it is not enjoyed. It is.

Religious mysticism is a delight of the God-consciousness in some form of fellowship, and is a delight that can be felt. Mysticism in the Upaniṣads has not this import. It denies the ripple in love. It denies the joy in beauty. It denies the concrete, it denies the common. It denies the vivid feeling and joyous consciousness. It feels that such mystical experience does not present the being as it is. It goes beyond such fine feelings and delights. The soul slumbers still in charms and attractions of the divided life; it feels a mystic intoxication in them and cannot break their fine spell and pass into the quiet. Even the adepts sometimes take fright at the Calm, for the joy of life is lost in silence and many stand aghast and fight shy of it. Rare among the adepts are those who have the training and insight to understand the import of transcendent Silence and the boldness to welcome it. The synthetic intuition has now to be displaced by the transcendent, and naturally therefore it looks like denying life and even consciousness.

The Śvetāśvatara promises liberation from bondage by mystic exaltation, but it has no direct reference to the identity of individual and Cosmic Being : it does not deny the cosmic feeling or intuition. The cosmic feeling may open the wider visions of life and consciousness. Such mystical consciousness, no doubt, gives us the perception of the infinite life in its fluidity of expression. Mystical exaltation in any form must necessarily overcome our usual experiences and induce a kind of direct consciousness of the supreme Existence. But this consciousness is not always the same, and cannot be always the same, for the psychical barometer of our being does not indicate the same level of penetration and insight. Hence, the usual objectivity in spiritual consciousness is not evenly maintained.

In the Śvetāśvatara Upaniṣad the mystic attitude is apparently devotional, and the initiate seems quite alive to the transcendence and immanence of Being. He takes shelter and protection in the Being which is the cause of all causes : he seeks inspiration from It.

It has a reference to Īśvara to which the seeker can completely give himself up for final release. Īsvara inspires Brahmā (the creator), manifests the Vedas. Īśvara is Jña, intelligence. The attitude is of reverence, admiration, and devotion, and complete self-giving.

The Śvetāśvatara does not reach the mystical heights of the Chāndogya and the Bṛhadāraṇyaka. It presents the intuition of the cosmic Being or the Oversoul running through the highest Hiraṇyagarbha and the lowest of the created existences. It repeats the conception of the Cosmic Puruṣa of the Ṛg-Veda, but does not clearly point to the stage where the individual consciousness oversteps its limitations and feels identity in the transcendence. The Cosmic Soul stands as the permeating essence of existence, the God of our search, the great redeemer. The theistic note here is dominant. But a finer vision and a deeper insight meets us in the Bṛhadāraṇyaka, where it is said of Vāmadeva that he began to feel that he was Manu and the Sun. And this feeling and realization is true of one who knows, "I am Brahman."

Even the gods have not power to prevent his becoming thus, for he becomes their self. The text continues : "Whoever worships another divinity than his self thinking he is one and I another, he knows not. He is like a sacrificial animal for the gods." (Bṛhadāraṇyaka, I, part 4, couplet 20.)

The self-opening has been almost complete here. The sense of individuality has been displaced. The cosmic sense has been established. The essence of existence is felt everywhere the same. The divisions of discrete space and time have been dispelled. The throbbing pulse of the cosmic life breathes in all existence, the expansive vision of the Oversoul illumines the All. The sense of a cosmic "I" becomes apparent in consciousness. The sense of the individual "I" is completely lost, and the adept has the uncommon sense of the "I" immanent in the whole existence, and the feeling and the perception of the "I" immanent in the Self. No sense of difference is felt between the Cosmic "I" and the individual "I". It is not the cosmic vision by the individual self, it is the cosmic vision by the Cosmic Self. The individual has no part to play, and is for the moment overshadowed; the individual self feels identified with the Cosmic Soul as permeating through the whole existence. Here is a profound revelation. It is profounder than the sense of a unity felt in external and internal forces. The Bṛhadāraṇyaka Upaniṣad says that the Ātman is immanent in psychic force as also in nature's dynamism. The former shows the spirit as Adhyātma, the latter as Adhibhūta; for this higher sense compels the deeper vision of the unity of the two. Even here the sense of identity is not complete. The restriction is still there. And surely the sense of my "I" as the Cosmic "I" is still not apparent. The cosmic sense is not fully established there. The sense of limitation still persists, and the sense of unity is established behind the apparent differences : but in the intuition of Vāmadeva the distinctions, internal and external, have dropped.

Vāmadeva's vision has this uniqueness that it has got over the distinction of the internal and the external and the vision of the Cosmic Self as "I" is unmistakenly clear. The consciousness of the Oversoul is transparent. Such a vision is precursor to the understanding of the final transcencence. The individual self has, therefore, the vision of itself as the Immense in which floats the whole existence. Such a vision displaces the time-sense. The finite soul enjoys the ease and the freedom from the oppressive time-sense and the history of development and growth. Such a cosmic sense brings release near, for it marks a great advance in spiritual life. Though the complete transcendence is not yet in sight, still the sense of the "I" being the Cosmic "I" is a great advance in spirituality and a fine asset for the final release. The unity of the Adhyātma and the Adhibhūta in the super-self does not give the finer experience of the Cosmic Self as identical with the finite self : this experience gives no doubt the thrill of the cosmic delight and the unity of the cosmic life, but it cannot give the self the exaltation of a semi-transcendent consciousness – the Self being the Cosmic Self. The cosmic intuition has therefore different meanings.

(1) It may mean the sense of the cosmic delight and existence actually felt and enjoyed by the recipient self. Here the mystic consciousness is not supranormal, save and except that its range of vision is wider, its feelings delicate, its perception subtle. It feels the unity of inner psyche and external forces and enjoys existence in its vastness and panorama.

The vision slowly and gradually proceeds to the appreciation of the naked spirit behind appearances. (2) And here follows the deeper meaning of cosmic intuition. The cosmic intuition here oversteps all distinctions between inner psyche and outer forces, and the even flow of joy is displaced by the serene calm of all-embracive intuition. The intuition is still confined to a centre, but the centre is not the confined centre of a finite consciousness. It is all-embracive, all-expansive, it transcends the distinctions of time, and hence it is possible to see the whole cosmic existence as reflected in the Self. The delight is almost transcendental, the shadow of the appearance still hovers round the transcendental consciousness.

The vision of Vāmadeva unfettered by the ordinary limitation of space and time reflects the whole existence. The vision represents the intuition of the super-subject. The finite subject and its limitation have died out. And therefore, it is indeed difficult fully to grasp the meaning and appreciate the exaltation of such a cosmic vision. The vision transcends the ordinary reciprocity of knowledge and has, therefore, an inexplicable elasticity. The "realistic" mould of our experiences passes into the fluidity of spiritual life and, what is more, an uncommon elasticity of being is felt by the self. The finiteness of the self is done to death and infinitude takes its place. And therefore the former self is overshadowed. A change takes place in the perception of time from the sense of a series to a sense of continuity, or perhaps the historical time-sense is completely erased by this experience. The restrictions have passed off, and the Self with its unbounded vision feels :

> "Divine am I inside and out, and I make holy whatever I touch or am touched from,
> The scent of these arm-pits' aroma finer than prayer,
> This head more than Churches, Bibles and all the creeds."

This cosmic intuition is neither synthetic nor aesthetic. In the aesthetic intuition, the presentation is objective. The recipient soul welcomes the vision as something independent of his being. It awakens melodious feelings and sometimes rapport in ecstasy.

Vāmadeva's vision has surpassed the objectivity of aesthetic presentation. It has surpassed the delight of harmony. It is penetrative enough to enter the Soul of existence which transcends the fine feelings and the sensitization of our subjective being. The experience is trans-subjective. But the vision is not yet completely transcendent. The cosmic intuition of Vāmadeva is not categorically different from empiric intuition. The two differ in magnitude and extensiveness, but not in character. The self-reference is present in both. In the former, the reference is to the Cosmic Self and not to the finite. But in the transcendent intuition, all reference to anything to the Self is lost. The Self alone is there in its complete isolation from all psychism, confined or unlimited. It has no reference, not the least, to space or time in any form, divided or undivided. It is unique in itself. It has no content.

The Consummation

Tattvamasi indicates, therefore, neither the truth of the individual or the Universal Self, nor the psychic or dynamic mutations that may have their place in them. It is not spiritual expansion or concentration. It is not even the poise of our psychic being. It is not even the supreme puissance, the undisturbed quietness which Īśvara enjoys in his superior detachment to the mutations in dynamic becoming.

Tattvamasi indicates the existence transcendental, the knowledge supramental, and the calm suprapsychic. It is not the panpsychic realization of the Cosmic Being. It is the supreme silence of Peace which reigns unnoticed in the heart of things. It is not, therefore a psychic feeling. It is not the joy of life which streams into the soul in its wise passivity. It indicates the *point* where the self realizes its identity. It is the conviction of the simple truth of Identity in spiritual life, and which can be in the complete detachment from the ever-expanding and growing life. The delight of Peace in the centre of our being can hardly be realized unless it is withdrawn from the surface. The expansion has its joy, it is engrossing. The soul in most cases is captivated by it beyond measure. It cannot carry the search further. But if the process of expansion is carried further, the soul loses itself. It undergoes a unique experience in the dropping of psychic consciousness, and herein the great Truth is realized. Thus, we are given the most assuring experience that, in the centre of our being, the spiritual life knows no division, no distinction, no gush of feeling, no taste, no experience, no giving up, no expansion, no tenderness, no majesty. It is what it is.

Tattvamasi is, therefore, no spiritual experience, no spiritual revelation, no psychic expanse and delight. No doubt, in the process of psychic expansion, the touch of the cosmic life at every part of our experience may be felt, but this cannot be the end of the mystic quest of the Upaniṣads. The psychic expansion is not the Truth. The Upaniṣads present the Truth which puts an end to the expansion and contraction of psychic life. Life cannot touch it, psychism cannot taste it. And the delight of psychic expansion which so often is the inevitable consequence of the mystic venture, and in which the feeling of akinness and affinity of all existence is the usual feeling, may be the precursor of the Calm, but it is not necessarily the end of the mystic quest. But in the life of search, the psychic expansion has a spiritual value, it gives the soul the uncommon experience of the psychic possibility which lies deep in the soul, and keeps up the struggle and pursuit. These experieneces are the twilights in the mystic life. They shed a flash of light amidst the covering darkness of the soul. They create faith. They excite hope. In this way they are welcome. But the psychism of our nature should completely vanish before the light of Truth can finally be established in us. A fine psychism is not necessarily spirituality. Spirituality lies in the cognition of Truth. The expansion of our psychic being, however fine an asset it may be, is not the vision of Truth. Hence, the supra-subjective psychic visions shold not pass for Truth. They are fine perspectives in the life of self-expansion, but self-expansion is really the expression of our vital and mental being, a move of the dynamism of our nature; but it is not the Truth that gives us calm and freedom from psychism. The "Paradise Regained" is neither far nor near : the seeking soul finds to his amazement that "Truth is his being", "Tat asi Tvam" (Thou art That). It is not a new possession, it is not a new claim. It is not even a new revelation. It is the simple truth which stands in its nakedness in the heart of things. The conventions of the intellect and the contrition of the heart should be set aside before the soul can be conscious of the possession. The greatest truth is always the simplest, the simplest is always the rarest. The hungers of the soul do not allow it that freedom from spiritual and intellectual conventions and illusions which can welcome the ever-shining Truth in the citadel of our being. Suddenly in what is called "mystic flashes" the great Truth dawns upon the spiritually fit.

The mystic flash that silently sheds its light upon the anxius soul strikes wonder with its unbounded light. Though this experience gives a contact with a world that finger-tips do not touch, a whole new universe of life and spirit, still this cannot be said to be the highest mystic consciousness. For one can travel free in this reign of ineffable light, deeply one can breathe in this world of peace, but the consciousness has not gone beyond the finer layers of existence enveloping the Great Mystery of the soul. The full peace comes when the flashes are strong enough to reflect the pivot of Being. The pilgrimage of the soul is liable to set-backs unless the Centre is reached, the Centre which radiates all light, and in which the soul has the sense of the highest security in the consciousness of being identical with the Eternal Light. It is an awakening on the Apex of Being from which thought and vision alike vanish. The distinction of mine and thine completely dissolves. The soul sails in deep waters. It is bound for "where mariner has not yet dared to go" and in the end comes to lose himself and all. But this is no loss, this is reassertion of the lost Peace in the Basic Being.

The mystic exaltation in the Upaniṣads is not confined to the passive reception of the life running through the myriad existences pursuing its march through the soul. It is not confined to the vision of the blessed peace that sleeps in the starry frame, it is not confined to the rare visitation of the living soul in nature and man. It gives the unique experience and the conviction of the Truth that resides in the heart of things and in the self : mystic exaltation removes the sense of difference and informs of a plane of existence wherein disappears the confined sense of the self and appears the limitless Being, the Plenitude of Existence. Such an existence has been erroneously called by Pratt "the infinite blank." True it is that neither purpose nor thought not self-consciousness can be ascribed to such an existence. Plotinus truly said : "The only one will neither know anything nor have anything to be ignorant of. Being one and united with itself it does not need to think of itself. You cannot catch a glimpse of it even by ascribing to it union with itself. Rather you must take away thinking and the act of being united and thought itself and everything else." But this certainly cannot make the one an *infinite blank,* it only makes it a reality which cannot be conceptually described and determined. It requires some other form and method of knowledge besides discursive thinking and conceptual understanding. The human understanding proceeds by concepts, and when they cannot be applied, a feeling becomes natural that what exists beyond is *negation.* It is *blank.* Blank it is not, though the thinking cannot conceive it otherwise, because of its natural limitation of apprehending by contrasts.[1]

This conclusion becomes irresistible from the texts. The Bṛhadāraṇyaka has it in Yājñavalkya's speech to his wife :

" 'Brahmanhood deserts him who knows Brahmanhood in aught else than the soul. Kṣatriyahood deserts him who knows Kṣatriyahood in aught else than the Soul. The world deserts him who knows the world in aught else than the Soul. The gods desert him who knows the gods in aught else than the Soul. The Vedas desert him who knows the Vedas is aught else than the Soul. Being deserts him who knows beings in aught else than the Soul. Everything deserts him who knows everything in aught else than the Soul. This Brahmanhood, this Kṣatriyahood, these worlds, these gods, these Vedas, all these beings, everything here is what this Soul is.' "

" 'It is—as, when a drum is being beaten, one would not be able to grasp the external sounds, but by grasping the drum or the beater of the drum the sound is grasped.' "

" 'It is—as, when a conch-shell is being blown, one would not be able to grasp the external sounds, but by grasping the conch-shell or the blower of the conch-shell the sound is grasped.' "

" 'It is—as, when a lute is being played, one would not be able to grasp the external sounds, but by grasping the lute or the player of the lute the sound is grasped.' "

" 'It is—as, when a drum is, being fuel, clouds of smoke separately issue forth, so lo, verily, from this great Being (Bhūta) has been breathed forth that which is Ṛg-Veda, Yajur-Veda, Sāma-Veda (Hymns), of the Atharvans and Aṅgirasas, Legend (Itihāsa), Ancient Lore (Purāṇa), Sciences (Vidyā), Mystic Doctrines (Upaniṣad), Verses (Śloka), Aphorisms (Sūtra), Explanations (Anuvyākhyāna), Commentaries (Vyākhyāna), Sacrifice, oblation, food, drink this world and the other and all beings. From it, indeed, have all these been breathed forth.' "

" 'It is—as the uniting place of all waters is the sea, likewise the uniting place of all touches is the skin; likewise the uniting place of all tastes is the tongue; likewise the uniting place of all odours is the nose; likewise the uniting place of all forms is the eye; likewise the uniting place of all sounds is the ear; likewise the uniting place of all intentions is the mind; likewise the uniting place of all knowledge is the heart; likewise the uniting place of all actions is the hands; likewise the uniting place of all pleasures is the generative organ; likewise the uniting place of all journeys is the feet; likewise the uniting place of all Vedas is speech.' "

" 'It is – as is a mass of salt, without inside, without outside, entirely a mass of taste, even so, verily, is the Soul, without inside, without outside, entirely a mass of knowledge.' "

" 'Arising out of these elements, into them also one vanishes away. After death there is no consciousness (Saṁjñā). Thus lo, says I.' Thus spake Yājñavalkya.

"Then said Maitreyī – 'Herein, indeed, you have caused me, sir, to arrive at the extreme of bewilderment. Verily I understand It (i.e. this Ātman) not.' "

"Then said he : 'Lo, verily I speak not bewilderment. Imperishable, verily, is this Soul, and of indestructible quality.' "

" 'For where there is a duality, as it were, there one sees another; there one smells another; there one tastes another; there one speaks to another; there one hears another; there one thinks another; there one touches another; there one understands another. But where one has become just one's own self, then whereby and whom would one see? then whereby and whom would one smell? then whereby and whom would one taste? then whereby and to whom would one speak? then whereby and whom would one hear? then whereby andn of whom would one think? then whereby and whom would one touch? then whereby and whom would one understand? whereby would one understand him by means of whom one understands this all?' "

" 'That Soul (Ātman) is not this, it is not that (neti-neti). It is unseizable, for it cannot be seized; indestructible, for it cannot be destroyed; unattached, for it does not attach itself; is unbound, does not tremble, is not injured.' "

" 'Lo, whereby would one understand the understander?' "

" 'Thus, you have the instruction told to you, Maitreyī. Such, lo, indeed, is immortality.' " (Bṛhadāraṇyaka Upaniṣad, iv, 7-15).' "

Again, the Chāndogya has it : "the expanse is the delight, the delight is not in this little." (Chāndogya Upaniṣad, 7th chap., 23rd part, couplet 519.) "Where nothing else is seen, nothing else is heard, nothing else is known, that is the Bhūmā, the unlimited; but where something is heard, something is seen, something known, that is the twisted; the Bhūmā, the limitless, dies not, the limited dies.

"My Worship, where is it located? In its own greatness." (Chhāndogya, 7th chap., 24th part, couplet 520.)

The Kena has it : "The eyes cannot see it, nor speech approach it, nor the mind comprehend it, it is different from what has been instructed into, it is not what we known, it is not what we know not."

Reference

1. "In *Sufism* two forms of mystic exaltation are noticed – abnormal and supernormal. Ibn-'I-Farid calls them respectively intoxication' and 'the sobriety of union.' The second is preceded by the first and does not necessarily follow it. In the first stage the distinction between creator and the creature has vanished, and in the second stage the creature is aware of himself as being one with the creator from whom he, as a Creature, is dintinct. While during the momentary intoxication of *fanā* all the attributes of the self are negated in the 'sobriety of union' they are restored with an increase, i.e. they are transmuted and wholly spiritualized. The highest mystical experience is positive and active in the sense that he who reaches it not only manifests the Divine attributes and actions in himself but maintains a personal relation to the God with whom he is one and who nevertheless transcends him". (Nicholson's *Idea of Personality in Sufism,* page 19).

It should be noticed that though the loss of personal consciousness is a feature in the mystical consciousness, still it cannot always be described as *intoxication*. The physical consciousness indicates the high range of consciousness; the more we get to the highest, the more becomes the knowledge dominant and life serene and calm. The loss of personal feelings is the standing testimony to the absence of all kinds of *intoxication* which is native to the life of love. The mystic approach in the Upaniṣads is more noetic than emotional, and therefore, the loss of personal consciousness in love or devotional mysticism should not be confounded with the eclipse of the personal consciousness as described in the Upaniṣads. The feeling attitude may have some experience when the universal consciousness is enjoyed as permeating Soul and nature when the mind is wide awake with its usual notions and ideas and when its vision has not gone beyond them and touched the fringe of the supernormal perceptions. But with the working of the supramental consciousness the *feeling of intoxication* must have been dropped, for here the ideative consciousness dominates and not the emotional one. And in the final stages the ideative or noetic element also drops, leaving a kind of experience which cannot be designated either emotional or ideational. Intuitions are of various kinds. There are instinctive intuitions, there are emotional intuitions, there are ideative intuitions. But these intuitions are included within the range of normal consciousness. The supramental intuitions proceed from the finer mentality, which is not accessible to normal experience. These are possible when the mind becomes very fine and elastic and is highly strung. These supramental experiences are strictly intuitions of the *Supermind* and cover the archetypes of the Soul. Nay, there are experiences which go beyond these archetypes of the Soul. Nay, there are experiences which go beyond these archetypal forms and the Soul rises in its complete independence of the mind and its limitations and possibilities. The Soul, bereft of its mental limitations, can only feel its cosmic essence and its acosmic transcendence. Surely such experiences cannot be identified with the usual *intoxication of ecstasy* felt in the height of love and devotion.

Chapter VIII

The Evolution of the Conception of The Ultimate Reality

The Upaniṣadic conception of Brahman sometimes bewilders the initiate because it is so varied. Brahman is identified practically with everything, from gross matter to the finest spirit. The search has been direct, and the initiate rises gradually to the appreciation of the finer and the finest. The finest cannot at once be felt and realized. The natural tendency is to welcome that which is directly felt and experienced as truth. It requires a long preparation to make the mind sensitive enough to truly appraise the being and responsive enough to live up to it. Naturally, the inner veils of the self should be removed one by one, not in the spirit of utter rejection, for rejection is beyond question. True rejection is mental and not actual. It is detachment to their functioning. This detachment becomes natural when their economy and value have been rightly assessed. They are then appreciated in their true meaning. Our psychic being is eased because of this right knowledge. Right knowledge gives right conduct. The mystic vision, therefore, is wide, it gives the knowledge of all phases of life. It leaves nothing aside. It is this penetration that makes it so bold an adventure and so fruitful a method. It does not dwell upon a particular perspective of life nor does it spin a theory out of it. Life in its completeness is revealed before it, and the makeup of the man and the universe in its elements are completely fathomed in the search. The Mystic is the Truthseer, not in the sense of enjoying ecstatic intoxication—that, no doubt, is his peculiar claim and privilege—but in the sense of an adventurous experimentalist who claims to see the exact constitution of the human *fabric,* the instincts, the vital urges, the impulses, the ideas, in their intricate blending and complete unison.

This kind of approach is evident in all the Upaniṣads, and the more intimate one is with the texts, the more deeply one is convinced of the scientific approach in them. The conscious interest and the discriminative attention are evenly kept up. Without them, the mystic approach is in danger of mistaking shadows for Truth. Understanding is a great asset in life; in mystic life it is necessary at every step to evaluate the new forces that are released, and the phychism that is stirred. A rich and fine discriminating understanding will be a power in the mystic, not an obstruction, if it is properly exercised. The law of contrariety finds its full play in the mystic life. Light and darkness, life and inertia, follow in quick succession. The higher the ideal, the greater the challenge. The higher harmony invites the greater conflict. And before the soul can pass into peace, it has to invite the deep struggle inherent in its nature. The struggle can be successful if the light of deeper understanding, which comes through living the life, does not suffer loss of radiance. It keeps up the faith when the soul meets confusion and darkness. Mystic life is a life of order, harmony, and balance. It draws out life from its confusion at its lowest limit, and introduces it into the realm of cosmic harmony. Our intellectual shortcoming and spiritual littleness read chaos in life and its expression; understanding alone can remove the sense of chaos and read everything in harmony divine. Mysticism is a life of illuminated understanding and enlightened adaptation. This understanding grows, and cannot be satisfied until it finds rest in Truth. The *Taittirīya Upaniṣad* gives a picture of this ever-growing understanding.

It begins with the conception that Brahman is Annam. Food is the sustaining principle, earth's creatures thrive on food, they are reduced to it (for Annam is also used in the sense of matter after death). This appeal cannot long satisfy.

The next principle is Prāṇa. Prāṇa is Brahman. From Prāṇa originate the Bhūtas (things and beings). They live upon Prāṇa. They pass into it (at death). (Taittirīya.)

The Taittirīya,[1] Śruti has twice referred to Prāṇa, and each time in the sense of a cosmic principle (ii, 3; iii, 3). Brahman is a Prāṇa, and in subsequent passages we are told Brahman is Manas, Vijñāna, and Ānanda.

But the Śruti is careful to add tnat the finer principles of Mana and Vijñāna function behind Prāṇa. They are more subtle, and they become effective through Prāṇa. Prāṇa is the vehicle of an effective expression of still more subtle forces. The Śruti, therefore, does not take Prāṇa to be a source of blind urge.

The distinctions of Prāṇa, Manas, and Vijñāna on this account are not to be minimized; what is the initial urge of self-expression is also a prāṇic urge. The gradual ascent to the centre acquaints us with the intelligent and creative nature of cosmic energy, and so long as the meaning and the creativeness are not explicit, the cosmic energy appears as a blind impulsion, which it is not.

Prāṇa is presented as the vital principle of gods, men, and creatures. The Upaniṣad does not go beyond this in the conception of Prāṇa. The stress laid on Āyu (duration of life) has made the inference irresistible that it is the principle which keeps up and sustains the individual beings, be they gods or men. It is their principle of animation.

The Praśna Upaniṣad gives us a better description of the cosmic Prāṇa (Mahāprāṇa). It brings out Prāṇa in the sense of universal energy, the primal force at the root of the whole creation.

The text reads : – "The Lord of Creation (Prajāpati), verily was desirous of creatures (offspring, *prajā*). He performed austerities. Having performed austerities, he profuced a pair, matter (Rayi) and life (prāṇa), thinking : These two will make creatures for me in manifold ways." The Āditya (Sun) is verily the prāṇa (life), Rayi is the moon (Candra), Rayi is everything here, both what is formed and what is formless. Therefore material form (Mūrti) indeed in Rayi (matter).

Śaṅkara takes Rayi to mean Ānnam (food), Prāṇa to mean Attā (the eater, the enjoyer). The author of the Ātmapurāṇa reaches the same conclusion. Here of course the literal sense cannot help us. Rayi is the creative matrix. Prāṇa is the creative energy. The analogy is this : Attā lives upon Annam and draws out the essence for the upbuilding of the body, so prāṇa (the cosmic life) energizes Rayi (the cosmic matter) to build up the creation. Both proceed from the form the dual nature of Prajāpati, the creator. Prāṇa and Rayi represent Prajāpati in the aspect of efficient cause and material cause of this universe.

We read in the hymn to the Prāṇa in the Praśna Upaniṣad : –

"As Agni, prāṇa warms, He is the Sun, He is the bountiful rain, He is the Wind. He is the Pṛthvī (the earth), He is the Rayi (creative matter), He is Shining God (Deva), He is gross (Sat), He is fine (Asat)), and He is immortal."

"As the spokes on the hub of a wheel, everything is supported in the Prāṇa – the verses, the Yajur verses, the Sāma hymns, the sacrifice, the nobility and the priesthood (the Brahman)."

"Thou art the Prajāpati, thou movest in the womb, it is thou thyself that art born again."

"To Thee, O Prāṇa, these creatures bring tributes – Thou, who dwellest in living creatures."

"Thou art the Chief carrier of oblation to gods; Thou art the first offering to the fathers (i.e. bearer of the Śrāddha).

Thou art the true practice of the seers, descendant of Atharvas and Aṅgiras!"

"Indra, art thou, O Life, with thy brilliance, Rudra, art thou as a protector, thou movest in the ethereal expanse, thou art the Sun, the Lord of the Lights. When thou rainest upon them, then these creatures of thine, O life, are blissful, thinking. 'There will be food for all desire.' "

"A vrātya art thou, O Life, the only seer,
A partaker, the real Lord of all;
We are the givers of thy sustenance,
Thou art the father of the wind
That Form of thine which abides in speech
Which abides in hearing, which abides in sight
And which is extended in the mind,
Make propitious! O leave us not!

"This whole world is in the control of life
Ever what is established in the third heaven,
As a mother her son, do thou protect us :
Grant to us affluence (Śrī) and wisdom (Prajñā)!"

The above brings out the cosmic functions of Prāṇa. It is the guiding force of the Universe. It is the basic principle of the whole creation. It controls and guides the devas, it grants affluence and wisdom to men, it moves the cosmic frame; it is the wonder of the gods and fear of mortals. Evidently it is the cosmic will.

Creation implies a bifurcation of the original energy—which, as active will, is Prāṇa, and which, as passive principle, is Rayi. Prāṇa is the positive element, Rayi the negative. These are not originally distinct, and therefore do not imply a dualism. The one being as the creative energy is Prāṇa, the same being as the formative material is Rayi. Rayi is the eternal feminine of the mystics. They are two aspects of one power—the first of which partakes of "the qualities of the thunderbolt, and the second shares with sentient nature 'that soft resistant force which defies destruction' "; the one masculine, centrigual, revealed and symbolized in igneous action, the other feminine, centripetal agneous action."

The whole creation is the amorous play of the two forces.

The Chāndogya also refers to Prāṇa in chap. iii, 18, 4, where it says : –

"Prāṇa is the fourth part of Brahman. It shines and glows with Vāyu as its light. He who knows this shines and glows with fame, splendour and eminence."

Again in iv, 30 : –

"Brahman is Prāṇa, Brahman is joy."

The Kauṣītaki Upaniṣad has a long sermon on Prāṇa. Indra said, "I am are breathing spirit (Prāṇa), the intelligental self (Prajñātman), Āyu (life) is Prāṇa. Prāṇa is verily Āyu, Prāṇa is verily blessed immortality, for so long as Prāṇa is in the body, so long is life. And, by Prāṇa, one obtains immortality, by wisdom unfailing determination (Satya Saṅkalpa). So, the who reverences me as life, as immortality, reveals the full term of life in this world, and obtains immortality, indestructibility in the Heaven-world.

"Prāṇa is prajñā. These together dwell in the body, together do they depart."

These quotations speak of Prāṇa as the cosmic energy.

The Kauṣītaki Upaniṣad does not conclude with the intimate association of Prāṇa and Prajñā. It goes further to show the supremacy of Prajñā and its omnipresence in the facts of existence and in the psychic and vital functions (iii, 5, 6).

Vāk (speech) is the one portion thereof. Name is its externally correlated existential element.

Prāṇa is the one portion thereof, odour is its externally correlated element.

This supremacy is finally contained in the following clear statements : –

With intelligence having mounted on breath with breath, one obtains all odours.

With Prajñā hearing moulded on speech with wisdom, one obtains all names.

With Prajñā (intelligence) having mounted on the mind (manas), with the mind one obtains all thoughts.

The flow of Prāṇa (life) is eternal. It is continuous and creative.

Time is one with Prāṇa, for time in the objective sense is a flow, and life is a flow. Intellect in its symbolic thinking distinguishes the two, but this distinction is not real; for time cannot be separated from motion, and Prāṇa is the motion with which we are familiar.

The objective time is dintinct from succession units, and is, in fact, the cause of these units. The succession supposes a flow, which in itself is undivided, and this self-creative flow is time in the objective sense. The divisions of past, present, and future impress the intellect, but the division is not real in the self-expressive effort, which is one eternal duration. Is the Akhaṇḍa Kāla, which is eternally self-reproducing continuity. Time is represented as a form of expression of reality. The other form is space. Space and time are generally thus used in the sense of forms of expression. But time in reality is not merely a form. It is the shaping, moulding force. Time is creative.

The creative principle because it is creative takes on it form, but this form is not separate from the principle; at least the sense of separateness is the creation of symbolic thinking. If we go far, we can see and feel that the sense of time begins when the creative energy takes a definite shape or form. The idea of time is associated with this, especially as generally understood. Time makes the idea of beginning and end clear, and in a world in which nothing functions, time has strictly no meaning and no sense. Time is then the creative energy on the point of expression, change, development, and progress. But, if these ideas are taken away from it, the sense of time as well as that of energy completely vanishes. The idea of duration as occasionally moulding and creating brings to us the conception of time, and apart from this moulding time has no sense. The sense of time as a form makes the idea and understanding of change as something different from energy and brings out the conception of space, time, and energy as the essential trinity of the phenomenal universe. But the fact is that time is not a separate category from energy. It is energy seen in its concrete and limited form of moulding.

Khaṇḍa Kāla (time in series) is time in the proper sense. Akhaṇḍa Kāla is time in the form of energy which is eternally creative.

The intimate relation between Prajñā and Prāṇa and Prāṇa and Vāk is full of meaning to the ardent seeker of Truth.

Prāṇa is associated with Prajñā. The dynamic element is the creative, the expressive, and the organizing power. It is the urge behind life, it is the urge behind creation. But this urge is not blind. It is associated with Prajñā, the illumination in the heart of the Universe. The dynamic element is the force and the principle of expression, the element which spins the whole creation out of itself. It creates the drama. It winds it up. But the comsic drama reveals a meaning, has significance; it is not, therefore, the drama of a blind force, it is not a capricious event. Definite beginning or end it may not have, the whole event may be spontaneous, but it is not blind. Hence Prāṇa is always to be associated with Prajñā (gnosis).

But Prāṇa does not function with a definite end or purpose. Prāṇa functions spontaneously.

Prāṇa is not the unconscious will at the heart of the universe. Prāṇa is the cosmic will behind the psychic and the cosmic functionings. It is the primal force. It objectifies in the form of ideas; since Will is unfettered, its creative ideas are also unfettered. Schopenhauer's will represents the Prāṇa more accurately, but the difference is that Schopenhauer would see nothing behind Will; the Upaniṣadic seers see the *Prajñā* behind it. Hence, there is no blind spontaneity nor telelogical finality in the functioning of the cosmic Prāṇa. The movement of the cosmic will cannot be reduced to any form of teleological purposiveness based upon the conception of finality, nor can it be reduced to the spontaneity of a blind will. The whole movement is an expression of the *effortless* and *purposeless* Ānanda.

Prāṇa functions without definite end, but this does not reduce it to a blind spontaneity. Its functioning is spontaneous, but not blind. And this clearly defines the relations between Prāṇa and Prajñā. Prāṇa emphasizes the dynamic aspect, Prajñā the essence of Being, and the two are one when Reality is represented in its creative aspect. When the adept cannot rise above the perception of an eternal fluidity of becoming, he has the vision of Prāṇa as well as Prajñā.

Prāṇa is referred to Prajñā and this reference distinguishes Prāṇa from *ēlan vital* of Bergson. Bergson's principle is alogical; so is Prāṇa, but Bergson's principle has no reference to anything else. It is the ultimate reality. But such is not the case in the Upaniṣads. The Prāṇa is the creative principle, but it is always associated with Prajñā. Prajñā in its creative aspect is Prāṇa. The fundamental reality is alogical but not unconscious.

Prāṇa is never free from a reference to the ultimate conscious princple. But Prāṇa has periods of occasional equilibrium in its depolarization, the *ēlan vital* has no such period of inertia or rest.

The association of Prāṇa with Prajñā does not make Prāṇa an idea-force. Prāṇa is not exactly idea-force. The latter presupposes the former. Idea-forces are the creative ideas which reveal themselves with the formation of a mind. They have a reference to a positive self. But Prāṇa implies the activity without reference to a concrete mind. The formation of a mind becomes a necessity when Prāṇa begins to function in concrete and definite form. It is evolved. It is shaped. But Prāṇa is the original dynamic reality, it is no effect of an idea, nor is it an idea, for the concrete mind is formed long after the evolution has traced its onward course. Hence, the thought forces cannot be identified with Prāṇa.

The Upaniṣads conceive an intimate relation between Prāṇa and Vāk. In Hindu Mysticism the first creative expression of Prāṇa is Vāk. Vāk is the Prāṇa personified into speech. It is the divine Sapience expressed in word. This Vāk is not the ordinary speech. It is the first concrete expression of wisdom which the elect alone can hear in the depth of their concentration. It is the medium of divine revelation. Prāṇa is impersonal, Vāk is personal. It is concentrated expression in a form. And it has the limitation of an expression.

Brahman is Conceived as Vijñāna

The primal Prāṇa is the creative force. But creation implies arrangement and order, and the shaping of forms. The effectual forms are moulded after the casual forms. Forms are inherent in the heart of the creative order. The non-differentiated becomes differentiated in creation, the non-manifest becomes manifest. Creativeness implies that the formless takes on it form, the modeless shapes itself as modes; the emergence of the world of forms is not possible unless there are the creative forms in the causal order. These forms are the idea-forces prevalent in the order of intelligence (Buddhi). Vijñāna is not merely the functional intelligence. It is the creative intelligence residing in the heart of things. The functional intelligence is expressive but not creative. The creative intelligence is dynamic.

The cosmic creative intelligence is intermediate between the cosmic Prāṇa and the cosmic manas. The cosmic Prāṇa causes the primal matter to stir,and this the cosmic intelligence shapes according to the objectification of the primal will in the forms of ideas.

The archetypal intelligence with its divine harmony can be felt in the world of Vijñāna, for the creative ideas exist in their rhythm. Rhythm prevails in the world when the one expresses the many, and the archetypal order represents the finest unfolding of the one into the many. When the peace of the one is disturbed by primal oscillation and polarization, the quiet or the silence is displaced by rhythm, the harmony or the beauty of the causal creative plane. This is the divine harmony, for it is the harmony in the heart of becoming undisturbed by the conflict and the confusion which arise as the manifestation flows more and more into the passive matter. There is harmony everywhere in a great or small degree, but the harmony is more towards the centre of existence than towards the circumference, for life becomes divided as it drifts away from the centre. Harmony prevails, therefore, more in the world of ideas and essence, than in the world of appearances.

Brahman is Conceived as Manas

Manas is creative. The rhythm of creation is the expression of the archetypal beauties, sublimities, truths, or values in a definite setting. It has, therefore, the sense of a limitation, and needs the exercise of a generic volition. The spontaneity of expression in the causal order—either in the world of the cosmic Prāṇa or the archetypal forms—is almost absent here, for the creative will is active, and is anxious to give a form of expression amongst others. The active and personal will first moves here. The will can be active when there is a question of choice between alternatives,and this choice is to be exercised in the order of effective creation. Active will is associated with a limitation of creation and mouldings of forms, and intervenes when the archetypal ideas receive definite and determinate expression. Between the spontaneity of the archetypal ideas and the spontaneity of vital life appears the dominant and determining will. And naturally so, for life is spontaneous in the realm of complete light and complete darkness. This spontaneity differs; one is the spontaneity of idea, the spontaneity of the super-conscious, the other is the spontaneity of the vitalism, the spontaneity of the insentient.

In one of the joy of rhythm and harmony reigns, in the other confusion, darkness, and inertia prevail. The order is not such as can reflect the truth and harmonies of the higher life.

(Hence, perfect rhythm is not possible even in the creative plane, for creation does not mean the origin of a new thing. It is resetting or rearrangement. It awakes rhythm in discord, infuses movement in inertia, creates beauties in ugliness. Manas represents the creative nature of Brahman).

Creativeness is self-conscious and self-directed activity. It is, as it were, to carve the slab of marble into a beautiful figure. The self as artist is revealed in it. The artist derives inspiration from the realm of ideas or archetypes. The inspiration may be spontaneous, but the execution is conscious. The artist plays his part half consciously and half unconsciously. Creativeness has reference to both. The cosmic artist in its creativeness cannot forgo this dual nature. It creates, and for creation the inspiration proceeds spontaneously; but, in its execution, it rises to the fully self-conscious effort, for it has to work out its design. It has to evoke life, harmony, beauty, and rhythm for the creative matrix.

Creativeness needs the active exercise of will. Manas is the active will. The will cannot create unless it be receptive of the rhythm of the realm of ideas; will submits to this rhythm in order to plant it in the "negative", the creative matrix. Creation shapes the negative element, and it is an endless process. Creativeness has therefore reference to a negative element, to a conscious agent, and to the world of harmony, rhythm, and ideas. It has not the ease, the purity, and the elasticity of the realm of ideas, since it has reference to an extra-ideal, extra-positive reality or thing. Hence, the sense of self becomes prominent in creativeness; the sense of an active creative, and necessarily self-conscious agent.

This *self-consciousness* is a limitation even in the cosmic sense, for it brings out the rhythm of creation more fully. It at the same time requires a conscious inteference and exertion to shape and mould the forces, to make them instrumental to the expression of the divine plan and idea. Creation is the rhyming of the forces in accordance to the divine will.

This process is continuous. It cannot cease. It will not. For creativeness can have no meaning, if it has a finality; the process continues to establish the divine rhythm and harmony–creation is, as it were, the rush of the divine life from its inmost recess into the world of receptive matter. So long as, the least difference between the shaping forms and ideas and the receptive matter continues, and so long as the lost equilibrium is not established, and the complete depolarization is not achieved, creation will never cease. The creative divinity is displaced, as it were, from the supreme silence and suffers limitation inasmuch as it is incessantly active to shape the forces and to release particular forms and types.

Creativeness then represents the picture of the divine in its limitation of a self-conscious idea or power. The sense of personality attends the creative effort. Take away this effort, the sense of personality dies away.

Hence, a difference is to be drawn between spontaneous expression and purposive creation. The former has no reference to a self-conscious agent and self-directed activity. The latter has. The former is consistent with the primal substance, the latter is consistent with the creative agent. The former does not consciously energize for creation, the latter does. Īśvara in that sense has no limitation of a creator, in the highest sense it enjoys the elasticity of an embracive being. It is equally present at every point of existence. It is Suprapersonal. Brahmā is personal, and has therefore the limitation of a creative personality.

Its delight is the joy of creation, the symphony of the formative life. Creativeness which attends the formation of self-consciousness may be individual and cosmic. But in each case there is the limitation of self-conscious formation. This self-conscious creativeness is represented as *Manas* in the Upaniṣads. Manas is Brahman in its creative aspect. And Prāṇa attends Manas to give effect to the creative purpose. Prāṇa is the cosmic energy which is instrumental to the creative principle and art. Manas is Prāṇa in its creative effort.

Brahman is Manas in the sense of the cosmic creative principle. Mānas represents in man the desire vehicle, the volitional self. Will is essentially creative.

Preservation follows creation. Self-consciousness comes out indistinctly in creativeness. It becomes prominent in preservation. If creativeness has a rhythm, preservation has also its harmony. Creation is the displacement of confusion and the emergence in harmony and rhythm.

Preservation is the continuity of this harmony. Rhythm is the soul of it. Preservation is more rhythmical than creation, for it is free from the internal opposition that meets creation. It is all melodious, there is no dissonance in it. Creation has to overcome opposition, and, therefore, the self-conscious life in its selective aspect is more prominent here, and the rhythm is therefore confined to the joy of construction. And the joy of construction is different from the delight of preservation. The former has a tension, the latter has no tension. It is the joy of life in its embraciveness and synthesis. There is no the least discordant note, and hence, the expression of life is the highest and the fullest. Hence, all the kindlier elements and softer beauties of the soul find expression in it. The life of preservation is very delicate. The least confusion immediately breaks and destroys it. It refuses all ugliness, all inertness. Life has here its highest delicacy and sweetness, its greatest attraction and charm. Hence, the sense of effort and restraint in creativeness is displaced by that of ease and elasticity. In the rhythm of preservation, self-consciousness has at times the low and high tide and has a tendency to pass into aesthetic forgetfulness.

This tension of maintaining the equilibrium keeps the soul active in this plane, but the equilibrium once established continues for a time, and in this interval there is the possibility of enjoying the complete concord, perfect unison, and harmony which occasionally lull the soul into the sleep of delight. It is really no sleep of self-forgetfulness, it is the sleep of self-awakening into the harmony of beauties and sublimities. The spontaneity of the soul becomes manifest, and in this spontaneity the self as the creative or preservative agent has an occasional respite. Hence, the perfect harmony of preservation is more attactive than the rhythm of creation, for here the self is freed from the limitation of creativeness and can enjoy the more expressive rhythm.

The soul can enjoy better the harmonies of the archetypal order in the rhythm of preservation than in the rhythm of creation. In the absence of the least dissonance, the harmony of preservation may approach the harmony of the archetypal order and the soul in perfect peace can have glimpses into the delight of the order. Hence, the beauties and the harmonies of preservative order can make it possible for the soul to gain access into the mysteries of the archetypal realm and pass into the temporary forgetfulness of the environmental surroundings. This access into the world of ideas – into the Buddhic plane – is not possible for the creative self.

The process of withdrawal has its own rhythm; creativeness has its special harmony; so has the process of withdrawal. The rhythm of creation is the special setting of the original negative substance, the rhythm of withdrawal is the breaking of all forms of special arrangement and grouping. If creative rhythm expresses the universal through the concrete, the ideal through the actual, the positive through the negative, the archetypal through the sensible, the rhythm of withdrawal represents the delight of the concrete passing into the universal, the actual into the ideal, the negative into the positive, the sensible into the archetypal. The cosmic drama plays a twofold function. It plays one part in the emergence of the concrete life and the concrete existence. It plays the other part in the disappearance of the dance of life in the eternal background. This disappearance is no confusion which attends the disruption of order and arrangement. It has its own rhythm, the rhythm which has the withdrawing effect of the particular and the concrete into the universal and the general. It is the bold invitation to the delight which follows the tracing of the cause in the effect, and the withdrawal of the effect in the cause. The rhythm of creativeness is the rhythm of expression of the caue in the effect, the rhythm of withdrawal is the indrawn process of the effect vanishing into the cause. The delight of the former is the delight of the concrete, the delight of self-production; the delight of the latter is the delight of the abstract, the self-inversion.

The self-inversion does not stop with the sensible and the actual, it also implies the withdrawal of the supra-sensible, the world of ideas and forms. The suprasensible world of forms may represent the causal, and in the process of inversion the effects pass into the causal, the actual into the formal. But the process does not stop there, it goes further : the archetypal ideas and values pass into the homogeneous.

There is a cosmic regeneration. There is a cosmic sleep. The rhythm of withdrawal becomes more and more intensive and delightful, the more it proceeds to the centre, to the supreme silence which reigns there. The rhythm acquaints the seeker with the positive and the negative element of creation, with the twofold aspect which reality takes upon it in its creative urge.

The adept undergoing spiritual evolution becomes acquainted directly with the positive and the negative principle of creation, for the bifurcation comes to our direct knowledge in the centre rather than at the circumference.

The cosmic withdrawal is the reverse of creation; and the forces are depolarized in it. Hence, it has a greater harmony and melody than creation; in creation a jarring note of a struggle is possible if the negative principle does not automatically yield itself to the positive principle. The opposition may create confusion. The rhythm cannot be completely established in creation. But different is the case with withdrawal—here the natural tendency for the negative and the positive is to merge their individualities in their original unity. This cannot be possible unless the mutual attraction is strong and the negative gives up itself to the positive completely. The rhythm of the withdrawal is more enjoyable because it helps to attain the finest equilibrium and poise of being. The eccentric tendency of creation is here displaced by the centric urge of the union, and hence, the soul experiences the unique delight of the perfect rhythm and silence. The least confusion mars the rhythm, the destroys the possibility of the perfect peace and silence in the merging of the forces. Hence, the highest delight of withdrawal can be felt when there is nothing to prevent the complete withdrawal of the negative into the positive. The rhythm of withdrawal is opposite to the rhythm of creation.

The more the process approaches the centre, the more embracive it grows, and the attraction towards the centre becomes the more manifest. The delight of the indefinite displaces the delight of the definite and the creative, and the soul has its dance of life drawn to a close in the delight of stillness and absorption. The rhythm of withdrawal gives the calm.

But this calm is to be distinguished from the calm of transcendence. This calm is the end of the withdrawal. It is the hushing of life's noise and life's dance into life's silence. It is, as it were, the occasional remission from the free expression of life in its creativeness. This silence is the precursor of life, it is the point where life returns after its period of oscillation and play. It is its initial point of emergence, it is the final point of retirement. Hence, the process of withdrawal is characterized by the absence of all activity characterizing creation, and requires for its establishment the wise passivity of the soul.

It has its peculiar feeling. Creativeness has its joy, withdrawal has its delight. Creativeness leads to the joy of equilibrium, equilibrium presupposes tension : if it supersedes the tension of creation (involved in conquering and opposing forces), it has the tension of maintaining the forces in proper adjustment, and for its continuity. Withdrawal has not the least tension, for it has neither to establish an order nor to maintain it. In withdrawal all tension dies out and the forces attain their original unity and neutrality. Hence, in withdrawal the self retires to itself completely – and this retirement is not *self-loss* in *self-creation,* but self-consciousness in self-immersion. Since, the mind is always habitually accustomed to the concrete, and is often led by the concrete urges, it cannot always consciously feel the higher level of self-consciousness in the withdrawal. It presents the often neglected side of life, and is often, therefore, thought ot be a blank and a negative. Blank it is not. Bliss it is. The Śruti calls it *Ānandam,* not the bliss of creation but the bliss of withdrawal. If creation presents the self in its creative aspect, withdrawal presents it in its cosmic sleep. It is the region behind the vital forms and the creative planes. The supraconscious intuition of the archetypal forms is superseded, for there are creative and active forms; they cannot be effective in the process of complete withdrawal. The archetypal aspect of life has its own delight, the delight of free movement and expression, the delight of perfect harmony.

The delight of harmony is here the greatest, since in this superconscious existence there is not the opposition that is met on the creative plane.

The archetypal forms are active in the supraconscious self – in the cosmic self – they are also withdrawn in the process of self-immersion. The delight of self-immersion is, therefore, higher than this harmony of the archetypal existence. It is the delight of reitrement of life into its source. It is the delight of the forms vanishing into the formless, of life hushing into the silence.

The archetypal forms of the Vijñāna-Maya Koṣa are supposed to be the finest in the order of expression, as they represent the ideal world of ideas and values which can be effective in the creative becoming and can give shape to the creative matrix. They are concrete formative principles. They represent the dynamic divinity in its supraformal expression. These, indeed, are expressions, but have no particular forms. They are more expressive than creative. Creativeness implies the duality of forms and matter. Where the cosmic life surpasses this duality of ideality and materiality, and has still an expression, it must necessarily be finer than the ideal forms. This, therefore, should be regarded as the formless form of the becoming.

Reference

1. Prāṇa in the Taittirīya Upaniṣad – A confusion may rise between Prāṇa as the vital principle and Prāṇa as the cosmic principle if sufficient care is not taken of the context in which they are used. Prāṇa as the vital principle cannot be superior to the finer forces

of desires and intelligence, and as such it comes next to Annam (gross matter). It gives the stay to the body, it organizes it, it vitalizes it. It is the stay of gods. It is the vital principle of all creatures. (Taittirīya-Brāhmaṇa Bod- 2, 3.) But when the distinction is drawn between Prāṇa and Manas, it draws out the gross and the fine nature of the urges. The urges on the vital planes have not the fineness of the mental urges. In mental urges the first stirring of psychism is felt, and here the vitalism is associated with the finer dynamism of our psychic nature. The distinction between vitalism and psychism is clear. Vitalism gives animation, movement, organization; psychism gives feeling, deliberation—in short, mentalism. Vitalism cannot reflect the light of consciousness, psychism can. Hence, the psychic forces appear as exhibiting greater loveliness, better fusion, and greater unity. They have a conscious reference to the psyche.

Prāṇa in the sense of force can be attirubted to the psychic forces, but Prāṇa in the sense of vitalism is the form of universal cosmic energy, or will assume a definite form for a definite purpose. When, therefore, reference is made to Prāṇa, its meaning as a cosmic principle cannot be lost upon us, though this principle be at times used in different senses, either of universal vitalism or of psychism; but vitalism or psychism is the limited conception of Prāṇa. It is the cosmic will, the *ēlan vital* of the universe. Hence the conception of Prāṇa is given better expression in the Praśna Upaniṣad, where the sense of the cosmic energy is more explicit. The universal energy is neither vital nor psychic, but something more, something that takes these definite forms, but in itself it is the principle of eternal becoming. It is neither biological, nor physical, nor psychical; but it has these forms of expression. The Taittirīya Upaniṣad has the following :—

"The gods do breathe along with breath (*prāṇa*)
As also men and beasts,
For truly breath is life (*āyus*) or beings,
Therefore it is called the life-of all;
To a full life go they who worship Brahman as breath,
For truly breath is the life of beings;
Therefore, it is called the life of all."

(Hume's translation.)

Chapter IX

Phases of Dynamic Divine

Brahman as Sat and Asat[1]

There are apparently two contradictroy epithets of Brahman in the Taittirīya Śruti. "Nothing he becomes who speaks of Brahman as nothing" (ii, vi). "There was nothing in the beginning and from the void the Sat comes into existence" (ii, vii).

This is no contradiction. The one speaks of Brahman, the other of the cosmos. Brahman is Sat. It is the primal existence. It cannot be non-existent. The cosmos, in the beginning of a cycle, is non-manifest. It is practically non-existent. The cosmos emerges, and so long as the emergence is not actually felt, it is thought of as non-existent, in the substance.

The nature of cosmic void becomes intelligible to us in the moments of introversion or withdrawal in deep sleep. Introversion gives us the idea of a blank, a void in experience before it can finally pass into the transcendent silence. The void is not really void, it is the point where the psychism of our being has a temporary remission from activity where the soul has risen above the ordinary experience, but is not in possession of the final vision.

The psychic mind is habituated to the content and the fluidity of life and it has a unique experience when it passes into calmer and deeper waters of life. The waves of life are withdrawn and naturally the soul of the initiate has the feeling of an emptiness and void beyond the noise of life.

The sense of a void is a great relief from the exacting and masterful urges of life. It discloses the complete independence of the soul. The natural tendency is to identify the urges with the essence of our being; but such occasional remissions from them speak in no uncertain terms of the freedom of the self and the deep repose of its being.

The Taittirīya has a string of contrary epithets for Brahman—Sat and Tat, Niruktam and Aniruktam, etc. These epithets indicate the relative and the absolute nature of Brahman.

In the cosmic life there is a periodical quietude and sleep—a periodical awakening and pulsation. Life starts afresh from the void. The void is the quiet repose in silence. It is the Sleep of Peace which the cosmic life enjoys after a period of activity.

Some think the void to be beginning of a new start in life. But void cannot give rise to appearance, even deceptive appearance. The apparent void is not void, it is the complete withdrawal of prāṇic urges. It is the state of cosmic equilibrium. The emergence of the cosmic process indicates that the cosmic poise is disturbed, and the positive and the negative forces are active.

The disturbance of the cosmic poise is followed by the finest prāṇic oscillation. This oscillation has its greatest rhythmic expression. And the duality of creative ideas and the formative matter is not yet formed. The dynamism is active in formless shaping and colourless vibration. The archetypal forms and colours become visible in the world of archetypes but not in the world of formless light and sound. Light and sound are the first expression from the void. These are first formations of the positive and the negative forces. They are fomless expressions.

Brahman as Śabda (Word)

The formless expressions of the Prāṇic oscillation are Nāda and Bindu.[2]

Nāda originally means a sound, a tune, a vibration. But not all kinds of sounds are Nāda. It is something that cannot be heard by the ear. It is the sound that reigns in the heart of the cosmos. It is the voiceless voice, the soundless sound of the deep. When the ear has lost the power of hearing, then it catches the harmony of harmonies, the delightful sound that is ever present in the soundless deep. It captivates the soul and withdraws it instantly, and with every cadence it breaks the chords that create ripples and disturb the equanimity.

Nāda is the first ripple of expression in the void, the voice of the voiceless. It is the first stir of expression. It is the first impress of the cosmic intelligence. It is continuous. It is akin to the music of the spheres.

"When now the wheel, which thou dost make eternal,
Desiring thee, made me attentive to it,
By harmony thou dost modulate and measure."

(Divine Comedy, Paradise, i.)

The music of the spheres is expressive of the rhythm that pervades the world, Nāda is the rhythm that pervades the causal world.

The harmony of the spheres acquaints us with the music that moves the universal forms. This enraptures the soul and sends it heavenward. The poet says in the Divine Comedy : "The newness of the sound and the great light kindled in me a longing for their cause."

The rhythm of the starry dance was set to the sounds arising from the motion itself and making unceasing music which was recognized and known as the harmony of the spheres (Gompherz : *Greek Thinkers,* Pythagoras).

The music of spheres is at best a reflection of Nāda. Life is music because it is harmony. The music of the spheres is the music of life through the starry universe. Nāda is the music with which life starts into growth. It is the eternal melody of life, the superb harmony we enjoy, when we have the most and the finest of life.

The original Nāda rises when the prāṇic urge meets the primal Ākāśa, the original ethereal expanse. The prāṇic urge vibrates the ethereal medium, and harmony is set up. This harmony is the first expression of intelligence, for before it the prāṇa was in equilibrium and no flutter could take place. This agitation in prāṇa and ether is rhythmic and is therefore delightful. The rhythm is sweet and attractive beyond measure.

Brāhman is the basic principle. Nāda is the expression. The first concrete expression is Nāda.

Nāda has two phases : (1) meaning, (2) harmony. The meaning becomes explicit when the harmony is deep. Meaning and harmony are co-eternal with Īśvara or Saguṇa Brahman, for Saguṇa Brahman has in it the constant stir of expression. The word "meaning" is used here only in the sense of expression, for in the highest realm of spiritual life there is expression. Meaning is always associated with personality. It is presupposed in finite expression and construction. But it cannot be so in the divine where life has its expression, but no definite meaning. The divine life is all harmony, free from the *contraries* of tension or relaxation, and therefore, in a sense, in it there is fine expression, but no meaning. Meaning is attributive to expression, where it is seen in a definite setting and distinct perspective.

Nāda is an expereince in the supramental or suprasensuous consciousness. It is supramental in the sense that it originates in the primal expression of Brahman in the void, and comes, therefore, prior to the evolution of life and mind. It is a unique experience which is received in the intense tension of the inner dynamism when it becomes sensitive to the suprasensuous consciousness.

Māyā is sometimes expressive and sometimes creative. It

is creative when it produces forms and modes. The creative activity, therefore, is more gross than the expressive activity of Māyā. Nāda and Bindu, therefore, belong to the expressive dynamism rather than to the creative dynamism of Māyā. And, therefore, they are beyond the grasp of the senses and mind. They are revealed in psychic intuition (in the Vedāntic sense). The word mind has a narrow limitation in the Vedānta, it means nothing but deliberative faculty. The supramental, therefore, implies here that which is beyond the reach of the normal mentation, beyond the normal functioning of mind. The suprasensuous psychism is continuous and reveals the dynamism of Māyā in its causal aspect, where no concrete formations or functionings take place. This phychism is therefore, something to be distinguished from the ordinary psychic activities inasmuch as it stretches itself out to the very core of existence. The sensuous mind is in touch with the senses, the suprasensuous mind is in touch with the core of our being. The former records the sense-impressions, the latter records the suprasensuous creations. Nāda is suprasensuous revelation. It is the fine cosmic vibration and has a great indrawing power. It can be received in the moments of psychic repose and withdrawing.

It requires to be aroused by the vigorous activity of the inner psychic dynamism. Its intuitions and receptions are immediate like the sense-receptions, though they represent the opening of the new powers of the soul.

The individual sense intuitions are displaced by the cosmic vibrations. But they are certainly distinct in character from the empiric intuitions by their being independent of the sensuous reference implied in the latter. The mind begins to exercise cosmical feeling and intuition.

The suprasensuous character of Nāda distinguishes it from empiric intuition. But it should not pass for transcendent consciousness. For, though it is supra-sensuous, it is not suprapsychical. It has a reference to the psyche of our being, and the psyche is different from the soul. When the senses and the lower mind are still and cannot function, the psychism reveals the inmost secrets which are otherwise inaccessible. And the realm of the formless becomes revealed to it.[3]

The mystic is the most sensitive of beings. He is hypersensitive, he is suprareceptive. He receives the flow of life in and out, in its expression through forms and expression beyond forms. He is the lover of life, and the life he lives is intensive. Hence, he cannot be irresponsive to life's expression in the world of forms as well as in the world of the formless. He feels about him the outpouring of life. He revers every expression of life "and any naivete, no matter how it is expressed, is more sacred to him than any phenomena limited by external form and prejudice" (Keyserling : *Travel Diary of Philosophy*, p. 104).

The mystic is keenly receptive to the play of life in the minutest living thing as well as to its depth in the core of being. His mentality cannot be exclusive. He enjoys the expression of spirit in the spatial and the temporal order. He is eager to break the bonds of space and time to enjoy life in transcendence; and, therefore, he can reject nothing. Spirit is his quest, and spirit he feels in the movement as well as in the silence of being. Such being the elasticity of mystic life, it refuses to see our categorical limitations. And the mystic spirit is essentially the spirit of acceptance, and not of denial. It can see the distinct value of every phase of spiritual expression, but it is always attentive to the unity and integrity of the spiritual reality. It is the truth of truths (Satyasya Satyam). And this unique insight enables mystics to unite the spirit of acceptance and the spirit of transcendence in their own life; while remaining responsive to the outpouring of the spiritual life throughout the universe, the mystic spirit cannot feel the fullest joy in the expression of life. The mystic is the lover of the complete and the eternal. The mystic appraises the beauty and the charm of life; but, since these can be better enjoyed in the spring of life than in its tidal waves, the mystic is anxious to get therein.

The charm of life invigorates and intoxicates the ordinary soul, but the mystic spirit cannot remain satisfied with any form of intoxication. Intoxication clouds the vision and disturbs the spiritual equilibrium which is necessary for appraising the Truth behind the appearance. In spiritual life the distinction should be drawn between appearance and reality. For there are spiritual phenomena, lights and sounds. They are the delights of fine psychism which can attire the soul with fine radiance and glamour, but the mystic soul should steer clear of them. Happily, there is in the spiritual life such conscious or unconscious self-evident indication of Truth that the soul cannot be deceived by the wayside attractions. Even if it, for the time being, be overpowered, it cannot remain long therein, provided it does not lose its psychic purity. The finest impulse in the mystic is the elevating impulse of knowledge, and, unless the psychic knots deeply laid in life be very gross, nothing can disturb theh spontaneous flow of life towards knowledge and Truth. The mystic is above all the lover of Truth. Freedom is the quest. Truth gives freedom. Hegel is perfectly right in his condemnation of common religious experiences, for they deflect us from the right objective truth.

L. De La Vallee Poussin says : "Vāk, the voice, is praised in some passages as another Logos, but this Logos is magical sound, not reason" (*The Way to Nirvana,* p. 24). This is a partial statement of truth, Vāk is the force which moves the universal framework. To say it is magical sound is to miss its import, it is the universal energy in its finest creative expression. Every creative expression, formless or with forms, has a meaning immanent in it, though the divine life must not be supposed to have a meaning akin to our own. The idea of immanence endows every move of expression with a meaning which is not otherwise realizable. Hindu mysticism in almost all its branches has laid stress upon Nāda as the most fruitful method of touching the heart of reality; and, if Nāda is only a magic sound, this possibility does not arise. Nāda quickens the warp of our being and, through its delightful music, the soul finds its easy entrance into the mysteries of creative dynamism.[4]

Confusion must not be made between the so-called mystic voices and mystic sights and the Nāda and the Bindu; the mystic voices and sights are sometimes due to the working of subconscious mind, and sometimes due to the "influence or possession from the finer world, due to agencies or incarnates" (F.W.H. Mysers : *Human Personality and its Survival of Bodily Death.*) The former bespeaks some forms of receptivity of the soul, and suprasensuous audition and vision—sometimes it may take the form of telekinesis. The latter, on the other hand, implies the suprasensuous vision of the deeps of the soul, in which the procession of introversion is almost complete.

In this height of being, expression and concentration are still impersonal and have not settled down to a *personal locus.* Īśvara as dinstinct from Brahman has a concentration, but not a personality in the usual sense of the term. Personality implies concentration, and something more, viz. spiritual fascination for fellowship in love and delight. Such personality Īśvara certainly does not possess. His is a concentrated being in a wide expanse; concentrated because the forces are centred round him, but this concentration should be distinguished from finite concentration.

Personality is identified with concreteness, for a concrete being is the centre of powers and qualities. But concreteness and concentration are different. Concreteness may imply and presuppose concentration, but concentration does not necessarily imply personality. A point has a concentration, but no personality; Īśvara certainly has no personality in the usual sense of the term.

Īśvara is more impersonal or superpersonal than personal. Personality implies limitation. Personality is a lower category, it implies not only concentration, but an outer-reference. The self and the not self must be clearly bifurcated before the sense of personality can emerge. In Īśvara such a division is not possible – and the expressions are spontaneous and impersonal. They are distinct from the personal creation. Nāda is one of such spontaneous expressions. It is therefore impersonal. It is no creation of a person. It has no reference to the creative order. It denies any personal interference. It has no personal origin. The independence of any personal origin makes it co-existent and co-eternal with Īśvara. Personal creations have beginning and end in time, for they are creations. Such is not the case with impersonal world. It is not a creation. It may appear and disappear. In the state of cosmic equilibrium and poise Nāda has no expression, for here the formless universe also disappears. It is a state beyond all urges and is realized only when the Prāṇa in us has the highest rhythmic movement, and passes through the quieter oscillations of Nāda finally into a silent expression. In this rhythmic functioning in its state of highest tension Māyā (the creative dynamism) gives rise to centres of light technically called Bindu. Bindu is the point of energy and light. The primal expression of the creative dynamism is the light that the eye cannot see, and the sound that the ear cannot hear. It would be wrong to suppose that the dynamic principle is ever inactive. There may be a falling off in activity when the two opposing tendencies – the centric and eccentric – meet in complete equilibrium. In such a state there can be no expression, no activity.

Expression goes with activity, with stirring – hence, the formal expression in *Bindu* is the shooting light of the creative function. It is not light that shines in the creative order. It is not the light that shines in itself in transcendence. Bindu is the light at the point of the creation of forms.

Bindu is the state prior to Nāda. It is the silent light that illuminates the causal order, the light that knows no darkening. It is the first in the order of expression and not of creation. Nāda silences by its delightful music, Bindu overpowers by its ocean of light. The one enraptures the soul, the other illuminates it. Bindu is Brahman transcending the creative order. It transcends the creative intelligence, the archetypal forms, for the archetypal forms have a reference to creativeness and as such they belong to Brahman as a creative power. But Bindu transcends all these. Māyā exists here in expressive activity. Bindu is beyond all ideative activity. Nāda is the initial activity of expression, the first breaking point of the equilibrium of the cosmic dynamism. Bindu is the dynamism in finest tension.

Bindu is Brahman with its Śakti in a state of expressive activity. Brahman is the transcendent being without the touch of Śakti. Bindu is the expression of Śakti, Brahman transcends Śakti. Bindu is the first expression of dynamism when it has not settled down to creation.

Before the world of concrete effects can materialize, the force of becoming has an abstract expression, and this expression is a move in being itself and may be freely called formless appearance. The emergence of forms takes place when the original impulsion settles itself down and the world of concrete causes and effects is therefore a world of distinct modes. But this world is of definite creation, and has a definite progress and end. This definite creation requires a focussing of intelligence and this intelligence is essentially architectonic.

Nāda and Bindu have their importance in this way, that they reveal to us and introduce to us the realm in which the first transformation of the dynamic divine takes place. They have, therefore, a charm and an attraction which cannot be experienced in the concrete creative order. The joy of the creative order is the delight of expression of values, it is essentially the delight of personal creation. The joy of the non-creative order is the delight of relaxation of the tension implied in personal creation.

The world of concrete effects is continuous in creation, preservation, and destruction. The one supposes the others. This continuous flux of becoming in the world of concrete effects does not touch the initial or the formless expression.

This world of concrete facts has a causal aspect, which is subtler and finer and can be immediately seen in the flight of yogic consciousness. Brahman as architectonic intelligence is therefore a definite form of consciousness, which is co-existent with the world of forms. As architectonic intelligence it has sure activity, but it is powerless beyond the world of form. The archetypal intelligence shapes, beautifies, and controls the cosmic order.

The formless world is non-creative, though it is expressive. The world of forms is creative as well as expressive.

Creative in the sense of having made a definite beginning can be ascribed to the world of forms. Forms originate, forms die out, but the formless world beyond the forms has no origin, no end. The world of forms passes into the formless when the cosmic creation comes to an end. Even in the world of forms there are higher and lower gods controlling them, and they differ from the cosmic creative and preservative intelligence in this, that they have not the cosmic sense. They are departmental agencies, fit for the minor ends of the department. This harmony of gods as creative or preservative intellingence has been fruitful to the panpsychic conception. The multitudinous gods are not independent or free forces. Their distinction has the look of a pluralism, still their ultimate dependence upon and resolution to an original unity takes away the shadow of pluralism.

In the world of forms, the mutual reciprocity among the gods or shining intelligence also speaks for the unitary hypothesis of being.

The Upaniṣads are not eloquent about the gods : and in them is noticed the three successive phases of being : –

1. The transcendent Sat-Brahman.
2. The formless and shapeless becoming, the world of formless expression.
3. The world of concrete forms and effects.

The same thread of lift runs through these stages, they differ only in condensation and concentration.

The delight of the first is the delight of transcendence, the delight of the second is the delight of expression, the delight of the third is the delight of creativeness. Mystics are often fond of the creative delight, but the deeper delight awaits them in the non-creative planes, which hardly can be enjoyed by any but mystics. The range of consciousness is not ordinarily so vast, nor its pitch so high. But the movement of mystic life is subtle, it touches the entire gamut of life in transcendence, expression, and creation. It appraises the values of life in its fathomless depth, in its utmost expansion, and in its concrete expression. This privilege is the mystic's because of the cultivation of a transcendent sense of appreciating reality.

Grace

The dynamic divine has other functions besides the cosmic activities. It is at work in shaping, organizing, and beautifying the cosmic order, it is equally active in beautifying, purifying, and chastening human souls by constant impresses from within. Nothing is free from its influence; but if the nature outside exhibits its creative and compelling power, the nature within exhibits it as shaping and chiselling human souls and making them fit receptacles for the secrets and mysteries of life, faith, and knowledge. It takes the human soul in its charge and carries it under its protection to the finest realms of existence. It widens its knowledge. It finally reveals the highest truth, which can conquer the fear of a divided life. This dynamic divine in its capacity of drawing souls exhibits a phase of its being which is not manifested nor called for in its cosmic activities. Grace exhibits the dynamic divine in its saving power and in direct relation to finite souls. This function is an additional one and can be exercised only in reference to beings conscious of spiritual values. Grace which beautifies the soul puts the dynamic divine in a better and higher form than archetypal intelligence, for the dynamic divine gives, here, care and protection. Therefore, in the function of grace it rises in finer activities and subtler impellings inspiring faith, hope and knowledge.

These are ends which are the finest expression of the spiritual ascent and towards which the whole cosmos is moving. The cosmic ends are the outward flow, grace is the inward flow of the divine life, and the dynamic divine in its finest activity is the carrier, protector, and illuminator of souls. This indrawn current of the dynamic divine is the source of spiritual and holy life, it removes the soul from the influences of the divided life, the natural clingings, and opens it to the spiritual influence which all along like the proverbial "mother bird" takes its charge under its protection, and delivers it to the ocean of light. (Katha, Kena, and Śvetāśvetara.)[5]

Hiraṇyagarbha, the cosmic Puruṣa, gains illumination from it. Hiraṇyagarbha is the first emergent Puruṣa that is conscious of the world of the concrete effects in its totality; in it the light of consciousness is focussed into a centre. It is supremely self-conscious. Its being is intensively self-concentrated. It is self-consciousness in excelsis. But this self-consciousness is its limitation. It can reflect the world of causes and effects, but it cannot reflect the formless and the shapeless world behind. It needs illumination. The light of knowledge is not its own. This also is acquired. Hence, it is in constant search of the light that does not meet the eyes, the light that tarries but changes not.

Hiraṇyagarbha has the inward light to reflect the cosmic totality, but it has not the light to reflect the dynamic divine and the basic being. It suffers in a sense from the limitation of a person. It needs light. It requires further illumination. This illumination proceeds from Īśvara which lies beyond the world of forms.

Christian Doctrine and Word and Nāda

Christian mysticism lays stress on "word." St. John identifies the "word" with Christ, "word" is reason of the philosophers. "The world is the poem of the word to the glory of the Father, in it, and by means of it, we display in time all the riches which God has eternally put within Him. 'The word was made flesh and tabernacled amongst us.' " (Dean Inge : *Christian Mysticism,* p. 46.)

"Word", be it reason or its expression, is supposed to lie at the base of creation. The world comes out of it, and, it is said, through it God displays all his riches and this expression is made definite in Christ. Christ, then, is the word or reason in concrete form. In this two implications are clear : (i) Word is reason; (ii) Christ is reason in flesh.

In Mīmāṁsā and Vedānta the relation between meaning and expression has been held to be eternal, and God cannot change them even if he would. The sense of an arbitrary fixing of a meaning to a word is not even within the compass of God, and as such to the Vedāntic and Mīmāṁsā teachers and Śabda has eternally a fixed connotation.

Śabdas may ultimately be expression of God, still God has no control over them, and, in the cycles of creative evolution, the same word has the same meaning. This connotative fixation is not dependent upon God. It is native with the words themsleves. In this sense the word is said to be impersonal. God cannot interfere with their meaning and expression. It comes to this, then, that the "Word" is a form of expression of God, over which He can exercise no control, i.e. which is another way of saying that God cannot change His own nature, and that there is no need of a change. This evades the doctrine of an arbitrary choice and power, but does not interfere with the all-embracive God. Word is power.

The Christian doctrine of "Word" is personal. Reason is personal. And word is reason. Reason and personality go together. Reason is a higher category than a mere impersonal fact or existence. For it embodies in it the creative rhythm and freedom. Word is, then, the divine Sapientia in its creative expression.

The Hindu doctrine of "Word" differs from the Christian conception. Reason is associated with personality and therefore, cannot be attributed to the super-personal Īśvara. Reason comes to be manifested with the creation of forms, it is the possession of the archetypal ideal. It resides in the world of ideas.

Hiraṇyagarbha is the Primal Reason, since it is the first person, the first individual emanation from the world of silence. The Upaniṣads do not pin their faith in the personification of word. The Brahma Upaniṣad has it : two Vidyās are worth acquiring : (1) Śabda-Brahma, (2) Para-Brahma. The adept in the fomer can gain easy access into the latter. The Śabda-Brahma is this initial and formless expression of the super-personal reality. It transcends the world of ideas; the expression of Reason, individual or cosmic. "Word" is, therefore, a great help to pass into the realm of spontaneous expression, to go beyond the creative realm of ideas into the ever-expressive music and harmony of the uncreate world. The world of creative reason has its rhythm, but it is a sham reflection of the former. It cannot be reproduced in the creative world. The voiceless voice has its absorbing and ehchanting music. It has a great indrawing power – for it really uplifts the soul from the delight of the creative order to the delight of spontaneous expression. The inevitable effect is that it lulls the creative functions to sleep and acquaints us with the realm of formless and spontaneous expression.

"Word," therefore, in the Upaniṣads represents higher reality than the *creative reason*. Hence it is commonly supposed to stand for the Para and Apara Brahma. Para-Brahma is the Nirguṇa aspect of the Absolute, the Apara-Brahma is its qualitative aspect, i.e. Saguṇa aspect. But the Saguna Īśvara is superior to Hiraṇyagarbha, who is the first personal expression of the Impersonal-Brahman. "Personality" of reason and word has not been emphasized in the Upaniṣads. They have an impersonal or super-personal aspect. But the super-personal should not always mean the transcendent. The personal aspect of reason or word is not yet formed and created. The "word" and "reason" have their super-personal character. "Word" in the Upaniṣads implies this aspect of the infinite. Om is the word. Om is Praṇava.

The divine life has an inconceivable stretch beyond the concrete personalities and architectonic forms which can be appreciated when the thread of life is pursued beyond its concrete expression. Then can the human nature feel no distinction between itself and the dynamic divine, and rites from the limitations of forms to the depth, subtlety, and overpowering life of the formless, and finally to the luminous transcendence pervading the supra-mental life. Nāda is the formless expression of the dynamic divine when in the pervading silence the dynamic divine has not diversified itself into functioning forms. The expressive urge has the finest thrill. This thrill of life has no definite functioning and is naturally pervasive of the whole universe in its finest aspect. The functioning intelligences can enjoy this fine thrill of life. Spiritual life has a luminosity all through, but the deeper it dives the luminosity passes from the luminosity of forms into a boundless, ceaseless, all-embracing luminosity. This realm extends far beyond and penetrates far deeper than the creative plane, and spirituality here is of a dizzy height which overpowers the soul.

The Brahma-Upaniṣad recognizes that the adept in the Śabda Brahma can have entrance into Para-Brahma. The tuning of our psychic being, after the harmony of the Śabda Brahma, makes it receptive to the mysteries of the Apara and the Para-Brahma. It transcends the archetypal beauties. It gets over the delight of the creative rhythm. It enables the soul to enter into the realm of peace. It enables the soul to cross the Rubicon, to pass beyond Hiraṇyagarbha, the first emergent cosmic Personality, and allows it access into the formless and the impersonal but not into the transcendent.

The "Word" has the redemptive force. It is the centric urge, which frees it from the earthly forces.

Word has the force of redemption. The creative force is also redemptive. The intiial expression is eccentric, it is also centric. The two are relative and interdependent; the creative is the self-expressive and the redemptive is the self-immersive. There is a reflex activity in the human soul. It receives, it gives. There is a reflex activity in the divine. It gives, it receives. The "Word" represents both the tendencies, but for the earnest seeker, it is the indrawn force towards the centre. And as such it is purifying, chastening, and finally redemptive.

The urge of self-immersion presupposes the urge of self-expression. "Word" represents these two urges. It has in it an expressive urge, it has in it the indrawing urge. The two forces go together. The one is the necessary consequence of the other. Had there been no expressive force, the redemptive force also would have been absent. In silence and complete equilibrium of becoming the problem does not arise.

But in this expression or immersion, there is no exercise of personal will, and the whole performance has the ease of spontaneity. But it is not mechanical.

This may sound strange, and naturally so. The higher is the pitch of spiritual life, the more attractive are the delicacies, the finer are the charms. The spiritual life in its unfoldment is a life of beauty, power, and majesty, and not seldom the soul is confined to those and cannot soar beyond, mistaking these stretches of spiritual expression as the highest experience. Spiritual life is often identified with power and creativeness, and when these have the highest intensity and potent expression a notion naturally gains ground that spiritual life has its acme of realization. When the life's pulse is vibrant with creative force, the adept has a new experience, a meaning, a new vision of life, and this sudden expansive feeling of power and the delight of creativeness have the effect of overpowering the spiritual ascent for the moment. And the underlying notion of life as intimately power and creativeness has the invariable effect of associating spiritual realization with the dynamic divine and of checking the finer course in realization for the moment. Unless the adept can pursue the attitude of complete detachment the mysteries of a still higher and finer spiritual life cannot be revealed to him. The detachment to the dynamic divine in its concrete expression gives the key to the higher expressions beyond creative forms and intelligences in supreme puissance in spiritual life. The word and the light extend far beyond the realm where the original mode of expression divides itself. The word and the light are therefore more affective powers than creative intelligences and forces. The former have no limitation, the latter have.

The "Word" is redemptive in the sense that it helps the seeker to realize the highest privileges attending the personal life, by evoking the finest and the richest possibilities lying dormant in the soul by allowing the soul to transcend its personal nature and its limitation and understand the impersonal truth. Religion here passes into philosophy. The impersonal nature of the "Word" together with the impersonal nature of Truth dawns upon the seeker and thoughts of personal joys and satisfaction become completely overshadowed by effulgence of Impersonal

Truth. "Word" wakens in us the understanding of the impersonal and inspires its vision, saves man from the masterful urges of personal self, and enables him to feel the sublimity of the Impersonal. It bestows the double privilege; the complete frictions of the potentialities sleeping in the soul, and finally its deliverance from them. It is redemptive in the sense of deliverance from the world of limitations and the final installing into the realm of silence. This is the true axis of spiritual life in the Upaniṣads. It is the life of spiritual evolution and final emancipation. Emancipation follows the finest development of a personality. Emancipation may be direct in the case of the fit, it may be indirect in the case of the less disciplined souls. But in the complete scheme the finest promise of emancipation goes with the highest evolution. Emancipation indicates that the spiritual illumination cannot reach its acme, unless joy of the concrete functions of spiritual life can be forsaken for the silence of the Impersonal and the Transcendent.

References

1. The word "Asat" according to Sureśvarācāryya, the author of the Vārtika, is the nameless and formless Brahman. The world as non-existent is the same as Brahman in existence. (Vārtika, pp. 1, 2, 5, 15, 16.)
2. Mention of them is frequent in the Upaniṣads. It is in the Kaṭha, the Praśna, the Chāndogya, the Māṇḍūkya, the Muṇḍaka. The Nādabindu and the Tejabindu are the special texts for them. What is implicit in the earlier texts becomes explicit in the later texts.
3. A distinction is to be drawn between soul, spirit, or psyche and mind (including the senses). The mind works in association with the senses. It is the lower mind. The higher mind works independently in the world of ideas and ideals. But it cannot penetrate into the causal world. Hence, it is advantageous to conceive the psyche or the spirit which intermediates between the soul and the mind.

4. *Vākyapadīya* (a treatise on the philosophy of Sanskrit Grammar by Bhartṛhari) has traced the successive stages of Nāda. The original sound is soundless sound (sound in quintessence). It has no verbal expression. It can have none. It requires a form before it can be expressed. That form is dhvani. This sfoṭa, the original sound-form, though one, has various forms. Sfoṭa is the original sound-form. Nāda is the expresion. The original form assumes many forms according as the expression is quick or slow, long or short, high or low (*evam nādasya hrasadīrghap lutatvodāttatvādi vidrutādivrttibhiśca stavanena sfoṭo vicitrām vṛttim anuvidhatta ityarthāt*).
5. On this point the Upaniṣads do not all give us the same impression. The Śvetāśvetara and the Kaṭha have explicit reference to the divine grace, the Kena has an implied reference.

   In this connection it will be profitable to remember that all spiritual illumination proceeds from the dynamic divine. He reveals the Vedas. He illumines Hiraṇyagarbha. He is the source not only of life but also of light.

Chapter X

Esoteric Realizations

The dynamic divine is rich in wealth of attributes. It is complete in its powers. The whole creation moves automatically in its wake, the Gods, men, beasts. (Kaṭha Upaniṣad). It is quiet and restful. It is sublime. It is the tree of existence with its root up and its foliage down. In includes all. It supports all. The text says, "that which is thus becoming, streams out of it..." The fire burns, the sun shines, Indra, the thunder-god, air, and death all move through its force. It gives delight. It inspires. It is rich in the contraries of qualities it exhibits. But its wealth of qualities and the delight consequent thereupon stand in marked contrast to the quiet of transcendence. It is not emptiness. The one exhibits its power, dignity, knowledge, majesty, the latter its impenetrable and mystifying silence. The former is infinitely rich in attribute, the latter is listless in self-effulgence.

The one exhibits its dynamic fullness, the other its immensity. Almost in all places, where references to Brahman, fullness, immanence, and transcendence are presented side by side, the Chāndogya (iii, 14) in the śāndilya-Vidyā points out the vivid presence of Brahman in the minutest of the minute existences and in the self. And that which throws light in the self is said to be larger than the earth, vaster than the vast ethereal expanse, vaster than the heavens, vaster than the Cosmos. That, which is in the being of seeds is in the self, that which is in the self is everywhere and greater than everything. It is intrepid activity, it is the essence of all desires and all tastes. The self is in one. It is Brahman.

The Śvetāśvetara also has it : "The deva, the effulgent one is immanent in everybody, it is all-pervasive, it is the inner self of all. He presides over destiny. He lives in all. He is conscious. He is alone. He is without qualities (vi, 11). None has ever seen His equal in Power. He has neither body nor sense. He possesses superior powers in knowledge, in action and in strength, and these are natural with Him. There is nothing in existence, from which a right inference about his nature can be drawn. He is the cause of all. He is the cause of all causes."

The Bṛhadāraṇyaka has it : "The great Ātman, who lies in the *heart-space*, is the Controller, the lord, the master of all. Merit cannot add to its greatness, demerit cannot subtract from its greatness. It is the lord of all, the preserver of creations and the stay of all."

The term "spiritual quiet or silence" does not fully indicate the realization. It looks poor inasmuch as it has apparently no content, and quietude seems to impress the blankness of spiritual life, and therefore, it is not uncommon that such a life is often taken to be the negation of spiritual life, rather than its fulfilment. Goaḍapāda truly says that even the adepts are afraid of so dizzy a height of spiritual life.

This apprehension betrays a timidity of spirit, since it refuses to ascend to the height of spiritual realization. The concrete spiritual life holds us so firmly that fear inevitably arises as soon as there is the least attempt to deny the basis of experience. But the Upaniṣads are most eloquent about the height and the spiritual life which does not allow any stir and division in it. The usual distinctions of the Divine and the human and their fellowship of the concrete spiritual life are lost in it. Since; the dynamic spiritual life in it is ever rich with such distinctions it naturally fights shy of transcendent approach. This clinging to the natural life is a bar to the appreciation of the depth of the calm in spiritual life. But the *calm* of transcendence is to be distinguished from the *quietude* in the dynamic spiritual life. Even in it there is an apparent quietude in realization where the seeking soul is overpowered by the dignity and the majesty of the dynamic divine. The soul also enjoys a sense of quietude when it realizes the impersonal aspect of the divine beyond the divine personalities.

It is the realm of the divine immense, where the divine powers and personalities do not exhibit themselves. The dynamic divine has an impersonal aspect. When the attractions of the spiritual oscillations do ont attract us, the impersonal aspect of the dynamic divine is realized. But this impersoanlity is not the impersonality of transcendence, it is the impersonality of the formless dynamic divinity. The dynamic divine comprises within it divine personalities as well as the formless divine. The divine life is plastic enough to express itself in divine personalities as well as to maintain the supra-personal vastness and immensity of existence in itself.

The immensity of the divine life oversteps the limitation of all activity; here the dynamic divine is realized in itself apart from concrete functionings which impose upon it a concreteness and a personality.

The Upaniṣadic teacher feels this and is, therefore, anxious to bring the quiet and freedom of transcendence to the fore as the end of fruition in mystic life, though it does not completely brush aside the claims of the dynamic aspect of spiritual life.

Dynamic fruition consists in enjoying the diffusion in spirtiaul life. It lies in opening the self to the impress of expansive life touching us both from within and without. The human soul is freed from the limiting and checking influences and is gradually given up to the divine urge in life and consciousness. This has the immediate effect of protecting the self from the instinctive urges of a limited personality and of putting it under the direct influence of the divine urge. An intimacy is established between human and divine urges, and the human urges are no longer supposed to be all-too-human : life is felt in its magnitude, depth and width of being. It gradually rises from the falsity of divisions to the appreciation of an all-encompassing life expressed in the urges.

The spiritual life in its initiation often welcomes such infusion of the dynamic divine as the end of the spiritual quest; but the more it advances, the more it feels that the spiritual life is not and cannot be confined to the personal life and to its harmony, rhythm, elasticity, and delight. Spiritual formation may mould the personal life in all its aspects and can exhibit correspondence in the divine life in its different personalities. The initiate may feel the expression of the dynamic divine in majestic and sweet personalities, in the wealth of its creativeness, in the terrific joy of its destructiveness, in the ease of life, and in the sweetness of its love and grace and preservation.

Nay, the spiritual life and its fruition may go so far as to overstep these divine personalities and feel the impersonal divine where the distinctions in felicity and knowledge are overcome by the intuition of an impersonal existence. This is the impersonal aspect of the divine. It is not transcendence. Personality and impersoanlity are comprosed with the divine. There is an impersonal aspect of the divinity superseding personal expressions. The personal aspect of the divinity is relative to the functions it exercises in creation, preservation, and destruction. But besides this Isvara has an impersonal aspect when it does not manifest itself in these creative functions. This is the stage when all the functionings are suspended and apparent sameness of the divine life is manifested. And exactly for the same reason the impersonal divine appears to be devoid of the richness of the creative content.

But this should not pass for the transcendent. The transcendent denies distinctions, the impersonal supersedes them. The impersonal is the main basis and spring of the eternal stream of life.

The analytic and synthetic concentration melts away, for this distinction is not absolutely real. And the elasticity of life speaks directly in favour of so expansive a being and life. That life has not this realization and is due to inertness. But this is given a direct denial by the elasticity of life and consciousness which the mystic enjoys.

The fruition in the dynamic spirituality has its stages : (1) The stage of an expanded receptivity. Here the initiate is the recipient of the inspiration from the dynamic divine. (2) Sooner or later this stage is crossed and the consciousness of a recipient is displaced by the direct consciousness of an expansive being. As soon as it is established the truth is felt that the division is a myth, and the spirit that throbs within is one that inspires life without.

The dynamic fruition, therefore, initiates man into the sense of divinity and endows him with divine powers, and as such gives him a control over nature implanted in him. It may sound strange indeed that wise passivity reveals the encom-passing life, but it is a fact and is the promise in mystical life. The mystic ideal is not merely to enjoy the divine life by remaining separate from it, but to enjoy it by becoming one with it.

But the dynamic fruition has still finer stretches and penetration, and the self-alienation in divinity is lost in the life of spiritual equilibrium *in Īśvara*. Here individuality completely drops out and is displaced by the effulgent light of the self beyond the stage of personal expression and personal being.

The aspirant for the dynamic spiritual life cannot remain satisfied with the partial expression of a concrete spiritual life. The uplifting and indrawing urge works incessantly and introduces the aspirant to the personal aspect of the divine. It enjoys the equable delight and the fine expression of the highest personality.

For it is still in the realm of the creative personality. However strong its urges may be, however sweet and soft its touch may be, however inspiring its influence may be, the seeking soul cannot take long to feel its limitation; the limitation of a person. The dynamic spirituality is still active and reveals the impersonality of the divine. The soul feels delight in the realm of the impersonal divine and enjoys the depth of its being. This delight is not the delight of a fellowship with the divine, it is the delight of an immensity of being in which personalities are not formed and expressed.

The being and the delight are alike impersonal. Such a consciousness intermediates between the delight of personality and the blessed Peace of the Transcendental.

And, therefore, the stretches in impersonal and superconscious life should not pass for the final realization and the mystic ideal of the Upaniṣads. Such a march of life has its value, attraction, charm, fruition, but this cannot install the soul in its calm.

There is a difference between the realization of the divine personality and the impersonal divine. These realizations are luminous. But the one radiates, the other does not. The one sheds rays vividly, the other does not. The one is life in its dance of expression, the other is life in its mute silence. All stirrings, all harmonies, all ripples of life have their source in this mute impersonal divine. It is more majestic because of its incomprehensiveness. It is mightier because of its inexhaustibleness.

But the terrific transcendence beyond the music as well as the silence of life, far exceeds the dynamic fruitions in richness of spiritual value. It presents a unique experience beyond personal and the impersonal divine. The former is life as well as illumination. The latter is illumination. The first is life in its cadence, the second is life in its silence, and the third is illumination. It is difficult to retain the fullness of this illumination, "the brilliancy of a blinding light," without any specification to be lighted up. It is a great revelation which frees the devout spirit from the oppression of existence and thought and from the intoxication of life and its fruition, from the jostlings of the psyche and her hopes and fears, delight and tears.

"The psyche is the intimate associate of the animal soul, but the home of the spirit is the desert." The psyche adjusts herself to the dance of life, enjoys its professions and gratifications, its progress and revelations, the fine tremor in the inner being. It enjoys the soft kisses, in the moment of rapport of union which the encompassing and vibrative life bears upon its blossoming soul.

But the fullness of psychic life and its delight is not to be mistaken for the transcendental calm and its dignity, for the former fills the being with finer delights of a finer sensibility. However fine the psyche being may be, it is associated with our higher mental nature; the psyche is born of spirit and matter, its delight cannot be the delight of pure being.

Its aspiration can be to enjoy the finest vibration of the creative urge in nature and in spirit, and, being a child of nature, it cannot enjoy the delight supernal of the spirit detached and transcendental. The finest development of the psyche makes it possible for it to feel the fine thrill of life and to develop finest intuitions into the wide stretches of existence, but it cannot endure the dazzling light of transcendence. It dies a natural death before that terrific silence of spirit. It cannot survive in the region of pure spirit, but through its finest development it can see the grandeur and the sublimity of Being in itself and can welcome its death knell, being aware and convinced of the victory of spirit over matter. The child that is born of spirit and matter realizes at the end of the life's journey the dignity of pure being—which is its Being—and casts off the history of its orientation and nativity in the realm of spirit and matter. This is Vidyā (the science, the superior wisdom which gives the final victory and the conquest of Truth over life, of Being over psyche). This truth enables us to cross life and death, the littleness of individuality, with its fears and anxieties. Life passes through completeness to silence, through fullness to calm. All partialities are shadows of death, the completeness should be sought through partialities, the sense of completeness gives the final promise and realization. The calm which is beyond time, beyond the ever-creative life, is Prajñā.

The extreme monism of Śaṅkara cannot accept that as the finest spiritual experience which has the least touch with relative life; and, though life grows in fineness, subtlety, inexplicable beauty and grandeu, Saṅkara would regard such a life as still a spiritual adventure, cut off from the height in the transcendent. Art, religion, and æsthetics, together with fine the play of the mystic sensibilities, are such experience, for they indicate the opening of a leaf from the sealed book of the super-consciousness. They might have a place in the inmost expression of being, stil they belong to the order of expression. But according to theistic reading they are truly esoteric, belonging as they do to the synthetic consciousness which is true reality.

Whatever the differences there may be in the interpretation of the texts—call some of these experiences esoteric or not, that is a mere matter of name and opinion—there cannot exist the least shadow of doubt that the mystic consciousness as it blooms feels the fine life, develops the fine receptive sensibility. It has stretch after stretch of subtler delights in finer vibrations of life, until such oscillations pass off into the silence.

These oscillations reveal the wider regions and subtler realms otherwise inaccessible. The mystic life is not to be confined to the silence of the inscrutable being which cannot be in any manner measured or followed.

The far-reaching stretches of the dynamic divine are equally claimed by all, but those who emphasize the joy and the transcendent attitude in mystic consciousness, do not set a high premium upon them. These, they hold, come on the way with deep penetration to which the inward nature yields and exhibits all the wealth it possesses. Therse are subtle delights attendant upon the fine oscillations and rhythmic vibrations of the inner being. They give out the inner wealth of becoming; the vibrations htat reach the mental plane in almost all cases are not swift enough to hold the vital and mental oscillation sufficiently high to feel and understand the ease, freedom, and wealth of becoming. In spiritual life such dance of life, with its exquisite beauty, inconceivable sweetness, inexhaustible wealth, unfailing vitality, swift action, sure power, and overcoming majesty, has an overpowering influence upon the soul, which not infrequently identifies the supreme puissance with such consummation. The dynamic divine is still His ideal and actual approach. But the texts do not stop with such delights and have clear indications of the transcendent, which naturally has a quietening effect upon the dance of life and offers the possibility in spiritual life of tasting the "Beyond".

Mysticism is the blossoming of life, and in the finest blossoming all the phases of life must find an expression. Hence, the mystic life has at times different tunes and different melodies. Sometimes the being is gently moved by aesthetic and love feelings, sometimes overpowered violently by the inrush of divine power, sometimes by the silence of Being. These expressions are the privileges of mystic life. They must come to the sincere seeker; but all of them have not the same value and hold in life. The mystic attitude is generally in the beginning theistic, it is in the end transcendental. Especially is it so in the Upaniṣads. The Upaniṣads do not at once begin with the stern attitude of a refusal of all experiences in mystic life, rather they seem anxious to carry the seeker through the widest possible elasticity and passivity of its being, which allows all possible experiences through the gateways of nature and the soul. Naturally, the value and the experiences which please the initiate cannot inspire the adept, for he has transcended them in the calm. This realization is unique. It cannot allow the assimilation of the experiences previously felt, for they belong to an order which has no access to the calm.

The calm, therefore, represents the highest Truth, and its realization the highest good, since it allows emancipation from life in its division, and enjoyments in their partialities. This emphasis has given the Upaniṣadic mysticism the character of transcendent mysticism, though it also exhibits experiences that invariably satisfy the less adventurous souls. The loss of the personal hold of consciousness, the evaporation of the history of life and its development, reaches so dizzy a height that many shudder at it and avoid it as the void; but the brave amongst mystic souls are pleased to welcome this void, as offering the greatest promise and the highest experience : promise, because it allows the uncommon privilege of enjoying the ocean of being behind the ripples on the surface; experience, because it gives the restive being undisturbed Peace. The loss of the personal hold, therefore, brings a new kind of experience which cannot be assimilated to any other kind. Even the peace of the void, which is the immediate consequence of a deflection from the personal consciousness or of a falling off in it, bears no comparison to the peace of truth. This deflection or this falling off has the resemblance of a sleep, a momentary overshadowing of or break in the personality. It is sometimes an obsession, sometimes an inertia of being; but it is not the wakening in the silence. The void, even when it is the precursor of the calm, can be only the negation of experience; it is in itself enjoyable; but life and our psychic being cannot long continue with the experience of a blank negation. It is the rest, the quiet after activity; but nature breaks equilibrium. The seeker must, therefore, proceed further and discover the light. The mystic consciousness feels the dark abyss of the soul and the void represents it. The sense of a "Void" haunts the soul that righlty follows the mystic urge to the end. This proves a terrible experience, because of its unfamiliarity and because of the suspended activity of the psychic self. The timid soul cannot welcome it, for it denies the normal and the usual.

The great charm of the Upaniṣads lies in impressing the truth and the peace of the transcendent at the same time, indicating thus possibilities both spiritual and effective.

In the presentation of dynamic and transcendent spiritual life the Upaniṣads do not encourage a life of progressive evolution in spirit more than a life of immediate transcendence. They only indicate that the soul in its receptivity and spiritual elasticity may feel the music and the symphony of life in its ideal and actual aspects and in its creative expressions. But the spiritual realization is not to be confined thereto. There are realizations that come on the way. They are the secrets which are disclosed to the aspirant and the seeker. And the seeking of the soul is not satisfied with these magnificent and sublime possibilities unless the final truth is presented, unless the silence displaces the music of life. Life offers the joy of creation, the blessings of love, the rhythm of fellowship. Silence offers the freedom of transcendence. The supreme relief of detachment gives the sure peace and strength of truth. This silent peace is the greatest offering and promise of *Parā Vidyā*, the esoteric wisdom.

Chapter XI

The One and the Many

The relation between the one and the many is a perplexing problem in philosophy. Philosopher are sharply divided. Some assert the reality of the many; some of the one. Some are anxious for an indivisible unity of the two. When the problem is approached through logic, such divergence of opinion is inevitable. Logic can at best give a *rationale* of relations and intellect is inherently incapable of transacting them. Whatever interpretation may be put upon the facts and their relations, it is almost impossible for intellect to deny them or to see facts as they are. Intellect, therefore, becomes involved in antinomies when it conceives the ultimate reality. Intellect is the best organ in man to understand the world of phenomena, but it is a doubtful counsellor in the spiritual life. Intellect stands quite dazzled by the elasticity and freedom of the spirit. Sometimes it appears as many, sometimes as one; sometimes as near, sometimes as distant; sometimes as great, sometimes as small. Intellect stands confused, it remains stupefied. It cannot square the inevitable contradictions that seem to be deep in the life of spirit. And naturally so. Spirit is too subtle an existence to be measured by the set categories of logic. The personality and the impersonality of spirit are problems that are raised by intellect, but do not belong to the nature of spirit. Spirit transcends both the descriptions; for are not these after all the attempt to define spirit, and is not definition a limitation?

True to the spiritual insight, the Kaṭha has it : "the one reflects itself as many."

Spirit has wonderful elasticity. It appears as smaller than the smallest, greater than the greatest. This elasticity is beyond the conception of set categories. Spirit appears to be many while it is one. It appears to be distant while it is near. This elasticity is a fact. And the beauty of it is that throughout all experiences and expressions, however contrary, spirit is not changed and never does change. Spirit is the one, spirit is the many, the many emerge from the one, the many emerge into the one. These are common places in the Upaniṣads and quite in conformity with the mystic spirit. The texts finally deny the many in the one.

To such affirmations none can take exception. Difference becomes eloquent regarding the nature of the many and its relation to the one.

The mystic is not disturbed by these differences. He views the problem in a different light. He is not anxious to deny. He is no tanxious to affirm. He stands above affirmation or denial. And therefore the mystic often appears as a contradiction and a conflict when he insists upon the sacredness of personality and at the same time seeks to lose it in the "Ocean of Being". The mystic feels life in its silence and expression, in its intension and extension. The mystic in his superior detachment can see and feel that personality is a temporary limitation of the soul, which it is urgent to put off by cultivating the inner vision and quickening the mystic illumination. Mysticism is anxious to retain the hold of personality up to the source, when it does not refuse a plunge into the deep. Personality is sacred, but personality is to be lost.

This contradiction runs throughout spiritual life when it is separated from the source. The contradiction cannot change its fundamental nature. It only shows the spirit in its expression. If there is an original contradiction in self-expression, there again rises in spiritual life a contradiction in fulfilment. The one is the yearning of the spirit to exhibit itself, the other, of the spirit to pass finally into the clam of its being. These tendencies are original, and no reason has been advanced so far or can be advanced for such a temporary expression and a calling back.

Logic has spent much energy in squaring these difficulties; philosphical imaginations are at work to evade them, but the facts stand there in spite of all human efforts to dismiss the finite form or to install it permanently in the scheme of things. The mystic fights shy of both courses; he accepts the finite selves, though he is equally anxious to get to the essence of being.

The fact is that the mystic is conscoius of an unfathomable deep or a beyond behind the finite and the definite; and his practical experiences tell him of the mysteries and the delights of the deep, and sometimes he experiences such depths.

Such experiences of the layers in the deep of our being have been the sacred source of inspiration and belief in such a life. The mystic naturally is anxious to give up the seen and to catch hold of the unseen—the unseen is his joy, the unknown is his quest.

Those who are anxious to retain the thread of personal consciousness all along in life have even to accept the magnitude of being in exalted states.

Naturally, in this height of being the adepts do not retain the thread of personality, and the Upaniṣads are clear and eloquent about it. As such they are ready to lose hold of personality, though they trace in the order of expression the successive phases of the creative order.

In later philosophy the apparent contradictions have been fruitful to the diverse philosophical constructions in Śaṅkara and Rāmānuja.

Both Śaṅkara and Rāmānuja draw their inspiration from the Śruti and both are anxious to read their theories in it. The texts are pregnant with rich suggestions that can lend their support to the theories of both. The Śruti speaks of a creative expression of Brahman and in the same breath gives a clear indication of everything merging into the Absolute. There are texts which clearly speak of the complete transcendence of the Absolute.

Spiritual life leaves no side of life untouched and unfulfilled. It gives full satisfaction to every part of our being. It touches all the chords of our nature. But this should not lead us to confine spiritual life to concrete realizations. Naturally the souls overcome with sufferings feel the weight of existence, and the first flashes of spiritual life are hailed with delight. The freshness and the case which invariably follow the spiritual awakening are not necessarily the fulfilment of spiritual life. The idealization of life and its relations in the wake of spiritual life has a fascination for the soul. It enlivens the normal experiences. It adds freshness to them. It makes them more enjoyable. It does not kill the expectations of life. It assures the fullest satisfactions of the hopes that spring constantly in the human breast. It promises everlasting life. It heals up the deep scars left in the soul. It makes life rich in experience, fertile in creation. Spiritual life is attractive because of its promises; and naturally, when its first fruits are enjoyed, the ardent spirit becomes overwhelmed in the festivity of delight. The psychic dynamism exhibits itself at its best, and the soul enjoys the rhythm and the harmony of spiritual life in their infinite varieties and inexhaustible shades.

Such spiritual experiences have a natural effect on our life, which finds in the harmony of life the key to unlock life's mysteries. And the universal harmony of the cosmic fellowship has been a commonplace among mystics. In spiritual life the value of harmony cannot be overrated. The more the soul is filled with harmony, the more clear becomes the vision of life that animates creation, the joy that dances in the heart of things. Harmony removes the spiritual dryness and insensitiveness of the soul. It reveals the unbroken unity of life. Spiritual harmony reveals the truth of the one in the many and the many in the one. If spiritual experiences have been confined to harmony, the truth of the reciprocity of the one and the many would have been the final truth.

The Upaniṣads, we have seen, conceive this harmony, but they are not confined to its truth and glory. Harmony is the law of spiritual life in its expression. It gives the radiant vision of the entire structure of existence filled with animation and the dance of life sustained in delight.

The Upaniṣads proceed far and welcome the calm in spiritual life. It is a unique experience. It reveals the Truth, silence beyond life, the poise beyond the dance of life. It gives the experience of the indeterminate in spiritual life. Spiritual life, therefore, completely changes its meaning when it comes to feel the indeterminate. It presents a new aspect, a new vision. In fact, this introduces so great a change in life and vision that no longer is any great value set upon previous experiences. The real spiritual life begins with the appreciation of the supraconceptual beyond the rhythmic oscillations of life. It presents the height which was not presented before.

The unique is presented in spiritual life. It is beyond thought, beyond words. This uniqueness gives us the sense of freedom in the place of harmony. Harmony breaks the rigidity of life and gives fluidity, affinity, and unity. It gives the inextricable blending of the different expressions of life. But it cannot raise us to the sense of freedom from all attractions of life.

The Upaniṣads give the conceptual and the supra-conceptual in truth, vision, and intuition; and, therefore, they are alive to the supreme elasticity of life and its experiences. Life presents a conceptual unity, it presents also a supraconceptual transcendence. It is keenly sensitive to the delights and festivities of the former, though it is no less receptive to the height of peace and silence of the latter.

The spiritual life may begin with the vision of a conceptual life, but it does not end there.

Its natural satisfaction lies in the systhetic intuition and the feeling of exaltation concequent upon it. The Upaniṣads do not deny such intuition. In fact they promise the blessedness of cosmic consciousness. But in transcendence spiritual life is installed in Truth. It surpasses all animal faith, all humanistic feelings, all divine inspirations.

Platonic mysticism finds delight in the supersensuous world of master-types or ideas. Santayana seems anxious to implant the supersensible world in the sensible, and takes away the sting from animal faith. The Upaniṣads do not deny the supersensible, though they think that this divison of the supersensible and the sensible proceeds from the animal faith; to the divine faith, there is nothing sensible or supersensible, for life is one and integral. It is divine. Its expressions are divine. Hence, there is no question of implanting the divine or the idealization of the actual.

Truth is there. It is simply to be known by freeing ourselves from realistic instinct and habits. The charm of the Upaniṣads lies in the transvaluation of the values in the light of the eternal truth and in reading every move of life in this light. There is no demand for the sublimation of animal faith. The spring of life is seized upon, and the shadow disappears, leaving behind the effulgent truth of life and silence.

Conflict between the sensible and the supersensible seems to be permanent in the Platonic mysticism. So, it is in the Christian mysticism, for the sensible has been thought to the permanently opposed to the supersensible, the flesh to the spirit; but the Upaniṣadic mysticism is singularly free from this conflict; for it does not accept the divison of existence into the sensibile and the supersensible. The sensible is the shadow, not the reality. It is not even the shadow of existence. The sensible finally resolves into the supersensible, when the mystic sense dawns upon us.

Chapter XII

Two Attitudes

I

The Upaniṣads present the full code of life. Though they are keenly alive to the glory of self-realization, still they present various other aspects of life which are certainly transcended in final realization, but which nevertheless exhibit themselves when life is mystically attuned. The final realization presupposes a great preparation, not only intellectually but also morally and spiritually; and it is a secret economy of nature that the highest cannot be installed unless the finest nature in us has been established. Intellectual discipline may decide in favour of one theory of the universe against another, but the conquest of Truth even in small measure requires a unique adaptation which can dispel the crude insistences of our vital and psychic being.

Intellect has its illusions, heart has its contritions, and will has its personal clingings. The illusions of the intellect, the heart, and the will must be set aside before the silent light of Truth can be visible.

The Upaniṣads, therefore, lay down definitely two paths : (1) the path of direct realization of Truth, and (2) the path of indirect realization. The direct path conquers the illusions of the intellect and the heart all at once in the final realization of identity. The indirect path is of the finest discrimination between the false and the true. It requires the highest philosphical acumen and transcendent insight which become possible with the quieting down of the urges of life. It gives us transcendental wisdom. The metaphysical search calls for the right philosophic attitude. It emerges when the life's equilibrium is not disturbed by the biological and the theological insistences. It is the correct attitude of approach that matters much in realization. Such attitude makes the realization easy, swift, and sure. But it is very difficult to adopt the right attitude. The pragmatic carries so much weight with life that the surface views have every possibility of asserting themselves. The heart sets upon an order of love and beauty, the will upon an order of power. Nay, when the truth of aestheticism and impressionism and the truth of creationism and energism have been superseded, intellect may make its own confusion by insisting upon the realms of truths and spiritual values encompassed within the unity of being. The difficulty becomes greater for the accomplished mind to approach the final truth of transcendence, since, it finds its intellectual satisfaction in the philosophical setting which does justice to all the sides of life.

It is for this reason we find that profound thinkers and writers like Keith and Santayana have not been able to appreciate and welcome the truth of transcendence. And it is natural. Probably a similar feeling has led F.H. Bradley to remark that philosophy supplies good reasons for bad instincts. The complete truth might not have been stated there, but there is not the slightest doubt that our convictions and prejudices do not allow the mind to reflect the complete truth.

The native instinct of man hastens to spin out a theory from the page of life that is open to him and has not the patience to wait for the full and the complete presentation of the mysteries of life. The side-lights are often too absorbing to allow of the calm pursuit of truth. And this can explain the theological conceptions that are found in the Upaniṣads. The inward perceptions are rich enough to offer possibilities and attractions, esoteric and exoteric, and these become real to the receptive soul of the mystic. The highest attainment can never be reached unless these charming possibilities can be sacrificed for the complete truth. If the psychic possibilities have no value either as presenting the truth or as offering the satisfaction that attends the realization of truth, yet they have value as exhibiting the esoteric mysteries, the subtle forces, inner and outer, and their correspondences. Nature is full of changes, processions, and troops of events, and the mystic is too sensitive a being not to receive their impress. And he enjoys the flux of existence better, for he can easily generate in him that detachment which sees more of life than is possible for those that are swimming in the stream of life. Life yields its secrets more to the detached than to the attached. The theological attitude cannot completely shake off the fine attachment to the subtler vibrations of life and cannot, therefore, claim that profound wisdom which follows complete indifference to the expression of life. The theological attitude cannot free itself from the illusions of the intellect and heart, and naturally finds delight in the realistic attitude of life. And these illusions cannot cease to be active in life. Though the Upaniṣads are not completely oblivious of the dynamic possibilities of life and its complete fruition in divine fellowship with its refined delight, chastened feeling, unobstructed vision, unrestricted wisdom, and undisturbed quietude, still they do not set high values upon them since they do not represent the highest truth of spiritual life.

Naturally they do indicate the two lines of approach and realization : (1) the line of philosophic and transcendent intuition to be preceeded by critical analysis, reflection, and meditation; (2) the line of synthetic intuition or synoptic vision to be preceded by the method of psychic penetration and contemplation. Contemplation can go with philosophic reflection, and can rear up the true philosophic attitude, but it is not necessary to final realization. And this difference in the approach is due to the difference in the conception of Being. Contemplation presupposes the reality of Being and its communion with the divine, intuition transcends contemplation and supposes the ideality of intuitions of practical reason. Contemplation presupposes the implications of practical reason. Intuition transcends them.

And these attitudes have been due to the esoteric and exoteric conceptions of Brahman.

These conceptions of Brahman bring to the fore two irreconcilable views, as non-qualified and qualified. The philosophic instinct which the Upaniṣads display for a soaring in identity can hardly be compatible with the theological attitude of the spiritual illumination through grace. The former denies the latter. Hence arise, the different attitudes of thought based upon the Upaniṣads.

II

There is no gainsaying that the two attitudes, transcendent and theological, are apparent in the Upaniṣads, and hence, the possibility of different teachings arises. Indeed, the Upaniṣads are rich in philosophic suggestions and possibilities. Life has never been separated from thought, and this mutual reinforcement of life and its intuitions from thought and of thought from direct realization, have enriched the Upaniṣads highly as religious and philosophic literature. It has also enriched the complexity of its concepts, for it looks like offering the satisfaction to the different attitudes of consciousness. Hence, a free reading of the Upaniṣads appeals equally to our transcendent, philosophic, and theological instincts.

The theological attitude finds satisfaction in the message of harmony, the harmony that runs through nature and exhibits nature's soul to the ardent seeker. The delight of the cosmic dance of life streams into the soul, widening its vision, till it comes to feel the pantheistic or panentheastic exaltation through nature. The superconscious vision gives the superconceptual realization of the divine, but it cannot surpass the inherent distinctions of the dynamic spirituality and cannot proceed beyond the vision of a dynamic divinity.

In the dynamic spiritual life the fine oscillation of our being, the fine feeling, the expansive being in deep sense of fellowship with nature, the sense of the universal unity are fine assets and even in such life the soul may lose itself in pantheistic exaltation, but still the superconscious vision is not to pass for the transcendent. The fulcrum of our individual existence is still there, and the cosmic vision and life are still felt at an individual centre. The theological attitude may give the cosmic intuition, but not the transcendent intuition. But this intuition has its value. It dispels the crude realization and prepares the soul for the higher reception of the transcendence.

The two attitudes in the Upaniṣads are not kept stricIty separate, and it appears that sometimes the theological doctrines run into the metaphysical conceptions. And naturally so, for the Upaniṣads give more an account of the spiritual realizations of life than a ready-made philosophy. The spiritual realization ultimately acquaints the seeker with the ultimate truth of Tattvamasi.

The spiritual realizations which follow the perfect discipline of spirit and the harmony of soul are not necessarily the final realization. Nevertheless they open the vistas of spiritual perspectives. And these the Upaniṣads in laying down the scheme of a full spiritual life, its initiation, growth, and consummation, cannot overlook the different phases that are covered by it. Hence, the two paths are recognized by Śaṅkara.

These perspectives have a place in the life of *Spiritual Immensity*. They have no place in the life of the *Spiritual Silence*. The immensities awakened by the spiritual harmony are immensities in power, in magnitude of existence, in knowledge, and in freedom. They may transcend even the relativities of the dynamic spiritual life—the relativities of the ascent and the descent, the relativities of death and life, the stirring and the progress, the light and the darkness, the realitivity of union and separation. But they cannot enjoy the peace of the Absolute.

III

Rāmānuja has been influenced by the sense of harmony and rhythm in spirit, Śaṅkara by transcendence. Both accept that the spiritual life is essentially a life of supernal delight; but while Rāmānuja emphasizes the dynamic aspect in spiritual life Śaṅkara emphasizes its transcendent aspect.

The Upaniṣads present both the aspects of spiritual life—the life in its endless perspective and values, as well as the life in its silence. The former gives us delight, the latter calm. The Upaniṣads feel that that both the rhythm and calm have their places in life, but they lay clear emphasis upon the latter. They feel in it the higher peace as the greater security and the absolute truth, inasmuch as it presents the spiritual life beyond the sense of relative values and truths.

To Rāmānuja personality is most sacred and most holy; and it is the basis of spiritual life. But the indication of the Upaniṣads seem to lie in the other direction. Not that the Upaniṣads are not alive to the immanental sublimities and immensities and the claims and insistences of personal life, but the Upaniṣads seem to be more appreciative of the significance of the transcendental truth.

The spiritual life is personal in its initiation and development, but supersedes the personal reference and touch at the end. And the development that follows the spiritual discipline is invariably associated with the subtle possibilities, free movement, and fine felicities. These dynamic fruitions in spiritual life generally capture our imagination. The subtle spiritual stir idealizes our normal experiences and inspires the vision of an all-embracing, dynamic unity. The fascination of the realm of subtle ideas and values captivates the soul and binds it to the attraction of personal life. But the Upaniṣads never fail to indicate the truth that gives Release and Freedom.

Śaṅkara's eternal glory lies in bringing to the front the value of the absolute as opposed to the relative in spiritual life. He is not blind to the joys and delights that rise in the oscillation of our being, but he sees farther and therefore emphasizes the aspect of spiritual life which is most likely to be neglected in the pursuit of joyous consciousness and personal delights. The merging of the personal self is no loss, is no surrender of the spiritual privileges of man. The charm, the ease, the freshness, and the grace of the elastic personal being bear no comparison to the feeling of relief, rest, quiet, and peace which the soul enjoys when the dance and oscillation of life are stopped in the impenetrable silence of our being. Rāmānuja is not alive to the significance of silence in mystic life. Śaṅkara emphasizes it and makes it the real quest of the spiritual life as it offers the highest privilege of transcendence. Personal experiences allow us the delights of subtle being, the promises of a chastened self, but they cannot give us the security which lies hidden in truth. The fine oscillations of psychic life, however agreeable and welcome, cannot give us the peace of truth. The Upaniṣads give us the religion of truth. Truth gives freedom. Any form of exaltation or ecstasy is not to pass for the final truth. They are psychic fits endowed with psychic possibilities.

IV

The Upaniṣads impress upon us the transcendent more than the spiritual (used in the common sense). The psychic life has different scales. These scales indicate varied experiences. And these experiences reveal themselves to the aspirant in their varieties. They are not confined to the inner harmonies and outward beauties, they are not confined to the majesty of silence.

They are not to be confined to the creative ideals of the soul. They are not to be confined within the radiant affections and rosy feelings that reflect sweetness and aroma in life.

These are the experiences of spiritual life, they are personal. They touch and vibrate the chord of personal life, but the Upaniṣads lay emphasis upon the truth. The truth is transcendent. The delights of the psychic self are not the mystical ideal of the Upaniṣads. And where psychism has no play, where life has no ripple, where the heart has no hopes, no fear, where the animal cravings and the spiritual feelings are all alike silenced, there truth in its transcendence becomes transparent and clear. A sense of vivid transparence and immediate luminuousness is the attraction of mystic life; but in the Upaniṣads the luminosity and transparence of being give us the feeling of the complete freedom. It is possible when the finest luminosity gives the highest detachment from the joys of life. Life is best understood in affectionate and appreciative detachment.

The former allows an easy entrance into the deeper secrets of life; the latter a fine understanding of them. The mystic life demands sympathy and discrimination. Sympathy unveils the secrets, discrimination makes a correct valuation. The theological attitude keeps up the sympathy, the metaphysical attitude keeps up the understanding. And the two together make the mystic life a source of unique blessedness and save it from the stiffness and the sense of separateness that dry up the joys of the soul, though never allowing it to be any longer dominated by human feelings and sympathies. The impress of the transcendent has a moulding effect upon the whole being. The heart vibrates no longer with human joys, but enjoys the uncovered blessedness of the soul and transfigures its demands in that light. It rejects none, it accepts none, but it loves all. It becomes free from all tension and relaxation, and enjoys life in its undisturbed quietude.

The sense of worship and humility, so much akin to the religious feeling, gives place to the delight of fullness and the sense of identity. It no longer remains in the realm of concepts but enters into the realm of feeling and evokes *Love* without tension, service without the sense of difference.

Will, love, impulse, and instincts change their character. Though the dynamic aspect of life is finally withdrawn, yet, so long as the concrete mould of personality lasts they are directed in a way which allows the enjoyment of their movement in an impersonal way. In fact, they exhibit their cosmic character when they are freed from their personal touch. The spiritual dynamism indicates the secret of *impersonal affection and service*, without the least touch of attachment. Affection without attachment, love without clinging, really make out their divine character, though in their expression life is not in the least deflected from the sense of transcendent freedom. It is indeed a wrong notion to suppose that transcendent wisdom denies all the expressions of life. Wisdom unfolds the divine character of expression, before the final passing into silence.

Spiritual life in the theistic sense has apparently the same effect, but it cannot there exhibit the impersonal delight of love and service. There personality is the greatest attraction. And intensive joy and bright felicities are enjoyed in the fullest development and expression of personality. The human feelings are mingled with the divine, but they do not lose their character, though they get a new lustre and colour by being associated with the divine. But they do not miss the reference to the axis of their being in personality, human and divine, and they cannot be expected to realize the impersonal character of the dynamic spiritual aspirations and feelings, hidden in the much deeper strata of divine life. These are revealed when the heart is moulded by the touch of transcendence.

Chapter XIII

Time and Spiritual Life

The relation of time to life is an interesting problem. The relation of time to spiritual life is still more interesting. The sense of creature-temporality due to the overpowering sense of time runs counter to the promise of immortality. But spiritual life is nothing if it cannot inspire the hope of immortality. The sense of creature-temporarility is to be surpassed and the finite selves must find a place in the eternal setting of life – not in the sense of a continuity temporarily suspended but subsequently recovered. Such a continuity the finite selves may enjoy in the natural course. Life is here guided by the law of alteration. Death may give the promise of resurrection, but such a spiritual progress through the occasional appearance and disappearance of the soul from the field of its activity and expression cannot be the inspiration of spiritual life. Life and death may play the role together to make life's attractions more vivid, life's joys more sweet. Death may prove to be not the enemy of life, but its inspirer. It may lose its sting, but this cannot withdraw the curtain of death and allow us to enjoy the continuous play of life. Death has an important function in the drama of life, but the secret urge in man has been always to enjoy the *perpetuity of life* without a temporary break and close. The secret of the attraction of mystic life lies not in offering currents of life but in offering its unceasing continuity with its fine blessedness. Hence, the mystic is always bent upon developing in him the insight which can rise above the discrete sense of time and appraise life in its unbroken continuity. The text says : "Knowledge gives immortality."

When the influence of time is set aside from life or even when the forced division between time and life anyhow vanishes, life presents a cheering aspect as its continuity is ensured, not in thought but is presented in experience, and immortality is no longer a promise but becomes a fact. The survival of personal life through time, and at moments the glimpse of eternity, offers the greatest joy and introduces us into the play of life undisturbed by occasional breaks.

The perennial life is the promise. The rise above the historic time-sense and the actual realization of the continued existence are great revelations and fine opening of our being. But mystic life is not confined to this alone. The more it proceeds to the source and spring of life, the more it rises from this sense of the continuous play of life through eternity to the realization of spiritual life as the timeless present, where the effort of expression is completely suspended and the delight of life's expression gives way to the delight of life's silence. Spiritual life at this height offers the uniqueness of transcending time even in its eternity completely, and life becomes free from the sense of time and the necessity of expression. Such kind of timelessness presents true *immortality*, for it is not the personal immortality. It is the immortality of truth.

The Upaniṣads conceive the continuity of personality so long as the final transcendence is not attained. Though in personal life there is the inherent promise and possibility of enjoying a continuity throughout time – and personality in this sense is co-extensive with time – still immortality is promised when the time-sense and personality are finally and completely eclipsed. It presents the Aspect of Existence beyond Time and Life. Such immortality is unique, for it dives deep into our experience and finds out the self not in any way related to them.

The Upaniṣads indeed in the progressing path of realization lay down a form of life which one may live through aeons in the present cycle of existence, but this is still a shadow of immortality inasmuch as the cycles of life have their start and finish. Hence, true immortality is not the continuity of personal life. The Upaniṣadic teachers see the limitation of personal life even in its exalted heights. Thoguh the occasional withdrawal of the discrete time-sense can effect a change in the outlook of personal life and can cause a redemption in eternal life. Still this intuition of immortality cannot satisfy. So long as personality continues, the joy of spiritual life lies in the impress of divine life through its ceaseless expressions; and this reception of eternal life is still confined to expressions. Spiritual life, therefore, cannot enjoy immortality beyond eternity. The temporality of life may be displaced by eternity. But eternity cannot present the aspect of life beyond temporal expression. The Upaniṣads consider such immortality as inferior to the timeless reality, for here the aspect of life is presented beyond the dimension of time. The immortality which the Upaniṣads impress upon us is the immortality beyond temporal dimensions of past, present, and future.

The intimation of immortality has, therefore, a personal and an impersonal sense. So long as, the spiritual life has an expression it naturally enjoys the blessings of personal immortality, it can enter into the finer realms of light, life, and power and enjoy the rhythmic oscillation of divine life. But the Upaniṣads lay their full emphasis upon spiritual life in the sense of time-transcendence. This they call true freedom, for it releases us from the time-sense and the limitation of personality.

Those who accept the phase of immortality through time enjoy spiritual evolution and come to realize divine fellowship. Though they assimilate the divine in them, they cannot rise above the limitation of cosmic changes – emergence and absorption. They pass into the cosmic death at the end of a cycle of existence, for they cannot rise above the cosmic transfiguration in time.

The Hindu Mysticism recognizes temporality of the cycles of existence. Every cycle has its *temporality*. And when the time is ripe for a new cycle of existence the souls realizing divine fellowship move cosmically in unison with the divine spirit. They disappear at the end of the cycle in the bosom of the divine. They wake up again with the stir in the divinity for a cosmic expression.

They no longer feel the limitation of personal orientation, they become associates of the divine. They make out the divine plan. They enjoy eternity as well as the temporality demanded by the cyclic expression of the divine life. Such kind of life indeed enjoys freedom from transience, but not complete freedom from time.

This kind of spiritual ideal has its charm. It offers simultaneously the eternity of life and the temporarility of its expression with the consciousness of eternity never dim. And the temporal-expression is never completely cut off from its setting in the eternal. The spiritual life is here seen in its historicity, without losing the eternal continuity. The historicity consists in dating of the divine expression in a particular cycle.

This kind of realization is, no doubt, a form of spiritual achievement, but it cannot be regarded as the final realization of spiritual life. It is, in the view of the Upaniṣadic teachers, a kind of pseudo-spirituality; for it does not put us beyond the touch of time, and give us complete freedom from it.

True spirituality lies in the complete transcendence of the time-sense and all its forms. The expression of life and spirit in time is a form of limitation, for it is a kind of self-alienation; for temporality or even eternity is the appraising of spiritual life not in itself, but through its cast in time.

The finer understanding of immortality arises from the

estimation of spiritual life transcending time, for time really and truly does not exist for spirit. Ouspensky has felt it and said : "There exist no personal and eternal appearance and disappearance of phenomena, no ceaselessly flowing fountain of ever-appearing and ever-vanishing events. Everything exists always. There is only one eternal present, the Eternal Now, which the weak human and limited human mind can neither grasp nor conceive."[1]

When man acquires the deeper insight into life independent of time, he has the deeper sense of immortality.

It is no longer affiliated with the continuity of the personal self, with its aspirations heightened, feelings idealized, and being God-centric. It essentially lies in releasing our consciousness from the historic sense. The historic sense deludes us with a false sense of timelessness. True timelessness consists in appraising reality independent of time. This is a great promise and saves us from the false fear of death and false hope of eternal life. Both these ideas of death and eternal recurrence are the creations of time, and unless we get over the time-sense, we cannot understand reality.

"Time is not a condition of the existence of the universe, but only a condition of the perception of the world by our psychic apparatus which imposes on the world conditions of time since otherwise the psychic apparatus would be unable to conceive it."[2]

If space and time are forms of our perception, as Kant has shown, "the roots of infinity are to be sought with us," for *infinity is conceived in relation to space and time*. But the infinity which is conceived is dynamical and it can be the historic infinity. This is also the reflection of reality in the mirror of space and time. True infinity is then that which is within us, which cannot fit in with psychic apparatus. And hence the method of appraising is different. The method lies in freeing us from the limitation of the psychic apparatus and to develop the sense of timeless perception.

From this is must not be supposed that the timeless becoming or duration is the true infinite life and that to appraise it in intellectual intuition is the essence of spiritual life. Though this sense of time releases us from its historic sense and imposes the sense of eternal life identifying immortality with Bergson's *Durēe-rēelle*—and allows us to see and welcome immortality of the *Durēe-rēelle*—and thus to get over the limitation of personal immortality, still it is not clear how the *Durēe-rēelle* can escape the limitation of being reflected through the psychic apparatus. Bergson, of course, breaks away from Kant in making time objective, but still his appeal to intuition as intimating the eternal duration is significant. He cannot make even this appreciation of the timeless continuity independent of the psychic apparatus; instead of appealing to the "inter-sense" of the sensibility, he appeals to the deeper sense of the mind to appraise the reality. Its appreciation is referred from the senseperception to the intuitive perception of the self. Instead of being the form of reception, time now becomes the principle of creative expression.

Since, time is the principle of change the eternal duration cannot possibly be intuited apart from the creative formations. Spiritual life in this sense will be the life of enjoying the eternal creativeness, but the intuition of the creative principle in isolation of the formations is neither desirable nor possible; for the heart of time lies in the presentation of the constant changes, and it is not possible to intuit duration independently of these changes.

The possibility or the actuality of changes does not introduce the least difference in the intuition of time, apart from its concrete reference to changes, either in actuality or in potentiality. The intuition of time, cannot rise above the concrete reference to events, hence it is not possible to relax the psychic concentration to enjoy the eternal fluidity of life or time.

If eternal duration cannot be intuited immediately as eternal duration, its very essence will be killed. Eternal duration has its fascination for finite minds for the infinite continuity of life, which attracts more by its remaining cut off from the horizon of our experience; its delight centres round the conception of progress in spiritual life. But spiritual progress in its initiation may endorse a distinction between the possibility and the actuality, and may always encourage the actualization of the possibilities in time. But this process of realization becomes interesting because of the eternal contrast between the life actualized and the life to be actualized. This is the delight of the uncertain, the delight of a plunge into the unknown. Hence, the fascination of the spiritual life in time lies not in the fullest but in the sectional presentation of the eternal duration of life.[3]

If the eternal duration of life is revealed to us in intellectual intuition, independently even of the actualities and potentialities, it loses its poetic charm as it is grasped in its total continuity. Its supposed infinity is no longer infinite, or the intuitive soul becomes itself infinite. The infinite duration, if it can be *intuited* immediately, must speak of a different character of time, beyond succession, continuity, and change. It must transcend the conception of time in ordinary sense.

Change and novelty speak of the new emergence in time, but the possibility of the intuition of eternal duration takes away all novelty and emergence from time and makes it rather a finished than an accomplishing process. Time must cease to be regarded as one of the attractions of spiritual life.

In fact, spiritual life cannot possess the same meaning in realization as it has in initiation; in initiation its charm essentially lies in its continuity through time, and in all its possibilities; but in realization it appears as essentially timeless.

Time has so deep a hold on us, that it becomes almost impossible to think of our spiritual life independently of it, but the essence of spiritual life independently of it, but the essence of spiritual life lies in its *timelessness*. The divine inpouring may exhilarate our being and intensify new perceptions of the finer and subtler movements of life; but its true attraction lies in revealing the essence of being as supratemporal. Time may suit the expression of spiritual life; but this way of understanding the divine life falls short of its true estimate. It loses its very essence. If spiritual life is to be lived, anyhow the sense of eternal duration must be a potent fact before us; but when it becomes a fact the sense of eternity dissolves. Eternity as a totality loses its charm for the sweeping intuition. Hence, the intuition of it really reduces it to a finite fact and refuses its essential character.

Spiritual life does not consist in the offering of the "moving image of eternity", i.e. time in its section, but in presenting eternity itself.

The former may indicate the growth of spiritual life, but its consummation requires the presentation of the complete picture of life and eternity. It is appealing only because it offers that possibility. The moving image of time may attract us, inspire us. It may awaken in us a dynamical aspiration for the same, but the aspiration is fulfilled in the intimate knowledge of eternity.

But it may be said that the demand for the complete knowledge of eternity really shows the lack of true appreciation of the spiritual life, which always is a growth, but never a finished product.

Quite so, but the dream of enjoying eternity and fullness remains a dream for ever. Hence, the seers of the Upaniṣads accept the objective in mystic life as nothing short of the full life, the sense of completeness; and, since it cannot be enjoyed in the idea of growth, they characterize the mystic life as essentially the transcendence of time-sense either as a form of our psychic structure or as the creative reality.

The sprightly play of life on the sands of time can satisfy the poetic instincts, but not the philosophic, not even the mystic.

The sense of the whole is essential. Indeed the greatest promise lies in releasing us from the sense of time. Though the spirit can reflect itself through time, its true nature transcends time.

Etenrity is but a form of temporality, for it makes spiritual life an expression and cannot allow it to reveal its timelessness. Spiritual life has its initiation when the soul has developed the faculty of timeless intuition or perception. Intuitions through time are intuitions of phenomena or of the expression of life or psyche, but not of reality.

The Upaniṣads emphasize the form of timeless perception and the formless delight as the essence of spiritual life. The joys of life, the transparence of purity, the luminous feeling of holiness, are all events in time, they are intuitions of the psyche and are its comforts; they have values in the revelation of the finer movements of life, but they cannot touch *the self as freedom*.

The Upaniṣads emphasize the conception of self as freedom. True freedom lies not in the unrestricted movement of life through time, but in the final release from the time-sense. This freedom from time really resolves all conflicts and exhibits life in its true spirituality, for spirituality is *freedom*. This release from the sense of time is unique in conception, because it gives us the taste of life beyond time. Life is usually so much identified with time, and our habit of appraising reality through time is so ingrained in us that it requires a new light, a new form of understanding, to realize immortality. It is indeed a blessed promise and inspiring hope to know that reality is not time and can be intuited independently of time. Appreciation of life and its events through time makes us slaves to it, and it becomes a splendid opportunity and privilege to open a new vista of realization independently of time.

There is a charm in the footprints of life left on the sands of time, there is a greater charm in the adventures of life, in its overtures, fights, defeat, success. The mystic enjoys them. The mystic enjoys life in its short and long duration. Life is joy and therefore everything, with a short or long history, leaves its unmistakable touch upon us. But the mystic usually is no respecter of time. Whatever he enjoys, he enjoys it by separating it from its temporal setting. The minute things please him, because he idealizes them and can raise them above time. This is the peculiar attitude of the mystic; and this attitude becomes prominent when the mystic insight becomes deepened. The everlasting and the enduring are the habitat of the mystic; and he cannot allow the time-sense to enter into him and tell the old story of life. There is in life the urge to get over *time*, and the urge is keen in the mystic. The mystic sees the more and the better of life because he has the unique fitness to flathom life without the psychic apparatus of time.

The objectivity of time requires an informative principle which intuits it, and it is indeed difficult to think this informing principle to be the creature of time. That which can appraise time, either as a psychic faculty or as a creative principle, must have an existence independent of time. The informing principle is, therefore, something not affected by the changes in time and belongs to a different category.

The appraising of events may be a phenomenon in time, but the intuition of time cannot be an event in time. It is true of the finite or the infinite duration; everywhere the appreciation of time must be different from the appreciation of events in time. This intuition of time is really timeless. It transcends time.

The way of thinking that life is duration, and this duration can be apprehended in intuition, is an advance in freeing life from its relational setting. It allows the fresh delight of enjoying the ever-creative life, but the intuition of such a life is no part of life itself. The intuition of motion cannot be motion. If it be so, such an intuition cannot see the whole of it. It suffers to be a restricted intuition, and becomes a process in time. A process in time is no correct appraiser of time. Intuition must be, then, timeless.

Spiritual life must not be satisfied with the fine oscillations of the psyche; these are also events in time. More often the final agitations and ripples of our being, apprehended through the frame of time, pass for the finest spiritual life, but to rise above time in its historic sense or in its psychic structure is the essence of spiritual life.

Great is the promise. Few are the souls that can feel, know, and enjoy it. There is no greater illusion than that the soul of man is always being entrapped in the wheel of time and in the trappings of sensibility and the charms of life; but, when the soul can rise above the psychical apparatus of time, the riddle of life is solved. The adept feels that nothing is truer than his self. To know it is the best wisdom, the highest promise, and the greatest freedom.

Life as the cycle movement of the divine Ānanda in time presents a great charm. It allows to enjoy the finer phases of life and makes every bit of life the spring of hope and the fountain of joy and eternally banishes remorse, strife, and discord from it. The Upaniṣads see in all forms of life the expression of Ānanda. But still, when it emphasizes the intuition of truth and Ānanda beyond its expression through time, it finds in it something unique. If the ideal in the Upaniṣads is to rise from the ignorance which sees in the movement of life nothing but the shadow of death, no less necessary is it to rise above the delight of the movement of divine Ānanda through its expression through life and time to the appreciation of truth and Ānanda, transcending time.

Those who are anxious to enjoy the divine life through its expression in time can have finer vision of the subtle movements of life through society, history and even through the finer stirrings, revealing the movement of life in the supra-mundane sphere. But these spiritual blessings and possibilities pale into insignificance before the transcendence in spiritual life. These are indeed high gifts of the soul, but they still belong to the order of spiritual expression through its cast through time, and cannot claim that mighty spiritual privilege and possibility attending spiritual intuition escaping time.

In spiritual life possibility may arise where we overcome the sense of the past and life can be seen in its completeness without being cut off by the discrete time-sense; the possibility may arise of the tangible presentation of life in its integrity and of enjoying it in its totality. But even here life transcends the influence of time, and sees and then enjoys the whole in the eternal present. But eternal present is not the sense of duration as commonly understood. The eternal present has no past, no future, nor any sense of continuity – it is, therefore, not time in the ordinary sense.

And, in the movement of life, the sense of the eternal present can be true of *Īśvara*, who enjoys *life* without the sense of *duration*, and everything for him is accomplished. There is no growth, no decay, nothing new, nothing old – no progress, no evolution. He sees life as expression, but without the sense of creativeness and evolution.

If the illusion of time can be anyhow shaken off, the sense of duration will give place to the sense of permanence. Duration may create the sense of novelty and the everpouring life, but its charm cannot hide its illusion. The delight of abidingness is greater than the charm of the novelty. Novelty gives us delight by the contrast it presents, but permanence gives us delight, because it is the soul of delight. When the soul has been able to dispense with the faculty of receiving impressions through time, it has a great ease, for it sees life not only in part but in its complete embrace and full presentation.

Indeed the attraction of the spiritual life is confined to the sense of permanence and the sense of completeness. Take away these, the spiritual life loses its charm and there is nothing to differentiate it from the ordinary life.

The mystic has the sense of the *eternal present*. This is unique. This gives the possibility of enjoying the whole without the limitation of time.

The eternal present displaces the historic sense by a cosmic sense. The former gives the idea of a continuity, the latter of an immediate awareness of the expanse.

The historic sense is the working through the subtle and the gross mind, the cosmic sense is the working of the causal mind. The cosmic mind where the roots of the phenomenal life and existence are centred has not the limitation of the finite minds; its light reflects the whole and the whole drama of life is revealed therein, and what takes the scientist and philosopher long to understand a particular truth, is evident to the cosmic causal mind, for it has immediate awareness.

The cosmic sense is free from the time-sense, for time even in its unbroken continuity is the setting for events. In fact, it comes to play when the spiritual dynamism or Śakti starts its play. Beyond this it has no use, no fountain. Time is the accompaniment of the divine Śakti in cosmic functionings, and the cosmic functioning is making actual or potent what is implicit or latent in it. And this actualization is a process in time and has a meaning for one who can see the play through time. But it has no meaning for the cosmic mind, for there everything is present, there is no latency or potency. Latency or potency is consistent with growth and development, and therefore with the gross and the subtle, but not with the causal, where there is no event but only presence of life and spirit.

The intuition of life this way has the advantage that it sees life not through its functioning but in itself. Hence, the reading of life independent of time opens a new vista in realization and understanding.

The sense of the eternal present is different from the sense of eternal duration. And the mystic spirit is fond of this eternal present, for it gives immediate awareness. The mystic is anxious to unveil the curtain of life and to see, feel, and enjoy the hidden secret of the permanent present beyond the screen of time. Hence, he cannot tolerate the time-sense and the compelling power of time.

The eternal "now" never vanishes. It is the background of the ever-creative "now". The mystic is the lover more of the former than of the latter. When the eternal "now" is realized, time in its three dimensions vanishes.

Life is not made perfect through time, and the mystic realizes this truth more than anybody else.

References

1. Ouspensky, *A New Model of the Universe*, p. 139.
2. *Ibid.*, p. 141.
3. The hope for immortality here has a greater fascination than immortality itself.

Chapter XIV

Esoteric and Exoteric Knowledge

Though the distinction between the esoteric and exoteric culture is now a commonplace, yet its importance seems not to have been fully grasped, its value still less felt and realized. This distinction is similar to the distinction between culture and realization, between talent and genius.

Talent lies in "the greater versality and acuteness of discursive thinking"; genius in the finest reception of the soul. The degree of receptivity determines the height of the genius. But in the Upaniṣads the distinction between Parā and Aparā goes deeper and further. Receptiveness is the common requirement in all forms of knowledge, and therefore the finest receptivity is not that which distinguishes Parā from Aparā.

Creative artist, constructive philosopher, and inspired poet are receptive in their own ways, but in the mystical life this receptivity has its uniqueness. It is not only an inspiration. It is the envisaging of truth. And, what is more, the being of the mystic is not deflected in the least from it. He consciously enjoys "Wonders of the deep" of which the poet and artist have but occasional glimpses. His whole being is rooted therein. And, consequently, in his case the receptivity is deep enough to carry the soul beyond the finest stretches of creative imagination. Mysticism is, therefore, the reception of the eternal life through all the avenues of the soul, thus receiving power to quicken all the faculties of our being and produce wonderful creative urges. The mystic may be the finest poet, he may be the acutest thinker, he may be the master artist. He sees the harmonies of life. If poetry and philosophy be expressions of life, the mystic can see more of the music of life and feel more of its cosmic settings. But his bent of being is centred in the intangible; his inwardness is directed to the realization of truth, the truth which gives unrestricted freedom, freedom even from the finest vibrations of life. He is anxious to go into the core of being where the supreme peace is not in the least disturbed by the ripples of life; Parā Vidyā connotes in its essence such opening and revelation.

Receptive illumination may embrace a wide range. It can extend from fine humanistic possibilities to dynamic impressions of subtle forces surrounding and inspiring life from without and within. It may penetrate into the supersensuous. It can possibly divulge the delicacies, the sublimities, and the harmonies of the supermind and finally it gives us the proud privilege of transcendental wisdom. Parā Vidyā is wisdom. Illumination is possible of the finer phases of life, but still it is not Upaniṣadic Wisdom.

In the Upaniṣads Parā Vidyā has, therefore, the implication of conveying the wisdom that gives freedom. The fine stretches in supersentient feelings and intuitions are realized in the process of the ascent to transcendence; they cover radiant spiritual experiences and intuitions revealing some aspect of the dynamic spiritual life; but still they cannot give us the intuition that can offer transcendent freedom. The Upaniṣadic wisdom connotes this freedom, which releases us not only from the snares of life but also from its richest fruitions. These fruitions, if they attract our attention, will naturally halt the progress of the soul; they indicate spiritual progress and, like lamp-posts, dispel darkness on the path; still they should not dazzle the soul, or hold it captive with their lustre.

It is necessary, therefore, to draw a distinction between the supersensuous intuitions and intuition. The supersensuous intuitions reveal the finer phases of our being, the stretches of the psychic life in its superaconscious immensities, the luminosity and the transparence of our psychic being, but they cannot give the security and the peace of wisdom. The enlightenment that proceeds from the psychic transparence is surely different from that which follows transcendent intuition. The one opens the endless vistas of spiritual and psychic fulfilment, the other gives the peace of truth. The former reveals the wonders of the dynamic divine in its interpid actvity, in its supreme silence, in its shining glories, in its majesties and powers. It can in short reveal the contraries of spiritual psychism.

Self-knowledge is wisdom. Self-knowledge denies distinctions. It is not self-revelation in the sense of a process. It is not the mystic quiet of contemplation. It is not the intoxication of love ecstasy. It is self-wisdom consequent on the mystic awakening from self-limitation. It is, the Muṇḍaka has put, the knowledge of the indestructible, the Akṣara. It is, as the Kaṭha has it, Amṛta the immortal. The Kaṭha says : "the self-created has spread out the objects pleasing to the senses, thus delivered the sense-objects are enjoyed, but not the inner self; the wise only see the inner self, being bent on immortality."

The Upaniṣads are alive to the value of spiritual life in immanance and its fine subtle delight, but still their finest wisdom is not confined to the expressions and felicities of the dynamic divine (Śvetāśvatara, Chapter VI).

They have not minimized their true importance. They have their vision still more extended. They appreciate mystic silence more than mystic delight. The Upaniṣads, therefore, have practically confined wisdom to self-knowledge and self-illumination. The mystic realization is, accordingly, not identified with any form of the super-sensuous experience. The luminous layer of our being extends far beyond the physical, the sensuous, the mental, the supermental, and even the divine.

The Muṇḍaka Upaniṣad has it : "Parā Vidyā is that by which the Akṣara is known and attained."

The Upaniṣads are alive to evolution in spirituality as well as to transcendence. Transcendence is the highest consummation in spiritual life, for it frees the soul from the illusions of the intellect. It frees the soul even from the illusions of spirituality. The evolution in spiritual life is the emergence of a finer life with dynamic fruitions in knowledge, power, dignity, and creativeness. They are sleeping potencies of the psyche, but they from obstacles to the final realization of truth.

The Upaniṣads never set high value upon these perfections, though they count them as indicating the stirring of the subtler layers of being and growth of finer perfections.

Fitness requires us to regard this fine movement of life as mystic, though it may not obtain in the acme of realization.

The Upaniṣad has it that "the heart-knots are broken, all doubts and the karmic-seeds are destroyed when Brahman is realized in its transcendent oneness and immanent unity." The direct realization of the transcendent is a possibility with the few, the high adepts. No doubt, the transcendent may be the desired end, but still the spiritual life cannot always be raised to this height. Spiritual life is often enjoyed in the concrete, for the transcendent is not always accessible, for less enjoyable. Though it offers an experience and realization which nothing else can offer, still it is in a sense the denial of concrete spiritual life. And, therefore, before the spiritual life can become exalted into the transcendent, it naturally should pass through spiritual possibilities of concrete life, not with the idea of being confined thereto but with that of realizing the orders of spiritual life in immediacy in the march of fulfilment. The seeker in this wise realizes the spiritual life in the world of concrete forms, causes, and effects, the world of the formless forms, the world of abstract spiritual expression, and finally passes into the silence of transcendence.

But it should not be lost upon us that, though the dynamic fruition is one stage of spiritual life is an attractive possibility, still it is not the culmination in spiritual life, And its possibilities and fruitions are nothing in comparison to spiritual consummation in the Absolute. The Upaniṣads are clear on this point. Hence, they emphasize more the direct knowledge of the Absolute than the indirect realization through the subtler consciousness of the dynamic spirituality. But in the spiritual life there can be no law of fixed antecendence and consequence, for our psychic being is so different. The fit soul can immediately aspire to the transcendent, his whole psychic being may be bent upon it, and he may not feel the least attraction to the finer evolutions in spirituality. The *brave* soul can welcome at once transcendence, since he stands convinced of the superficialities even of the finest concrete spiritual experiences. It, no doubt, speaks of the greater transparency of his being and the finer psychic fitness to be able to welcome the terrific height of realization. To the timid spirit this terrific height in realization cannot immediately be vouchsafed, for it is so singularly remote that it cannot fit in with his being. Hence, he has to make way by the process of progressive realization. He must satisfy the first dynamical aspirations before he can think of realizing the highest in spiritual life.

Parā Vidyā, therefore, is the super-wisdom of Brahman. It naturally calls for unique adaptations which can so fit our being as to reveal truth to us directly. It may comprise within it all forms of esoteric culture, which can prepare the way for the ultimate realization.

But in esoteric culture there are different forms. Some give us the direct way to realization, others introduce us to the indirect path.

The direct path is the path of wisdom, the indirect path is the path of progressive assimilation of life and delight. The former is based upon understanding and intuition, the latter upon sympathetic vibration of the psychic being. The one is the eye-doctrine, the other is the heart-doctrine. In common technique they are called Vidyās. The word "Vidyā" has the sense of science, knowledge, and wisdom. It indicates sometimes the discipline, sometimes the fruition. In "Brahma-Vidyā" the sense of fruition is greater than the sense of discipline. But in "Dahar-Vidyā" (conception upon the heart-space) the sense of discipline is greater than the sense of fruition. "Vidyā" chiefly denotes a physical attitude which unfailingly endows the adept with wisdom. But the "Vidyās" in the Upaniṣ ads have not the same meaning

They do not generate have not the same meaning. Some "Vidyās" give direct knowledge, others make our psychic nature susceptible to fine influences and subtler powers. The latter may be called Upāsanā, which word has the literal meaning of "sitting near" in the communion, and expresses contemplative meditation. Upāsanā endows us with life and receptivity. It makes the being stir with graceful vibrations, revealing to us the subtle forces of nature and self. It raises our vision to the expressions of life's beauties and sublimities, and finally gives sympathetic understanding of the eternity and the all-pervasiveness of life. It may draw us into the softer expressions and the finer phases, but these enjoyments of the rhythm and the delicacies of life do not speak much of the spiritual life. The texts frequently refer to the freshness and the joy that the initiate feels from the sympathetic vision of life, but this is only the surface-effect of spiritual opening in Upāsanā. The fine and pure psychic self, however, can gradually rise to feel its unity with the cosmic psychic power. Upāsanā can give the union of the individual psychic self with the cosmic psychic life. And the tension and the intensity of our psychic being can so increase as to leave no difference between the two. The individualized psychic self becomes the medium of radiation of cosmic psychic forces. But this richness in psychism is not only the effect of Upāsanā. It also endows the seeker with knowledge, the knowledge of the dynamic divine in its activity in creation, and in its immanence through every atom of existence. Upāsanā can place the self in tune with the cosmic life. It opens the soul to the urges of the infinite life, and the oscillation with which they vibrate in the heart of things. When the soul receives the vibration of the infinite life a new consciousness of the all-pervasive power and wisdom dawns upon it. But Upāsanā does not only give the intimation of divine power life, and being. It has indrawing virtues. The soul catches the influence of the infinite life and is lifted up from the abyss of darkness and division. Veil after veil is withdrawn from its view before it can fully realize the formation of the divine life through the hierarchies of existence. But this is not enough. Soon the revelation becomes clear of the unity of life that runs through existence.

The contemplative receptivity can acquaint the soul with urges of cosmic life, it can give fellowship with the divine, it can even reveal the impersonal aspect of the divine, but it cannot endow the soul with the knowledge of transcendence, for it cannot tear off the psychic individuality. It rotates round this axis.

Hence, it can never rise to the height and enjoy the privilege of transcendent wisdom.

Even in the meditation that follows Upāsanā the self may free itself from the theistic attitude of mind and realize the magnitude of its own being. It feels the cosmic self, and the cosmic life as its being. The sense of exclusiveness and individuality is to be overcome in spiritual life.

Corresponding to these kinds of knowledge, the distinction has been drawn between the Parā (superior) and Aparā (inferior) Brahman. The path of the realization of the former is necessarily distinct from the way of realization of the latter; but the realization of both requires a fine psychic being. The psychic fitness required for the realization of the one may lead on by making a still finer opening for the realization of the other.

Chapter XV

Two Paths

Śaṅkara in his commentary on the Chāndogya distinguishes the paths of spiritual evolution from the path of native seeking, the path of light and the path of darkness.

The path of darkness is the path is unrestricted impulses. It allows the gratification of the natural man. And the consequence is the morass of entanglement in the crude impelling of nature. Śaṅkara says : "Misery of a degraded life is the consequence." (Commentary on Chāndogya, Introduction.)

The path of life is the path of restricted habits, disciplined will, and chastened being. When the discipline is restricted to the formation of habits and acquisition of merits in the performance of sacrifices only, the fruition is not high. It allows of enjoying life in a subtler plane of existence. But it cannot give a radiant and shining self which is the promise of a life not only of sacrifice but of scrifice helped by the finer prāṇic culture and devaworship. (Śaṅkara.) Naturally the promise in mystic life is consequent upon the emergence of fine consciousness. The fineness of insight and being due to sacrificial rites cannot compare favourably with the fineness of being and insight reared up by meditative effort. The former does not go so deep as the latter. The latter acquaints the seeker with the movement of fine life and consciousness.

The performance of sacrifice cannot allow us the free flow of spiritual life, because the ideal strictly sought is not spirituality. The direct end is gratification, and hence, the sense of agency cannot be lost. Karma still entangles the soul. Where Karma follows a sanctioned path. It can produce a fine sensibility and some merit. Merit yields subtle gratifications but, since the initiate cannot get above the conceit of agency, he naturally becomes bound to an active psyche which does not become chastened by dedication and wisdom. The sacrificial rites may chasten the soul and generate some merit, but it cannot make the soul and the psyche the recipient of the deeper currents of life. The main attraction of spirituality is the freedom it allows from the self-centric move of life by breaking the chords of individuality. Karma has been denounced because, it instead of relaxing, always deepens the sense of individuality. Nay, what is more, the sacrificial rites lend a deceptive attraction by the promise of subtle gratifications.

Knowledge gives freedom from the sense of an agent, and Karma cannot free the soul from psychic impellings and susceptibilities. True freedom comes from the dissociation of the self from the psyche. And even when this ideal of freedom is not achieved, the higher psychism can make the soul the recipient of the finer currents of spirit, if the sense of the agency is lost. Karma can compel nature to yield us gratification, but spirituality is not mere conquest over nature. It is transformation of nature. But Karma cannot give us this. The sense of agency is the creation of nature; and, unless man can be denaturalized, it cannot rise above it and possess true spirituality.

Karma in the Upaniṣads has a wider significance. It includes both sacrificial rites and Upāsanā. Both imply some form of activity. The one rears up fine and powerful will, the other fine concentration and penetrative mind. The powerful will together with the merit acquired by the sacrificial performances bring fruitions to the agent. Such Upāsanā gives us glimpses into higher mentality. It is a free form of activism. Though the end of such activism is a revelation of knowledge, power, and delight, a fine expression of being and consciousness, still it cannot be confounded with Jñānam. Jñānam gives transcendence : Upāsanā fine mentality and rich powers.

The Upaniṣads give preference to the Karma which becomes spiritualized, so to speak, by being associated with prāṇic culture and deva-worship. But this is not strictly Karma. Here the activism of Karma is displaced by the receptivity of dedication and devotion, and the Prāṇic culture.

It has no longer the crude impelling of Karma : it can now exhibit its purer and freer nature, its finer receptivity. The moment the psyche becomes free from the sense of agency, it feels its unbounded receptivity and expanse, and the serene, free, spontaneous delight of spiritual life. The free flow of Prāṇa is indicative of the fine life in spirit, for the spiritual life is infinitely plastic and endlessly receptive. A time comes in the history of spiritual life when the sense of active agent is displaced by the sense of passive recipient, and the flow of life is felt uninterruptedly.

When Karma becomes associated with cosmic Prāṇa, it is no longer Karma : for the prāṇic culture frees us from the sense of agency. The infusion of the cosmic or Mahāprāṇa into our being effects a tremendous change in it.

It starts varied intuitions, according to the degree of the receptivity of the refined psychism which it produces. The Upaniṣads lay great emphasis upon the Prāṇa-Upāsanā. Prāṇa-Upāsanā puts us in intimate touch with the complexities and subtleties of the cosmic life as expressed in the physical, the biological, and the psychic planes of existence. Nay, it carries the soul through the finer psychic planes to the root cause of the whole existence, the Mahāprāṇa.

The regulation of Prāṇas establishes prāṇic equilibrium, but we cannot long stand there if we have earthly attractions.

Śaṅkara in his commentary on the Praśna Upaniṣad (vi, 8) identifies Prāṇa with Hiraṇyagarbha. And the adept in the prāṇic culture naturally has the fitness to reach Hiraṇyagarbha (the being with inner effulgene). Prāṇa is pervasive of the whole existence. It is operative in every atom. It carries the adept from the realm of effects to the realm of causes, from the realm of causes to the realm of the first cause. But Prāṇa cannot carry the soul beyond that. It can give a forward move and an upward lift; and the adept may rest in safety. He can stay in the realm of the first cause to gain the final illumination and to attain the calm.

The adept in prāṇic culture becomes aware of the subtle connection between the Mahāprāṇa and the Prāṇas, and getting hold of this connection he can merge himself into the Mahāprāṇa, and can have its rest and quiet there. Prāṇa is the world-soul, the thread of life that keeps us and the world in being, and naturally the adept in Prāṇa can have direct intimacy with the world-soul.

To shake off the yoke of individuality, a deeper realization and understanding is necessary. The prāṇic dynamism, however finely attuned with the cosmic dynamism, however inwardly drawn, cannot shake off the sense of individuality. There may be occasional overshadowing of individuality. When there is the sudden inrush from the cosmic dynamism, but this cannot permanently remove the sense of individuality. The seed of individuality still persists.The occasional silence felt in the prāṇic culture is due to the depolarization of the forces—centripetal and centrifugal : but this deplorization cannot be permanent. For the contraries of polarization and depolarization are constant in the dynamic divine; and a complete depolarization is only possible when there is the cosmic withdrawal at the end of a cycle of existence.

To link oneself with cosmic Prāṇa—to feel its infusion and vibration—is a desirable end. It endows the adept with powers. It reveals the richness of the infinite life, and finally the adept comes to understand Prāṇa as the divine energy. The indrawn urge of the Prāṇa establishes an unfailing association between the finite and the infinite. It can free us from the conflicts and can introduce to us rhythms and melodies of life. It can introduce us to the spring of life and acquaint us with the dynamic aspect of spiritual life. It can give us ever-broadening vision, but it cannot give us the final wisdom of transcendence.

We shall draw at this stage a distinction between Upāsanā and Jñāna. Upāsanā is a finer form of psychic activity. It has its terminus in knowledge. Śaṅkara puts it thus : "Upāsanā is to keep up the even flow of mental consciousness upon some object, as prescribed in the Śāstras, and to keep off the disturbing stream of consciousness, quite different." He goes on : "these form forms of discipline because of promoting *sattva* are helpful to the final knowledge."

Upāsanā is the meditative strain. It is psychic concentration. It is sometimes inspired by devotional feelings. Upāsanā places the soul in a receptive attitude. It fosters fine mentality which can obtain easy access into the mysteries of life and nature. It frees the mind from the subjective preoccupations and desires. It affords a great relaxation of our being from the insurgent impulses and fosters the physic attitude which allows communion with the heart of reality.

Its great task is to acquaint us with the divine and to convey us to its charge. It puts us in direct connection with radiant life. It makes us vibrate with forces of spirituality. It introduces us to a new life. It oscillates our being with new hopes and aspirations. But these hopes and aspirations follow new perceptions and realizations in the finer setting of life, which reveals itself as the chastened notes of life are touched upon.

But the Upaniṣads do not lay so much stress upon the music of soul. They lay stress upon wisdom. The finer currents of life exhibiting in the devotional mysticism are not much noticed, since they are supposed not to represent the highest end of the mystic life.

Hence, even in Upāsanā they emphasize the attitude of attaining freedom and not the attitude of enjoying finer delight and freer movement.

Vidyā in the former sense is transcendent wisdom. Vidyā in the latter sense is artistic or poetic intuition. But all is not said when we characterize Vidyā in the latter sense as artistic intuition, for there are many Vidyās, which give us knowledge not only of the divine setting of existence, but carry us with analytical penetration from the fine to the finer realm of existence. Some Vidyās present the synoptic vision of the immanental existence, some supply the analytical presentation of the details of existence and enable us to appraise them in their true colour and proper estimate. But finally the knowledge of them is blended in the whole, for the bent of mystic life is to be in tune with the spirit of the whole.

The greatest asset of mysticism is that it sees the whole in a moment. The mysticism in the Upaniṣads shows the decided tendency to appraise the whole in the great and the small, and even when there is the possibility of concentration upon the different aspects of existence it never deflects from its central tendency. A cursory glance is cast upon the points of existence to appraise their setting in the whole.

Upāsanā conveys, therefore, the sense of complete melting of our former being and a re-moulding of it in divine harmony. This rebuilding of life gives a direct access to the lights supramental and power supranatural. And this harmony builds for the final knowledge. Upāsanā goes naturally midway between activism and transcendence. It transforms human activism into divine impelling and adjusts the relation of life in its supramental light. But it cannot lead us beyond the enlightened vision of the facts and forces of life in the cosmic setting. To this end we require the Vidyā of the first kind. This Vidyā is fundamentally different from the Upāsanā, for it carries us beyond the realm of life to the realm of silence.

The Upaniṣads prescribe various forms of Upāsanā. Their object is to carry the seeker from gross to fine truths, with the sharpening of intellect and fineness of feelings which they foster.

Upāsanā reveals truth to us by making our whole being rhythmical. It is a spiritual art. It sets our being in a definite way and moulds it in a fashion such as would make it communica-tive of spiritual truths lying hidden in the soul.

The various Vidyās are forms of Upāsanā. They put the mind in a psychic attitude to realize truths. All the Vidyas cannot give the same kind of truth, for they do not foster the same psychism. Most of the Vidyās are confined to the sectional presentation of the truth in immanence. And, therefore, when the texts read that Vidyā gives us immortality, it must not pass for the ordinary psychic intuition. A distinction is, therefore, to be drawn between Vidyās. And it generally falls into two divisions : (1) Vidyā in the sense of transcendental wisdom; (2) Vidyās in the sense of psychic intuition giving us the immanental secrets of spirit reflected in nature.

It generates a state of will-lessness. This freeing of the self from will gives it a rest, a calm, and a relaxation which offer it the right receptivity for the higher knowledge of the object.

It raises the "consciousness to the pure will-less, timeless subject of knowledge." This attitude of the subject at once makes a corresponding change in the knowledge of the object.

And if the subject in Upāsanā is elevated to a pure receptive being, the object is also drawn out from its environmental setting. Its objectivity in the ordinary sense is dissolved, for this "objectivity" lies in being an element in the order of the relatives. Upāsanā helps us to see the objects in their bareness and not as space-time events. It wants to free them from the law of final causes. It wants to see them in their ideal aspect, in their inner rhythm and harmony. Its charm lies in the presentation of "objects" as "ideas" set in a fine harmony.

This idealization of the objects at least frees them from the pictorial time-sense and allows a timeless perception. This placing of ideas beyond the order of realistic space and time is what captivates the soul, for along with this kind of perception the soul also enjoys a unique freedom.

Upāsanā has, therefore, a transcendence. But this transcendence is akin to the transcendence in aesthetic intuition or perception. There is transcendence of space and time. Sometimes there is transcendence of the subject, the subject being absorbed in the object. In Upāsanā, there is a clean forgetting at times of the subject—and a complete absorption of it in the idea or the object.

In this clean forgetting of the self and its tendencies there is the possibility of the object or the idea being impressed fully upon the receptive mind. A sort of aesthetic absorption follows.

Aesthetic absorption carries us into the heart of reality and one returns from this with the impress of knowledge about the reality; if one is not completely overcome. Hence, Upāsanā has also an informative aspect. It introduces us into the causal aspect of existence and reveals the immensities and beauties hidden therein.

But to characterize Upāsanā as aesthetic intuition will not be to represent the full truth. In Upāsanā in its best form and fullest intensity, there is a sense of identification of the subject with the object; at least the subject becomes so much possessed of the object that its clear impress is left upon the subject. Nothing is dead and inert. Upāsanā brings this truth to us. And, therefore, naturally the meditative self feels the dynamic forces of ideas and powers. Absorption is followed by knowledge and power.

The worship of even the creative matrix (Prakṛti), the worship of Prāṇa, all come under Upāsanā. These Vidyās are always sources of some power, for they give knowledge of Prakṛti and its forces, and teach us how to regulate them to our advantage and control them for our purpose. Such Vidyās cannot give us complete freedom from subjective impulses. They can stir forces in us and the corresponding forces in nature to attain some definite ends by the help of the law of correspondence. Even when definite ends are not taught, these Vidyās can at best acquaint us with the causal aspect of Prakṛti and allow a riddance out of the conflict of the divergent forces of nature. It can give an apparent equilibrium when the centrifugal forces are calmed down.

Upāsanā in all its forms acquaints us with the truth hidden in nature and in the psyche, but in its finest form it breaks the original polarization of reality into Prāṇa and Raye, and restores the original calm. But here it takes a different form and is no longer a kind of mental absorption. Yet its character is not lost. This depolarization also reproduces the original equilibrium. It is a state where all activities of nature and mind are suspended. The end is to recover the lost self by quelling momentarily the forces of creative expression.

Upāsanā in this form is a source of power and rest; power, because it gives control over the forces; and rest, because it produces equilibrium by depolarizing the original forces, with which creation begins.

But this depolarization cannot be permanent, for there is the constant cosmic tendency of creativeness and expression; and, however effective the process may be, it cannot produce the eternal sleep of the forces in the creative matrix (Prakṛti). But even this sleep is not desirable, for it is not the quiet of the soul. It is the enforced quiet produced by the inversion of the process of creative expression. It appears as a state of will-lessness and as a desirable freedom from the insurgent impulses. But this Will-lessness is not a state of complete freedom from tension, since, the seeds of desires lie inherent and break the momentary calm. Life moves within tension and relaxation, and, besides the natural relaxation in sleep, the self enjoys relaxation in Upāsanā. It can establish silence which cannot be subsequently disturbed by the inrush of unenlightened impulses and desires. It can connect it to cosmic vitalism, and can give us effective manhood, but it cannot give us the final enlightenment. It cannot make us ready for wisdom and calm. This shortcoming must accompany all forms of approaches that are without the kindly rays of knowledge and understanding.

Hence, the Upaniṣads do not subscribe themselves to any form of worship, which has no bearing on knowledge. Even when the forces of nature or even Prāṇa have been accepted as the medium of worship, they have been looked upon as reflecting some power of Brahman. This attitude throws saving grace upon Upāsanā.

The Vedānta says that true superiority is attained in Upāsanā by concentrating on the forces as Brahman. This superiority lies in directing our attention to wisdom and is not natural to the unenlightened self. The unenlightened self seeks power from the forces, the enlightened self looks upon them as reflecting the cosmic being. Religious consciousness frees us from the thought of the self and the delight of religious consciousness lies in this freedom from all forms of subjectivity. Subjectivity in religion sits upon the soul as a nightmare, and unless the soul can rid itself of this oppression, it cannot understand, enjoy the meaning and touch of religious inspiration. The religious instinct in man is essentially an impulse to forget the blind insistencies of the self and religious inspiration is a blessing because it allows the enjoyment of the disinterested delight.

The disinterested delight cannot be realized if there is a subjective touch in our attitude and seeking. This disinterestedness makes religion a subject of absorbing interest. The thought of self at once pulls us down from the height and stifles the possibility of spiritual life. It requires, therefore, a fine training in philosophy, a deeper understanding which can free us from the thought of self and invite the stream of supernal delight into us. Happily if our being is in right tune, all the necessary requirements follow. True spirituality cannot leave any point of our being undeveloped, since the response proceeds from the whole being.

The religious sense transfigures our thought and being, and frees us from the native disposition. Religion requires a complete transformation, for it is a new life based upon a new understanding.

The reading of the phychic and cosmic forces in the light of the supreme light changes the nature and character of our attitude in Upāsanā from the seeking of power and privilege to the serene joy of harmony and mystic exaltation consequent on the fine perception of the radiant soul in nature and man.

The worship of the Devas can at best give some subjective satisfaction. It cannot carry us further. In the Īṣa Upaniṣad emphasis has, therefore, been laid on all the forms of Vidyā as helping us to penetrate into the mysteries of our being and Prakṛti; but it distinctly is anxious to carry us forward to the knowledge of Ātman, since the Vidyās cannot give us freedom. These Vidyās, Sambhūti, Asambhūti, etc., are after all methods and disciplines to gain access into the finer and causal aspects of becoming, and hence, they fall short of true mystic insight. They may carry through the different planes of existence, but they cannot give the wisdom transcendental. They satisfy the subjective claim and have the impress of religious empiricism. True spirituality cannot be traced in them, religious intuition excels in its synoptic vision of reality, hence, the Upaniṣads lay more stress upon the form of Upāsanā which forsakes the path of satisfaction and fosters æsthetic and spiritual intuition. The Kaṭha truly says : "When the heart becomes free from all clingings to desires, then the mortal becomes immortal and attains Brahman. When the heart-knots are all sundered, then the man attains immortality." These texts put forward are true character of spiritual life.

The fruit of highest spirituality is wisdom. Wisdom gives freedom. Brahma-Vidyā is to be distinguished from other Vidyās or Upāsanās in this, that it enables us to overcome impellings of natural insistencies or even supernatural aspirations and enjoy the calm beyond natural or spiritual dynamism.

Forgetfulness of the actual into the ideal has been the saving grace of religion; forgetfulness in the contemplation of the music, the beauty, and the dignity of life has been the attraction of aesthetic life. It is life's fine expression in life's grace and beauty that attracts in the life of contemplation (Upāsanā). But the secret of attraction in Brahma-Vidyā lies in even going beyond this. The soul must rise to the height of seeing the face of silence. It is not the silence where the noise of life is hushed in its music. It is the silence where the music of life melts away.

The music of life is deep-laid in silence; those who are not lost in the raptures of its music can feel the dignity of its silence. Silence and music are interwoven in the texture of our being; he who can see the silence can better understand the music.

Chapter XVI

The Five Sheaths[1]

The Upaniṣads lay down a training and a discipline which can give the direct knowledge of the psychic and vital forces and the powers that function in us and can make us cosmically active. This, no doubt, is the path of powers which can be fruitful towards wisdom and knowledge by wise detachment.

The inward search for the highest truth is psychological penetration into the subtler forces active in man and nature. The penetration is keen and analytical enough to distinguish the principles and their functions, either psychical or cosmical. The Upaniṣads lay down a course of concentration upon these principles. This makes it possible to realize their nature and appreciate their functions.

Concentration intensifies their functions and magnifies their being, for the inner has a correspondence with the outer, and the thread of life is the same within and without. The inner penetration enables us to feel their cosmic functions and the initiate thiswise develops in him cosmic powers. The concentration upon Manas, Vijñāna, Citta, Saṅkalpa, etc., makes us feel their cosmic character. Intensive concentration is effective not only in giving the inward being a poise and a calm, but also is fruitful in moving these forces cosmically. The range of vision, therefore, extends the unity of forces and the adept soon begins to feel, not frequently, but occasionally, the wave of cosmic life, mentality, and intelligence.

The meditative strain has the immediate effect not only of

developing a finer insight, but also of moving the finer being. The finer vision is followed by a wider being.

The great hindrance to expansive life is the clinging to a finite centre; and concentration helps the assimilation of the fundamental unity of life by dispelling the limitation of being and the restriction of functions.

The sense of separateness is detrimental to the fostering of the universal sense, and the Chāndogya, therefore, enjoins the removal of thin distinctions of principles and functions to foster right understanding.[2]

These faculties can be divided as belonging to either higher or lower mentality. Ānanda and Vijñāna are superior to mental vital-complexes. They are not expressly active in all. They have scarcely any touch with the animal being. They are forces of bliss and intelligence; intelligence which gives us superior wisdom and philosophic penetration, bliss, which is consequent upon the transformation of the lower self and upon quietude.

Manas and Prāṇa are mental-vital complexes. They meet the needs of the animal self. Manas is the seat of desires. Desires move Prāṇa to activity. Manas under the influence of Vijñāna can function is a subtle way, and then it becomes freed from the demands of the lower self.

Ordinarily these forces do not work harmoniously. The vital-animal nature is generally dominant, and it is active in most men. Only in the philosophers and in the artists, the flashes come from the higher nature. Even then a conflict is felt between the demands of the higher and the lower self. The great point with the mystic is to put the whole nature into harmony by gradually transforming the lower nature. When the lower does not any longer present its own demand, when it loses itself in the blending fo the whole, in the peace of the soul, then alone the divine harmony is established in us and our being moves in perfect rhythm. The more the texture of our being is set is fine harmony, the more the correspondence between the inner and the cosmic life becomes a fact of our knowledge and the secrets of life come to be realized to the full.

Nature has its saving grace. Through conflict and tension it rises to the higher harmony. When we have passed beyond tension, we shall have harmony. Tension is the helper, tension was the bar. When we have done with desire, we have the secret to power. Desire was the bar, desire is the helper. The forces of opposition offer real help when the deeper harmony in which they are laid out is realized.

The Mystic is, therefore, anxious to establish a tune in the psychic being in order that the lower urges may not disturb the calm and frustrate the search; this becomes possible when the pranic and mental urges no longer seek crude satisfaction. To this end, concentration is to be sustained, so long as detachment is not completely established. Detachment is helpful in two ways : –

(1) It gives the fuller knowledge which is not otherwise possible; (2) it opens the possibility of realizing the unity of these principles, in their psychic and cosmic functioning.

Nay, the greater the detachment, the finer becomes the vision. And so long as the detachment continues the self receives the impress of the cosmic urges. This inflow of cosmic energy gives us more life and greater freedom.

This kind of meditation acquaints the seeker directly with the forces forming his composite being and infuses into him subtler vibrations of these forces.

The seeker does not enjoy them in a personal sense. At least a personal touch puts a restriction upon the free exhibition and display of these forces.

The more the cosmic functioning of them becomes clearly evident, the more the self becomes dissociated from the personal limitation. How the restriction of forces comes to take place is difficult to envisage, but the mystic bent is to destroy their inertia and increase their elasticity, and finally to break through the false divisions that exhibit their limitation. The Upaniṣads are eloquent about the final transcendence of the soul, and, to foster this understanding, it is necessary and helpful that the centralization of the finite should be dispensed with, and the understanding of an identity of the dynamic divine and the finite being should be built up.

The finite consciousness and powers are embraced by the infinite consciousness and powers, and it indeed goes a great way when the meaning and the reality of this distinction are lost upon us by quickening of the forces, for this really exhibits the potential divinity of man. Man is enmeshed in limitations, but his limitations are not eternal. The divinity sleeps in him and a realization of this divinity is possible. His divinity becomes apparent when the restrictions of his being and powers are withdrawn by awakening in him a divine psychism. This implies, therefore, a discipline and a culture to energize the forces; and nothing is more fruitful to that end than the concentration upon them as Ātman.

The withdrawal of the distinction between the dynamic divine and man which is the promise of Upāsanā can, therefore, be at best a yogic discipline with the acquisition of supernatural psychic powers. It can give an occasional stirring of the dynamic divine in us and can occasionally suspend the native functioning of the individual self; but such an opening cannot be permanent from the nature of the case, for man, constituted as he is, cannot long enjoy the ingress of divine powers. He is not fit for it owing to the limitation of his physical and intellectual systems. The stirring of his powers gradually fits him for an effective expression of the cosmic life through him, but that becomes possible only when the acquired tendencies of the vital-mental being have been displaced by the inflow of the dynamic divine. Whatever is looked upon as Brahman acquires a significance and a power, which is not otherwise accessible. Such seems to be the conclusion of the Chāndogya.

The meditative penetration brings us to the realization of Prāṇa as the finest force located in Ātman. Prāṇa gains expressiion in longing and desire (evidently the desire for creation). Longing begets remembrance and mentality. Now, the cosmic creation begins. Mentality begets Ākāśa; Ākāśa, Teja; Teja, Āpas; Āpas, Anna. Next begins the psychic creation. Anna gives Bala (strength and vitality); Bala gives Vijñāna (Śaṅkara writes in the commentary : "Balam gives the power of understanding of the objects presented to the mind"); Vijñāna is superior to Dhyāna; Dhyāna is superior to Citta, for Dhyāna makes Citta collected and receptive. Citta is superior to Saṅkalpa, for Citta makes Saṅkalpa possible.

Conclusion

This stage in the process of spiritual fruition is necessary. By removing the conflicts of our vital and psychic nature and by purifying our inner nature it shows the rich possibilities of the spiritual life.

The coarseness and grossness of the sheaths round the self do not allow its light to be fully reflected in us. Spiritual life is a life of powers, elasticity, movement, and freedom; and, unless the psychic forces are keenly active in us, the potentialities of dynamic spiritual life cannot be fully realized. The psychic forces acquire strength, when their inward nature as ultimately cosmic forces is made clear.

Every centre of existence can wake up his potential divinity in him by creating a harmony in himself. And this inner harmony ultimately reveals the greater harmony between the psychic and the cosmic forces. Man is installed this way to his divine heritage of power, plenty, and peace. The psychic centres become the transmitters of divine will. Wider realization in the plentitude of being is the natural result of the complete divinization of our being. But to this consummation nothing is so conducive as the removal of the ego and egoistic claims and insistencies. Nature abhors a vacuum. The dynamic divine fills our beings when the little self is removed from the scene of activity. To die is to live, to forget is to know, to be emptied is to be filled. Such is the mystery of the spiritual life.

If the Upaniṣads give us the different forms of meditation, they also indicate the most sensitive and receptive centres in our psychic being. The Chāndogya enjoins to concentrate on the heart-cave, the Maitra on the bliss-cave. The former is known as Dahara-Ākāśa, the latter as Ānanda Guhā. The Brahma-Vindu also prescribes concentration on the heart-centre.

Meditation becomes easily intensive and swiftly expressive in this centre. This centre at once gives a sublime feeling and an expressive calm. Concentratioin on this centre gives the wide stretch of illumination. Raṅga Rāmānuja regards it as the culmination of spiritual seeking. This is the centre of our being. There are many centres, but the one which can be most agreeably helpful is the heart-centre. This centre can respond to the finer oscillations of the whole being, and can ultimately arouse the cosmic vision. It reveals the secrets of silence. With this centre is connected the subtle passage through which the adepts escape at death which finally enables the adept to pass out of thebody. (Śāṅkara Bhāṣya, Chap. VIII of Chāndogya). The Yogis have command over this path of exit from and re-entering into the physical body. This is the path which directly connects the psychic with the cosmic being, and allows the psyche to pass out of the physical envelope and directly envisage the different strata or planes of subtle existence. This is a possibility, however, that can be developed by very few initiates. Śaṅkara says in his commentary : "Brahman, the light of knowledge, is reflected in the transparent mirror of concentrated mental being of the Yogis."

There are many psychic centres. They have distinctive

functions. They awake and originate different kinds of psychic forces and powers. But the forces are to be harmonized, for they are forces of the dynamic divinity. The Upaniṣads have laid stress upon the heart-centre because it is the pivot of our being and concentration on this can reveal to us the blending of existence in the divine.

Śaṅkara has raised the question whether the Brahmapura, the Dahara-Ākāśa, is a convenient centre of meditation or Brahman itself. He goes on : "Since Brahman is felt in this heart-cave, therefore the centre usually stands for Brahmapura. Indeed this Brahmapura is Brahma." Ānanda Giri has it that Brahmapura is the centre of the knowledge of Brahman.That which is the locus of all existence, cannot have strictly any locus, and this location can only be figurative. But the sensation of an illuminative calm marks out this centre as the special seat of delight. This also suggests the theory of spiritual space.

Raṅga Rāmānuja takes Dahara Ākāśa to mean Sūkṣma Ākāśa or subtle space. Again he says that Ākāśa suggests Paramātmā.

The texts describe Suṣupti as a state in which the self passes into a natural calm, being freed from desires and clingings of the self.

The text has it that "when the soul has its agreeable peace in sleep (being freed from the impure impress of the sense-objects), it dreams not, when it enters into the nerves; then no sin can touch it, as it is then possessed of light". Raṅga Rāmānuja says : "Tejas is here indicative of Brahman, because of its illuminativeness." Śaṅkara has also in his commentary on the text : "Merit or demerit does not touch it, as it is possessed of truth." (VIII, vi. 3).

The texts here describe the suspension of the mental and the sense-activity and the natural withdrawal of the soul in Suṣupti where it sees not the worlds of waking and dream.

The entrance into the nerves is indicative of the entrance into the mystic centre with a location behind the heart. This path is the mystic path and is revealed to the adepts.[3]

In deep sleep the soul passes into this centre, and the texts say that in this centre it feels no individuality, it is possessed of light.

Śaṅkara comments : "This is surely the entrance into Brahmaloka... by that passage the wise pass into Brahmaloka." The text reads : "This is the satisfaction that Ātman gets out of the body and attains the superior light and gets to its own truer being." (Chāndogya, VIII, 3,4).

Suṣupti has no psychic oscillations of the waking and the dream. Natureis inoperative in Suṣupti. This inaction gives the soul an advantage, enabling it to see itself independent of the psychic activities. This discriminatioin is a great help to mystic consciousness, for it takes long to impress this distinction between the psyche and the self.

Dahara-Upāsanā fosters that attitude which can give an easy isolation from the vital and mental insistences and acquaint the soul with the stream of light that scatters its silent influence in the deep recesses of the heart. Suṣupti also gives a temporary release from these insistences.

The utmost concentration in meditation and the utmost diffusion in Suṣupti have in the end almost the same result. Concentration tears the veil, diffusion makes it inoperative. When our being becomes fully attuned, it can keep up its conscious discrimination in deep sleep. Here diffusion gives a natural quiet and the habits of concentration keep up discrimination even in the quietude of sleep.The natural relaxation of Suṣupti combined with the habit of concentration produces a kind of psychic sleep. Such sleep may be called yoga-nidrā, for to speak in terminology of Śaṅkara it is not sleep in which tamas dominates, it is sleep in which sattva dominates. The sāttvic dominance produces an outward inaction of the mental being, but keeps up luminosity all the time. Psychic sleep is to be distinguished from natural sleep. The normal functions of the mind become inoperative in both. In normal sleep the psychic being is quiet, attention is diffusive. In psychic sleep the physic being remains active. But in both sleeps there is a fall or lapse of the active and logical self—the lapse of historic continuity and the sense of time. The one implies complete relaxation of psychic being, the other its utmost concentration. The fine psychic possibilities which follow purification are to be distinguished from psychic oscillations in Suṣupti. The former give penetration and power, the latter a foreshadowing of the self's independence and freedom from psychic life. Suṣ upti frees us from the sense of relativity of the normal and the supersensuous consciousness.

The experience in Suṣupti is unique. It almost gives a new dimension of being. It foreshadows it. In the highest tension of the psychic being there is, in the dropping of the normal, epistemological duality; but still the access into the finer stretches of life has its charms and more of them. The vibrations from the suprasensuous heights often pass for the great spiritual fruitions but the normal experience of Suṣupti has a great educative influence; it suggests a new opening in the spiritual life and indicates it as without any dimension. Conscious life has its dimension, so to speak, in its normal and supranormal stretches. But its existence without a reference to any dimension is what is indicated in Suṣupti and is realized in Turiya.[4]

The disciplines referred to above are fraught with finer spiritual possibilities in the life of concentration. These possibilities are the evolution of the finer consciousness and the subtler movement of being.

References

1. The Taittirīya directly and the Chāndogya indirectly have touched upon the Five Sheaths and have gone so far as to regard them

not only as psychological principles, but also as cosmological. The Chāndogya gives us a similar account.

Prāṇa is put at the top, next to Brahman. Next to Prāṇa is Āśā (hope). The first wave of Prāṇa is the wave of creation; hope and desire —Āśā and Smara—are initial urges to creation. They originate Ākāśa; Ākāśa originates Teja; Teja, Āpas; Apas, Anna; Anna initiates strength; strength (it must be psyche and physical strength) begets Vijñāna, which is superior to Dhyāna (because concentration begets knowledge); Dhyāna to Citta (Dhyāna is Citta on a point of concentration); Citta to Saṅkalpa; Saṅkalpa to Manas; Manas to speech; speech to name (because name is the concrete expression of speech).

2. This is implied everywhere in the Chāndogya Upaniṣad in the promise of a free life and power as the result of intensive concentration upon these principles.
3. "The nerves of the heart are a hundred and one, the one amongst them passes through the brains." (Chāndogya.)
4. Fourth state of consciousness.

Chapter XVII

Symbolism

Symbolism is apparent in the texts. Apart from nature's forces used as symbols, the Upaniṣads lay stress on *Om*. Natural forces are used as symbols to inspire an animated vision of nature. The location of Brahman in nature's forces, the sun, the moon, the fire, is the rudimentary awakening of spiritual consciousness. Though, in this vision of nature, spiritual consciousness is animistic, still this is an advance upon the naturalistic outlook. But this animistic vision does not long persist. In animism a kind of dualism – matter and spirit – still lingers. But spiritualization runs swiftly, and the conscoiusness of nature as different from spirit is displaced by the idealistic vision of nature. Nature is supposed to be the play of spirit. And at this height of consciousness symbolism gives way to spiritual perception.

The symbol *Om* has deeper significance. It unfolds the finer sensibility and perception. It can move the inner spirituality of man. It stands for the cosmic harmony. It presents the rhythm deeply laid in spirit.

It helps to transcend the discord of life and exhibit its harmony, a harmony which is not otherwise accessible. In a sense it represents the impersonal life in its expansive being. It helps the supramental opening as it touches the generally untouched layers of the deeper consciousness. It stirs the finer being the frees the self from the instinctive urges. This clear consciousness of the self as separate from instinctive urges, from the vital-animal propensions, is the secondary effect. This secondary effect has its use. It discriminates the gross and the irrational from the fine and the rational. The want of discrimination has been the fruitful source of the error that spiritual life can be shaped out of the non-spiritual.

This duality between nature and spirit, between the outward forces of the organism and the senses and indrawn force of spirit has been well illustrated in the Chāndogya (Chapter II). The "natural" man has his senses and faculties directed to natural ends. They satisfy animal ends. Unless the faculties and the senses can be spiritualized, the birth of spirit within becomes impossible. The story goes that the senses, including the vital-Prāṇa, the Manas, and all other faculties, took the protection of Udgītha (*Om*); they were then freed from their grossness and impurities and obtained the elasticity and penetration natural to spiritual life.

When the inner being catches the influence of the higher rhythm of life and soul, it together with the organs of the senses undergoes a change and a transformation.

The divinity which is immanent in us manifests itself as we grow clean. The senses and the organism vibrate with fine urges and become open to fine influences. The senses feel the elevating inspiration of the new life. They feel the touch of divine life inwardly and outwardly. Spiritual life is indicated as freedom, ease, and freshness; the fullest current of spiritual life cannot make its way unless the physical body and sense-organs are spiritualized, so to speak, i.e. unless they are impelled by the fine Sattva and become free from the inertia of Tamas and the impetuosity of Rajas.

The first effect, therefore, of the spiritual awakening is (1) the discrimination of the material from the spiritual and (2) the gradual spiritualization of the organs of the mind and the senses.

This, no doubt, sounds strange, but spiritual insight tells

us that so strong and effective is the dynamic current of spirit, that though the complete spiritualization of the body is not possible from the nature of the case, yet the body under the higher influence is purified of its dross in such a way as makes it a fit vehicle of effective spiritual expression. This implies no change in its physical nature, but the dominance of its Sāttvic constituent which engrafts it with a transparent being. It feels easy, highly vitalized, and quick to receive influences. These changes take place not directly but indirectly, for the spiritual influence has immediate effect upon the mental being, it purifies and chastens it and, indirectly, its vehicle of expression, the senses and the organism. When the subtle body is influenced by the impressions of the senses, it can hardly be sensitive to the higher influences of spirit, and it is threfore an almost imperative necessity for the spiritual seeker to keep the subtle body free from the influence of the flesh.

The greatest difficulty is experienced here for in most cases the tendencies of the flesh are dominant and imperative, and the dweller of the soul puts up an inefficient fight against them as a rule. The silent currents of the soul should be effectively moved that the tendencies of the subtle body may be freed from the influence and impress of the gross body and be brought under the direct impulsion of the spirit.

Spiritualization is, then, strictly possible of the finer bodies, and it becomes swiftly possible when the genial current of the soul has its free activity. To this end the elimination of the darker elements is necessary. And a rejuvenation, because of the inrush of the dynamic spirituality, is the immediate consequence.

Spiritual life in its unfolding is a twofold process. It rejects the obstructuve elements and forces. It influences vitality, mentality, and intelligence. The last is the process of rejuvenation. This rejuvenation makes the spiritual initiations, for it is here that the spiritual life in the concrete is directly felt. Spiritual promise is nothing if it does not bring with it a new awakening, a novel stir in our being.

This stir is the positive fruition in spiritual life. Rejuvenation is possible because of the divine inflow. The human system is receptive and elastic enough to hold the inflow of divine life, and truly speaking the heightened being is possible only when the divine inflow overshadows the personal being, and the vital and mental being moves on with divine impulsion.

The native impulsion and powers are displaced by the divine impulsion and, in the heightened intensity, the being attains and feels identification with the dynamic divine. The identification is not of powers, but of being. The case of natural intelligence can never allow identification to be effective for long. When the inward rhythm has its full play, the identification becomes almost complete. The distinction between the finite and the infinite is no distinction of being, it is a distinction of magnitude and power. And the finite magnitude and power are not rigidly finite, they have elasticity. The finite can occasionally transcend the limitation and assimilate the dynamic divine.

"If speculation tends to a terrific unity, in which all things are absorbed, action tends directly backwards to diversity. The first is the course or gravitation of mind, the second is the power of nature." (Emerson : *Representative Men* : Plato.) Spiritual life is essentially an inward impulse to gain rest and quiet in the central light of the self. This centripetence is what characterizes true philosophy and true mysticism. "In the midst of the sun is the light, in the midst of the light is truth, in the midst of truth is the imperishable being" – so say the Vedas. This inward seeking is facilitated by the rhythm of cosmic life.

The cosmic rhythm is powerful enough to break even the outward bent of our being. In the life of expression the indrawn force is checked and the outdrawn self-alienative force has its way; and, in the contrary movement, the indrawn force has its way, and the out-drawn force becomes inactive. But this indrawnness becomes only occasional unless and until the forces are depolarazied.

Om is the symbol of the higher and the lower Brahman. The former is the promise of the final knowledge of the Upaniṣads, the latter is a stage accessory to the former. The syllable "Om" starts in us a centripetal current. It lays bare the component parts of our being and finally stirs our spiritual nature and sets up the spiritual current. It reveals our true spirituality.

The unity of the inward and the cosmic life is a favourite theme of the Upaniṣads. It is a kind of spiritual correspondence, the correspondence of Adhibhūta, Adhidaiva, and Adhyātma. If it moves the powers within, it also moves the powers without, and nature is compelled to reveal her secrets. This correspondence is not the correspondence of the spiritual and the physical. It is really the correspondence between psychic and cosmic powrs and forces. The inner psychic opening reveals this correspondence, and the thread of this cosmic life is felt and realized as identical with the pulse that beats in the centre of our being. This explains the power of the mystic. The active energizing of the inner psychic being puts the mystic on a superior plane from which he can feel and see the ripple in the universal dynamism.

So long as the final transcendence is not attained, the quickened inner being enjoys the vistas of the wider life and feels the finer planes of existence where the life's flow is easy, delight, even, and being subtle. The Kaṭha-Upaniṣad says : "The position which all the Vedas long for, that which all the disciplines speak of, deserving which, Brahmacarya is practised, I will tell you in brief; it is *Om,*" (I, ii, 15). The symbol is here represented as the end. It is the path and the end alike.

"Where the heavens, the earth, and the pervading space

are, and the winds with all the prāṇic-force have their stay, know that Ātman. Meditate upon *Om* as Ātman."

Really it is so. In spiritual life the two cannot be separate. The end is immanent in the means; the means, however external it may appear, is really inherent in the end. Otherwise the symbolism in religious worship would lose its charms and meaning. In Indian Mysticism symbols do not serve merely as a convenient and agreeable object of meditation, but also as the carriers of potencies and powers which finally reveal the truth by removing the veil of ignorance. Hence, a distinction is drawn between kinds of symbols : (1) artificial, and (2) natural. The artificial symbol is something which is selected for the moment because it excites some psychic interest in us. It has the power to relax our being. But such artificial symbols cannot have any deep effect upon our psychic nature. They touch its fringe of life, but cannot effect a total change in it. Natural symbols are those that can really stir the coiled-up spiritual dynamism in our being and set us a spiritual current. They represent the finest dynamic forces sleeping in nature and man, and therefore their effect is inevitable in awakening the fine powers and in making our being more finely receptive and more fruitfully active and gracefully expressive. They initiate cosmic vibrations in us.

Symbolism has, therefore, a deeper meaning than what is attached to it. And seen in this light *Om*, just as all other forms of symbols, is not to be supposed, a mere convenient form accidentally adapted for spiritual ends. (As a convenient makeshift for swift and sure concentration, it would not have the same importance which is attached to it.) Things which create some spiritual interest can serve as symbols in the life of spiritual seeking. Some end they do serve, for they stand for and evoke some noble feelings and sentiments; but they cannot produce that kind of psychism which makes us the fit recipients of spiritual wisdom. Unless they represent spiritual powers in us they have neither any meaning nor any importance in mystic life. *Om* is significant of a meaning and indicative of a value. It is a source of arousing the spiritual possibilities. It represents the essence of spirit and is therefore powerful enough to move the spirit to intense activity in us.

In this indissoluble union of power and meaning, meaning and object, can we see the true significance of symbols, especially of *Om*. Without this supposition no satisfactory explanation can be given of the subtle mystic powers and experiences it evokes and the encompassing vision it commands. The knots of psychic life are torn asunder, the waves of the lower being are quelled by the spiritual influence of *Om*.

In this sense, it is the symbol of the dynamic divine. This dynamic divine has its expression in the rhythm of Nāda. Nāda is not different from it. *Om* wakes up the delightful harmonies. It unties the complex knots of our vital and psychic life. It frees us from the doubts of a reflective mentality. It gives us the surety of intuitive consciousness. It removes the complexities of our psychic being. It makes it transparent and vibrative enough to reflect true spirituality.

Besides *Om*, the Chāndogya speaks of other symbols, e.g. *Gāyatrī* (III, 12). Gāyatrī is a kind of metre; the Taittirīya Upaniṣad (I, 4), also speaks of the metre. The two Upaniṣads emphasize the importance of metre on life. The metres have a great psychological significance. They play with tremendous force on our emotions. And the correspondence between the kind of metre and the nature of emotion is a captivating subject. Still more attractive is the relation between the metre and the spiritual life – the specific character of the metre and the specific spiritual oscillations in our being. This is a fascinating subject which has been later developed in the Tantra. The matter is important from the spiritual standpoint, for it helps the setting of our being in such a way as to make us fit percipients of truth.

The different harmonies and melodies play upon our emotions. But not all of them can move spiritual forces in us, unless these harmonies have direct connection with the cosmic harmony.

Different harmonies execute different moods. But this is not enough. Not all of them have the same kind of influence. Short and swift harmonies can hardly evoke spiritual feelings. Our nature is to be deeply moved before we can aspire to be spiritual; the deep stirrings are possible ony when the harmonies proceed from the very heart of the universe and touch the core of our being. The universe them melts into harmony. And the more we can draw on the higher and the subtler, the finer is the revelation. Even amongst cosmic harmonies there is difference. Every one of them does not evoke the same feeling, move the same chord in us.

If the harmony is deep it is cosmic, or at least in touch with the cosmic life. Such harmonies make for spiritual illumination. Spiritual life is all the more attractive because of the fine harmony it sets up in our being, and it promises the melting away of all conflicts. Life is harmony. It is best enjoyed when the lost harmony is fully restored.

All harmonies have not the same effect, since, they represent different aspects of the divine life. Not all of them can reflect the divine life fully, though each one of them plays its part in the cosmic harmony. Hence, not every one of them can carry the soul to the same height of spiritual realization.

There are harmonies which awaken dynamic spirituality, there are others which move roseate feelings, there are others which favour a calm and pensive mood. But their spirituality can be judged by the effect they leave upon us. They must above all produce a transparent and chastened being and make it more vivid and responsive to the finer life currents. There are times when the sense of harmony takes us unawares beyond the range of human feelings and leaves upon us the divine impress, and reveals to us the supramental secrets of the dynamic divine. But even here every form of harmony cannot bestow the same privilege and blessing. Some give powers, others knowledge. The harmonies which give knowledge must be finer than those that can endow us with powers. They vibrate deeper chords. The former can carry us into the inmost recesses of being, the latter cannot. The Upaniṣads lay emphasis upon harmonies that can foster intellectual intuition. *Om* is the symbol of such a harmony. They emphasize harmonies that may foster cosmic sense and cosmic feelings and acquaint us with the radiant beauty and light of truth reflected in the cosmic spheres. Gāyatrī is such a harmony. The Chāndogya enjoins us to worship Gāyatrī as Brahman.

The word "Gāyatrī" literally means that which, if chanted, saves. Every harmony has not this saving grace. There are, broadly speaking, two kinds of harmonies : (1) Creative harmonies, (2) Redemptive harmonies. The former bring out the best creative power, the latter give freedom. The difference comes with the different kinds of modulations. There are modulations which make our being keenly penetrative and finely active. There are modulations which make us completely indrawn. Gāyatrī represents the former, *Om*, the latter. Gāyatrī chastens us, purifies us, and initiates cosmic vision in us—it acquaints us with the radiant spiritual current that is in the orb of the sun, that penetrates through the spheres of existence. It strikes out a rhythm on our psychic being which feels the wider rhythm and the radiant current through the mundane and the supramundane existence.[1] Gāyatrī gives fine life and radiant light; Praṇava (*Om*), silence through life and light. Hence, their rhythms are different in character and possess distinct spiritual values.

Reference

1. Chāndogya, III, 12, 6.

Chapter XVIII

Rhythm of Life and the States of Consciousness

The rhythm of life has its direct effect upon our consciousness. Conscious life is affected by the rhythmic oscillations of life. They can produce different mental states by freeing the mind from the tension of life. Rhythm of life effects relaxation of our being. And relaxation allows finer and deeper penetration.

Conscious life cannot exhibit its finer expression in immanence and its essence in transcendence unless it is freed from the tension of the mental being and the senses. They put limitation upon consciousness. The great task which awaits the initiate is not only an intellectual understanding and satisfaction of the permanence of soul and its difference from the vibrative mental being, but also a luminous vision and a consequent conviction of the force of indrawnness and the truth of transcendence which can set aside the eccentric projection of the mental being to enjoy the privileges and possibilities of sensibility.

Relaxation is effective in freeing the senses and the mind from the boisterous activity and the conflicts of contraries of the theoretic and practical life. The psychic being enjoys a poise. It becomes free of all sense of attachment, all sense of strife, comparison, struggle. It enjoys tranquillity, a wise passivity.

But this relaxation has its degrees. Nature provides us with the law of alternate assertion and relaxation. Life drawn to the conflicts and the contaries naturally suffers from tension, and this tension becomes so deep-seated that our psychic being cannot relax itself even when nature calls for it. This is why world-stricken souls cannot enjoy the rest and the leisure which nature in its course provides for every being. The spiritual initiate, on the other hand, waits for relaxation provided by nature to help him to develop his spiritual possibilities, for this occasional respite and lapse can be utilized freely by the seeker to dissociate himself from the active urges of nature. And this relaxation not only facilitates spiritual detachment, but also goes a great way in exhibiting the reality and the play of the finer forces of the mental being.

The value of dream and sleep can be realized only in relaxation, for the pressure and the demands of waking life are too heavy to allow of a dispassionate survey of the inner mental life.

Sleep, too, liberates. The waking consciousness can hardly relieve itself of the tension created by the relations of life and free itself from the conscious attention steadily kept up by them.

The Māṇḍūkya Upaniṣad brings out the full implication of rhythm and its correspondence with the different phases of our conscious life. The psychic life has its waking, dream, and sleep, and corresponding to this there are the gross, the subtle, and the causal aspects of the cosmic consciousness. The psychic life runs parallel with the cosmic life. The rhythmic vibration of the Praṇava (*Om*) impresses us with the knowledge of this correspodence.

The same being puts on these appearances or dimensions as it is seemingly identified with the Upādhis, the gross or the fine. The gross can ill reflect being, the fine can reflect it well. The latter has therefore, a singular dimension and better expression than the former. The gross can touch the fringe of conscious life as it is reflected through the senses, and the vital-mental self. It is true individually as well as cosmically. In the latter the reflection takes place through totality; in the former, through an individual. The delight of this dimension of existence is the crude joy of the sensible. It has no reference to the super-sensible. When the senses become inactive in dream the higher dimension of conscious life appears. Dream exhibits the spontaneous creativeness of the soul, its power of free creation and free projection; this aspect is not presented in the waking state. Therein the soul is the recipient or percipient, in dream it is creative of its only universe throughout its own forces; and as such it has its delight of creation in place of the delight of reception. Even as recipient in waking it enjoys the gross, the actual; in dream, it enjoys the finer, the ideal.

In dream the self is free from the limitations of the vital – the physical self; in waking it is not free from the limitations of the mind, its desires, thoughts, and ideas.

Corresponding to this individual dream-consciousness there is a subtle consciousness in cosmic life which reflects and exhibits the subtle cosmic life and mind. Here the free spontaneity of the soul is presented in its highest, for the range of dream consciousness is really freer, wider, and higher than the range of waking consciousness.

Waking consciousness is a limitation, for in the waking state the senses become active with the mind, and, therefore, the sense of individuality becomes keen. Individuality draws a screen before the commonalty of cosmic life. The dream does not represent therefore a lower grade of consciousness; the truth, on the other hand, is that the waking consciousness is the dream-consciousness restricted, because of its expression through the sense and the sensible. If, by the power of withdrawing, the soul can completely separate itself from the senses it can realize the freedom, the freshness, or the elasticity of the dream. The dream life has less tension and greater ease than the waking. In dream there is relaxation, in waking, constant tension.

There are dreams which are the reproductions of the waking experiences; they are automatic groupings of the psychic impressions caught up in experience and left in the hidden chambers of the soul.

But there are dreams which are the expressions of the soul freed from the fetters of the waking state and its associations. These dreams exhibit the power of free creation of the soul. The web of the psychic life is intricate. Its threads pass into one another, and, therefore, it becomes difficult at times to distinguish the dreams which are the revival of the waking experiences and the dreams which are the creations of the soul in its freedom from its association with the sense. There are dreams associated with our instinctive self, but there are dreams different from all these. They proceed from our causal mind, free from all reference to the empirical self. Such dreams really shoot forth from the self. They exhibit the creative power of it.

If such dreams reflect the freedom of the individual soul, the more do they reflect the spontaneity of the cosmic soul. Its freedom is greater because of its dimension and range of being. It reflects the subtlety of cosmic creation, the finer world of the causal forms and ideas. It includes even the archetypal forms, for they are creation in the finer world and ideas. And ideas are let loose in unfettered activity in the relaxed being.

Dream is more comprehensive in range than waking. The cosmic consciousness in dream has, therefore, a finer being and experience than cosmic consciousness in waking. If one embraces the subtle world of ideas, the other comprehends the gross world of actualities and facts. The dimension may be the same, for consciousness in the phases of expression must have identical dimension.

But, owing to the dissociation of the psychic and the mental being from the vital-animal-self, cosmic life can function with its natural ease, freedom, and elasticity. The dream-consciousness is more unstrained in its activity and wider in scope and being than waking consciousness. From the Upaniṣadic or Vedāntic standpoint the dream-consciousness is a higher grade of existence than waking, for the spontaneous creative power of the soul is more evident in it.

In waking this spontaneous creative power is displaced by the conscious creative power. But this one is associated with personality or individuality. Its creation is the expression of will. Its motivation is formed by the influence of inner inclinations and the environmental forces. The personal will is shaped by these. It is not entirely free. It has a pointed reference to the ego, to its satisfactions, to its timely expressions in the order of events and purposes. Its creativeness is restricted to the inception of a purpose, an order, harmony; in the natural flow of events, it cannot completely override the external influences and the shaping forces. It has to overcome opposition and resistence. But such is not the case with the creativeness in dream. The formulation of an eventful history is evidently absent there. In dream the soul is unfettered and has its free enjoyment of spontaneous expression. Values and purpose are the delights of the personality. Free expression is the delight of the soul. Such delight is evident in dream. The soul enjoys here, therefore, a wider range of being and expression, unfettered as it is from the compelling sense of a personality. This free and spontaneous self-expression in dream exhibits the self in its detachment from the sense of personality and discloses an aspect which is not always presented before us. It makes clear the difference between self and personality. It enables discrimination to be made between the wider self and the limited personality. The constant association with the reference to the external order makes the sense of personality dominant in our waking life, and hence possibility does often arise to understand the supra-personal character of the self.

Personality is associated with will, will lapses in dream. But the lapse of will does not mean the loss of activity. Activity is there, but is not self-directed activity towards an end. The dream-consciousness, therefore, presents the self not as a person but as a spontaneously creative reality. This form of creativeness and expression, too, are not personal in the ordinary sense. It is creation without purpose, it is expression without meaning. Meaning goes with purpose.

The dream universe has greater fineness. Its range is wide, its functioning is subtle. It acquaints us with the creativeness of free ideas, ideas without desires. And naturally, therefore, it is a unique phase of our physhic life. This is a great truth, which is not often realized. Creation in dream is ideal creation. The ideal creation in it is more impersonal than personal. Activity of desires is to be distinguished from the activity of ideas. Desires always refer to personal satisfaction. Ideas are free from such satisfaction. Desires are mental-vital urges. Desires are personal. Except in higher abstraction it is not possible to distinguish desires from ideas in waking consciousness. But in dream the ideas are set free from desires. Ideas are forces. So are desires. But desires have reference to the mental-vital self. Ideas have no such reference. Hence, distinction is to be drawn between the dreams in which suppressed notions and repressed desires are released and dreams which are expressive of the spontaneous creative activity of the self.[1]

The former have a sense of personality which is completely absent from the latter.

The sense of "I" continues in the dream consciousness, but it is not of the nature of the "I" of the waking-consciousness.

The sense of personality is dropped, but not the sense of

"I" It continues, not in its ordinary sense of reasoned energizing, but as the freely-expressive creative activity. It builds its ideal universe, which is not necessarily less real than the actual. The actual appears real because of its enduring satisfactions. The ideal appears real because of indifference to and transcendence of these satisfactions. It presents the semi-transcendence of the creative self. The actual is the limitation of the ideal. The senses together with the Rājasic Ahaṅkāra create these limitations, which are not present in the dream.

The former has an explicit or implicit reference to the personal self. The sense of gratification is also present. The personal touch is absent from the former, as also the sense of gratification. The moment they appear on the scene, the character of the dream changes. Dreams which are creations of ideas (not necessarily of suppressed ideas) are really enjoyable, for they read as a new chapter in life, a new expression, free from all personal inclinations and references.

This dropping of the active personality introduces us to impersonal creation in dream. There is expression. There is experience. But there is not the active agent, not the active experiencer. Such dreams are just like the floating appearances of which the self is the onlooker, and not the personal enjoyer. Next comes the deep sleep. Both in waking and dream the self, as it were, has projection out of itself and has a reference to presented actualities, or revealed idealities. Consciousness appears, therefore, to have an apex in either case, an extra individual reference, be it presented or created. Consciousness has, consequently, as it were, a bent, a concentration, a focussing in waking or in dream. Dream may impress us with the free creative activity of the self, but it cannot dispossess it of this concentration. The spontaneous activity is there.

But in deep sleep consciousness is free from all psychism, all references, all actions, all creations. Here the subject disappears, the object disappears, the percipient disappears with the perceived. The psychic life has a rest and a calm. The dynamism of life and experience becomes still. But it is not to be supposed that the self is immersed in darkness and gloom. The self is still awake, it is still conscious. But there is no functioning. Here is knowledge, but no bipolar reference. Similarly in Samādhi we have knowledge without bipolar reference; but there is a distinction. In Suṣupti attention is completely diffused, in Samādhi it is in its highest concentration. The psychic being in Suṣupti is in the highest state of relaxation; in Samādhi it is in highest tension. The result is apparently the same, the complete dropping of the personal consciousness.

The complete relaxation of the psychic being in Suṣupti does not make the self completely free from it, though for the moment it remains inactive. Hence Suṣupti presents the self without the psychic activity; it is a natural state.

Suṣupti is not to be looked upon as a state whence consciousness has dropped. Suṣupti acquaints us with consciousness in its winder dimension, which is restricted in the waking state by the creation of a personal reference. It is, therefore, unique. Even in suprasensuous consciousness the personality is active, in the high efforts of meditative indrawnness the self may feel its supramental nature, but the supramental self is not free from the fine revelation of a superior psychic dynamism. A fine psychism allows higher vistas of consciousness and life, but cannot exhibit the self in its detachment from them. Suṣupti presents that possibility. The supramental revelations are in time. The presentations may not be discrete. They may be presented in panoramic majesty in a single act of intuition, but they cannot be free from the psychism that remains still active. The supramental vision is, therefore, confined to space and time. It is different from empiric intuition in this, that its range is wide, its knowledge unfettered and continuous. The time sense in it is not discrete, but continuous.

But the intuition in Suṣupti has nothing concrete to reveal. It reveals the total absence of all concrete things; the absence of all psychism; it reveals a blank negation of concrete presentations. It is nature's retirement into rest. The psychic dynamism remains inoperative for the moment. It attains a neutral equilibrium. This at once differentiates Suṣupti from waking and dream. In waking and dream the psychic being has its disturbed equilibrium, but in Suṣupti this psychic being is not the least disturbed. This difference on the psychic side of life often reflects a difference on the conscious side.

Should it not be supposed that Suṣupti is all darkness? It is not darkness. Light still burns; though its focussing to a centre and illuminating a field are for the moment shadowed. Thus, the absence of the psychic functioning makes us feel that the conscious life in Suṣupti is a life without knowledge. It is not concrete knowledge. It cannot be for obvious reasons. But Suṣupti has its form of intuition or illumination. Its freedom from the bipolar reference makes it categorically different from the usual form of the knowledge. It introduces a new form of experience, illumination with negation. It is knowledge of no concrete things, it is the knowledge of a void, though there is no functioning indicative of the void. The knowledge is direct, immediate, and intensive.

The psychology of Suṣupti is an important factor in the life of a mystic, for it exhibits the self in detachment from instincts, urges, and experiences. It exhibits it in its freedom from all tension of psychic and vital life.

The soul, also in Suṣupti, becomes free from the sense of time. Time attends psychic and vital formations, and, when the soul is detached from the psychic dynamism, it naturally becomes free from the overpowering time sense.

This independence of time sense allows it a unique freedom, freedom from all dynamism. The discrete time sense cannot exist, for this is associated with memory, and memory plays no part in Suṣupti. The sense of continuous duration drops from Suṣupti, for the sense of duration is also relative to a percipient and in Suṣupti there is no active percipient.

Duration is a formative agent. Such a formative agent does not exist in Suṣupti – Suṣupti is the state of intense withdrawnness.

Time in its eternal duration can be felt in supramental perception, when the picture of the whole world would reveal before the adept the continuous functioning of time through the past, the present, and the future.

Time is the ordinary sense as the measure of events does not exist for the supermind; it exists as the principle of duration and creative energy. Time in the discrete sense is the creation of our logical intellect.

The supermind is conscious of this eternal duration. It knows it by an intellectual intuition. The intuition of the supermind differs from the intuition in Suṣupti. The one has the time sense, not in ordinary sense, the sense of duration – the other has not. In Suṣupti the psychic self, the ego of desires, memories, remains in abeyance; and, though the process of passing into the oblivion of Suṣupti and emerging out of it is a process in time, still Suṣupti is no process in time. Psychism does not function in Suṣupti, nor does the creative principle. And time, without creative functioning, cannot exist. Suṣupti therefore exhibits a state of existence free from the compelling force of time. Suṣupti represents the complete withdrawnness of the creative dynamism. It remains in a state of suspended activity. And this suspension is natural. Consciousness, therefore, can have no concentration or projection.

With the time sense, the sense of space also drops. Space implies the possibility of co-existence. But this is a possibility for concrete facts and relations. Such a possibility cannot exist in Suṣupti. The sense of space is not evident there. The whole dynamism retires into the background, the self.

A sense of immensity is there, but not the sense of space. Space and time are the inextricable framework of the concrete effects for the dynamism, the world of causes and effects. But the dynamism is inoperative in Suṣupti, the spatial and the temporal order both disappear therefrom.

The self alone remains, along with the actively dynamic principle suspended. A tendency is marked to identify supraspace with Brahman. Brahman is space. The spiritual space is conceived to exist side by side with the creative dynamism; but this spiritual space is the immensity which is the self. Ordinarily the psyche is identified with the self and the disappearance of the active psyche seems to leave a void behind. But this is no void. It is the immense. And Suṣupti allows the possibility of passing into the immense; when the psychism and the dynamism are withdrawn the self in its immensity alone remains. This immensity carries no idea of space, it is beyond space.

Suṣupti is a state of natural withdrawnness. It cannot be voluntary withdrawnness, which rises from understanding and discipline. This natural withdrawnness does not help us to see the distinction of self from the dynamism. It cannot afford the opportunity of enjoying the self in complete transcendence.

The rhythm of Nāda, it is affirmed, has a reference to the four stages of conscious being. It makes our being psychically sensitive and receptive. It makes it receptive to the four phases of conscious life, not only in its individual but also in its collective sense. It withdraws the soul from the surface view of things and unties the knots that bind it to the body and the mind.

At any rate, the soul finds itself in the mazes of mind and body. It is necessary, therefore, to rear up in body and mind a receptivity and a keen discriminative sensibility which can distinguish the urges from the soul. But this cannot be possible unless our psychic being is made fine and records with exactitude the subtler vibrations and urges of the vital and the mental self.

The delicate psychic being with its efficient sensitiveness can distinguish between the waking consciousness and the waking state.

It produces a withdrawnness which makes the soul the silent percipient of the urges, meanings, and relations of life. And the indrawnness may be so nearly complete that the soul can feel the natural transcendence of the cosmic intuition distinct from the cosmic forces that are playing all around.

Similarly, this process can be effective in withdrawing our attention from the facts of life to the subtler forces of Saṁskāras and idea-forces it may introduce into the world of free creative ideas. Spiritual life persupposes a release from the realistic sense and its limitations. The waking life is generally hedged round by limitations, and cannot feel the free creative powers of the spirit. The more freely the seeker can realize the creative power of the soul, the more it is possible for it to produce such a state in waking-consciousness by concentration and withdrawal. The senses may be kept inactive, and the mind can move freely in the world of its ideas.

Between the world of dream and the world of such meditative creation there is little difference. In dream the psyche is dissociated from the sense organs and their activities. By dream here we mean the kind which is neither produced by the peripheral activity nor by personal desires and the vital mental urges. This dissociation is natural. In waking it is produced when the mind works under absorbing ideas. The dissociation from the senses may be occasional and temporary.

The more the mind is indrawn the more it can feel its creative power. It can also feel that its creation are spontaneous and do not necessarily refer to any personal need or satisfaction. A new world is revealed in which the distance and the difference between the individual and the collective self are resolved; and sometimes the ideas gush forth from within, and the pictures that are cast upon the mind's mirror actually come to be true in the factual world. This correspondence cannot be explained unless there is a correspondence between the ideas and the facts.

This correspondence is a proof that the whole creation is ideal and not real. The realistic sense of creation causes bondage, its idealistic sense makes for liberation.

The more the waking consciousness is released from its realistic sense, the greater is the possibility of realizing the creative and the projective power of the self; and if, perchance, the correspondence between the individual and the universal consciousness is felt in waking life, the ideality of the world becomes a fact and a realization.

But the least tension of being that remains in this meditative strain produced by the psychic thrill of Nāda is completely removed when Nāda sends the soul into a spiritual slumber. It is not slumber. It is the removal of all tension from the psychic being. Tension is due to the working of the opposing forces, and the least tension in the soul does not allow the psychic being complete rest and silence. The high office of Nāda is to carry the soul to the peace which effertless meditation gives. Nāda in its highest intensity frees the soul from its crude association and its free creation, and enables it to pass from the world of ideas and facts into the world of light and illumination.

We rise from the illusion of experience, we rise above the space and the time sense. We rise above the insurgent urges of psychic life. We transcend the dimension of psychic life. A new revelation completely changes the meaning of life and experience, and sets us in a novel adjustment. A new freedom is in sight. It is not the freedom of grace. It is not the freedom of delicate and subtle being. It is not the freedom of extensive vision. It is the freedom which follows the perception of truth. It is the freedom of enlightenment. Such a freedom is experienced in Turīya, the fourth state of our conscious being when it is exhibited in its complete dissociation from all forms of psychism.

The slumber of the soul produced by Nāda and the slumber of sleep are different. The latter is natural, the former is produced. Psychism is diffused in the latter, it is concentrated in the former.

But the slumber of Nāda is a form of psychic slumber and self-hypnosis. This gives the soul uncommon ease, elasticity, and knowledge of the creative dynamism; but it cannot give the blessed transcendence. It can give the finest delight of exquisite harmony. But it cannot itself carry the soul to transcendence. The rhythmic vibration of Nāda can make us receptive to the finer oscillations of life, and embracive consciousness gives us cosmic feeling by making our being more elastic and responsive.

Though the highest elasticity and delicacy of being make it a fit recipient of the absolute truth, and a responsive and receptive medium of it, still the highest truth cannot be reached by Nāda, for, although quite effective in the creative plane, it is not effective in the non-creative order. Nāda is the finest expression of the creative dynamism. It can carry us the root of the cosmic life, but it cannot carry us to the Absolute which overshadows the cosmic sense. The peace it gives is the peace of blessed harmony which unties all psychic complexes. It can widen our normal consciousness by making it elastic and by freeing it from the ego-centric reference and reveal the divinity sleeping in man. It can give access into the supermind, the source whence it starts, and acquaint us with its exquisite harmony and unfathomable depth, but the thread of our life and consciousness is not lost in this ascent of the supramental heights from the normal self-consciousness. Life moves, as it were, in the same scale of psychic life. There may be differences of fineness and subtlety, but there is no fundamental difference in the composition of experience. But the whole history of life is changed in the fourth state of knowledge. The subconscious, the selfconscious, and the superconscious are the three scales in the gamut of life, but the transcendent does not come under any scale of life. It is a unique experience whence the music is displaced by silence.

The fourth state is unique. Our knowledge in it has no dimension, no magnitude. Knowledge in sentient or super-sentient form has an expanse : it may be reflectng a small or a huge universe. The whole universe, with its myriads of existences, can be reflected in it, or it may reflect a speck of dust or an atom of existence. But there is a state of knowledge which does not reflect anything : hence, it has no magnitude. Knowledge itself has no magnitude. It has a field like a magnetic field, which it illumines. It may range from hell to heaven. Knowledge reflects the movement of life, subtle, gross, earthly, divine, as the case may be. Generally mysticism points to experiences which are supernormal or superconscious, and the mystics become fond of them, since, they exhibit chastened life with its purity of delight. And at times the vision of a circle of angelic beings inspiring and giving protection to the seekers is vouchsafed and the privilege of conversing with them is conferred upon the seekers. The supersensible realm of spirits has been the hope and the promise of the mystic life.

And the experience of a perfect order in which the parts are interlocked in the harmony of the whole has been the inspiration of the saints. It is an order which is a living poem.

Everything is divine. "The universe is a gigantic crystal, all whose atoms and laminae lie in uninterrupted order and with unbroken unity." This unity is represented in different ways. Some make it a centre of love, some of life.

The life of spirit feels the perfect unison, freedom, harmony, and perfect peace; but this feeling of immensity and the life of perpetual divine communion is not the end of the mystic search in the Upaniṣads. The Upaniṣads strike a singular note in transcending even this glorious and joyous consciousness. This note aims at the pivot of being and the focal unity of consciousness. It has no field to illuminate. It has nothing to reflect. It produces a revolutionary change in the outlook of life, for it changes the centre of attraction from the immensity of the superconscious being to the stillness of being.

The fourth state of consciousness, generally called Turīya, is therefore not to be confounded with the super-conscious stretches of life and consciousness. These stretches are enfolded in relative experience, they are the finer experiences which are revealed when the centres of spiritual experience become active in us. They, therefore, imply a continuity with the normal psychic consciousness, though their range is vast, their experiences deep and wide. Their charm lies that way.

But the fourth state of consciousness transcends these experiences and intuitions, howsoever fine. It has no reference to any kind of psychism and relativity. It indicates a new turn in life, for it has nothing in common or in continuity with other states of consciousness.

It is not to be regarded as the state of being in which lie hidden the roots of life and the urges of becoming. It may be the underlying canvas on which life's footprint can leave no mark. It is always with life, but it always escapes the touch of life.

But it is not the cosmic envelope of life, for it has no relation to life. It indicates, therefore, a phase in our conscius life lying beyond all implications of relativity. Consciousness has, as it were, three dimensions, in waking, in dream, in sleep. Turīya is the consciousness without any dimension.

Reference

1. In the terms of Indian psychology the waking and the dream present the Ahaṅkāra in its Rājasic and Sāttvic aspect; the former is creative, the latter is expressive. In the former Ahaṅkāra is associated with Manas and the senses, in the latter with Manas. But the Sāttvic Ahaṅkāra with its Rajas dominant is creative in the personal sense. Ahaṅkāra with Sattva dominant is expressive but not creative in the usual sense.

Chapter XIX

Abode of Brahman

The Upaniṣads conceive different planes of subtle existence. The more we can enter the subtle spheres, the easier is the life, the freer is delight, and the more elastic is the being. The finest life is reached in Brahmaloka.

The word "Brahmaloka" has a double significance. "Brahma" may mean Brahman, "loka" implies abode. Brahmaloka thus may mean the abode which is Brahman. Here no difference is left between Brahman and Loka. Or it may mean a plane of existence in the order of spiritual ascent.

The Upaniṣads conceive the planes of finer existence which are hidden from our clouded vision, but which reveal themselves to the illumined souls when they rise in the scale of purity, fineness, and freedom from earthly desires. In this upward ascent life becomes free, and knowledge intuitive. Only the shining transparence of our being can reveal the finer flow of serenity and delight encircling life. The notion of septenary planes of existence is ultimately the vision of the finer life current which enfolds the soul, but of which it has not knowledge so long as it has not the yearning for freedom and chastened being. Sometimes under rare conditions and in inspired moments the soul is favoured with rare glimpses. These planes stand revealed before the supermind, and the supermind fills them with its supramundane expressions of beauty, dignity, fineness, and symmetry. Life is more easy, delight more serene, intuition more free. The finest of these super-sensuous planes of existence is the Brahmaloka. The spring of life on this plane is the finest, for it is the first expression in the process of the formation of the cosmic spheres, or we may say more consistently it is the spatial-temporal expression of Īśvara, for the ideal of "loka" suggests a spatial expanse in which the throbbing life is active. Brahmaloka, in this sense, is not Brahman, but is its expression in space and time. It is luminous and transparent and endures for a cycle of existence, i.e. so long as the cosmic withdrawal does not break it up for its re-emergence in the next cyclic order.

Brahmaloka is the centre of existence, where life has its fullest play, delight its greatest expansion. Nothing can be in common between this summit of existence and the lower planes, for the move of life in the power planes is gross, restricted, and determined, and therefore access into this finest realm is invariably associated with experiences incompatible with the experiences of divided life, however fine and subtle. In the Chāndogya Upaniṣad the word "Brahmaloka" has been used in the sense of Brahman.

These planes should not be mistaken for *Bhumis* of Buddhistic Mysticism. The latter represent the progressive stages in the career of Buddhisattva. They are essentially psychical perfections. But the planes of the Upaniṣads are cosmical. There may be a correspondence between psychical perfections and cosmical planes, and psychic receptivity may feel the correspondence.

The different planes of experience and existence reflect the spiritual light in varying intensity. The spiritual current is not everywhere the same. Reflection is proportionate to the transparence and purity of being.

The stream of spiritual inspiration may visit and enter into the soul from majestic heights and can produce fine modulations.

Brahmaloka suggests the theory of spiritual space. Though the Upaniṣads are not definitely expressive of it, still it cannot be doubted that a spiritual space and time are suggested in them, for the experience of a shining expanse is undoubtedly hinted at in many planes.

This space and time are to be distinguished from space and time of ordinary experience. The ordinary space is pictorial space and ordinary time sentimental time. Spiritual space and time are original expanse and duration co-eternal with Īśvara and coeval with it. They are, therefore, the finest expression of Māyā, and are a part of the dynamic divine. The first expression of spirit in concentration is associated with them. The mystics are conscious of such expanse in rare heights of inspiration and spiritual life. The original space and time are one with spirit. Spirit is space because it embraces all, it pervades all. Spirit is time, because it is the ever-creative. Nothing can limit it, since it is the original expanse and therefore the stay of all existence. Nothing can destroy it, since the expression is perpetual, it is eternal time or duration. Space and time are intimate with the spirit in concentration. The expression of spirit is continuous, and the range of spirit is pervasive. Continuity and pervasiveness represent spiritual time and spiritual space.

This is the sovereign edifice of the world, in which the whole world is included and outside of which nothing is. It is not in space. It is the last heaven, the Empyrean. It is the primal mind, which the Greeks call *Protone.*

The delight and the expanse of Brahmaloka are enjoyed by the seeker who finds no essential distinction between the finite self and Īśvara. The finite does not at once vanish. But still the feeling and experience of a wide diffusive life becomes clearly evident in this height of existence. The idea of difference dissolves away and the spiritual life in essence is felt everywehre the same. The ever-expressive and ever-effulgent nature of spirit is a pleasing experience, and the sense of an uncommon elasticity of being and spontaneity of expression is a happy realization. The spirit has its initial expression. There is no sense of restraint in the spirit, though it is ceaselessly creative. And hence, moral merit and demerit cannot trouble the soul installed in this height.

Our merit and demerit, our knowledge and ignorance in the relativities and the contraries of life cannot approach the realm of spirit. The least sense of difference in the concept of truth has a crushing effect upon ourselves. The discrete or individualistic sense produces the sense of an agent. It creates a false centre and attracts it by pragmatic values. Truth realization requires the transcendence of the pragmatic values and the discrete sense of events and things. To put it in another way, the life of Karma is a life of tension, for it creates in self a false individuality and raises false hopes. Upāsanā gives relief from the tension of individuality; and this relief is displaced by the rhythm and harmony of spirit pervading the order of expression. The lift of the soul in its ever-expressive meditative strain breaks the spell of Karma, because meditation generates and fosters true understanding. Understanding kills the individualized sense of our being, for individuality is the child of ignorance. Individuality breeds the sense of rigidity, which cannot see the plasticity of life and superabundance of spirit, and fosters values and ideals which seek the gratification of the individual. And unless, therefore, there is a better understanding and deeper vision of life, it is indeed difficult to rise from the possibilities to the life of activism to receive the message of harmony, unity, and dignity of the ever-expressive life of spirit.

A life of activism is not necessarily opposed to the spiritual life, but a life of conscious activism certainly is. It cannot rise above the concentrated sense of an agent and feel the truth of the deeper law of spontaneous expression of life and its beauties. It at once changes the course of life from the seeking of values, ethical or moral, from the life of satisfaction, physical or biological, to the realization of freedom, ease, elasticity of spirit. But this elasticity of life is disturbed in the physical and the biological planes of existence, and cannot be felt in its fullest expression unless our being becomes spiritually strung. The conception of planes of existence through which the flow of life and spirit infiltrates is a commonplace amongst the mystics, and a correspondence amongst these planes and the different layers of our psychic being and consciousness is also generally accepted. These planes reveal immanental truths to the seeker according to his inner purification and perfection, especially of the psychic being. The psychic self has degrees of perfections, and corresponding to them spread out the finer realms of existence, promising finer life, speedier movement. And the sensitive soul of the mystic can discover the infinite shades of blessedness. Nature always fulfils herself. The forsaking of the joys of life endows the mystic with the delight of the finer currents and they carry the soul to the still subtler delights and make it more and more receptive to the gifts of the heaven-bent life. Life can be felt by life, life develops fine insight and direct intuition. They are luminous experiences of the soul.

The delight of spiritual fellowship is not so prominent in the Upaniṣads as the security and elasticity of being and widening of consciousness. The security is sought in the wide dimension of being and expansive feeling. Spiritual life is essentially seeking the magnitude of being and Upāsanā secures this by the concentration of the identity of being, running through expression. Upāsanā does not merely give the communion. It reveals the akinness of nature. Communion speaks of akinness. But it cannot establish the complete identity. It can heighten up the magnitude of our being and make us understand that the distinction between Jīva and Īśvara is not eternal. Jīva can appropriate the powers of Īśvara, though it cannot interfere with his power and control over creation.

Upāsanā secures for us a control over the natural urges and finer play of natural forces. The least difference is denied, and hence the adept enjoys in Brahmaloka not so much a fellowship as an akinness in being and nature. The finite soul is finite. In the course of the ascent, the soul enjoys the highest plenitude of being in the Brahmaloka; it has a kind of identity with Īśvara. As such it has its undisturbed quietude of being, untarnished vision of the immanental truth. The dimension and the magnitude of Īśvara may differ from those of the seeking soul, but the sense of akinness which is sought in this height of existence has its desirable effect. It fosters the enduring sense of the spirit, in the place of the transient and sick soul hedged round by Karma and its transient creative ideals.

In the realm of values a distinction is to be drawn between gratification and appreciation. Gratification is the satisfaction of crude sensibility. It is the satisfaction of the vital self and the lower mentality. It does not offer the delight of fine self-expression and the chastened oscillation of being. Appreciation is enduring felicitation that follows the fine movement of life. It springs from the mind free from the impelling of the senses. It affords quiet joy of contemplation. The sense of worth is manifestly clear in appreciation. This distinction has a bearing upon the fruition of Karma and Upāsanā. In active pursuits of gratification here or hereafter through the performance of sacrificial rites, the self has a confused vision of itself and is led by the lower instincts of sense-gratification. It is, no doubt, creative, but its creative ends do not rise higher above the engrossing vital satisfactions. Upāsanā is more contemplative than creative, its purpose is to open up the possibilities of super-sentient realization. The self in Karma is the agent, it dominates over the circumstances and puts them in a new setting to realize its end. The self in Upāsanā is the recipient, it does not produce any new setting, it sympathetically enters into the fine oscillations of life and the symmetry of the cosmic setting and enjoys their rhythm, delight, and joy. It reveals the deeper truths not always revealed to the senses.

But when we speak of value in mystic consciousness we mean subtle movement and delight consequent upon the upbuilding of the subtle existence.

Value in mystical consciousness is not necessarily a creative urge. The true joy of life is the joy of completeness. Poetry and Art enjoy glimpses of the creative life and give expression to it. They cannot get a glimpse of the transcendence. The value of mystic life essentially lies here. It presents to us the aspect of life which is not exhibited in the creative expression of the soul. It is not reducible to aesthetic or ethical activity. It may suggest them, but it transcends their value in a state of being, free from all urges either of knowledge or activity. It is free from all tension. When our being becomes free from all tension, it can then only enjoy its own nativity. The breathless calm lies at the centre of our being and the true value is set upon it at the heart of things.

This truth has been clearly established in the Upaniṣads when they point out the supreme value of transcendence and its superiority to all other fine expressions and urges of life. The Upaniṣads recognize the path of progress of the soul through the subtle realm of existence, till it reaches the plane where life bestows its highest blessing in the form of unceasing flow of delight and expansive existence. The Upaniṣadic saints appraise the highest truth in the centre of existence and the highest value is given to it inasmuch as it offers a unique experience which gives us release from the entanglements, attractions, and distractions of a divided life. Nay, it offers an experience before which every other experience is as nothing. The joys of life fade into insignificance before it. The subtle delight of the fine psychism, the active stirrings of life, the dance of creation, pale into insignificance before it. It is so majestic in its transcendence that nothing on this side of life can either compare with it in value or describe it.

One point more. The heights of majestic life have a unique character—the absence of effort. Mystical life may have many expressions—silence, contemplation, or action, but every move of life in the mystic is easy, natural, and spontaneous. The least effort for an ideal is not there. It cannot be there, for the mystic enjoys life beyond tension, resistance, and conflict. The creative ideals in life attract us by the sense of obstacles conquered, resistance overcome.

The sense of the self as the victor is there. Creative ideals attract us because of the height of self-consciousness brought out in the struggle. But in the mystical life there is no struggle, no resistance, no tension. Life at this height has its gracious smoothness, even and quiet flow. Activity or contemplation here are natural and easy. They form the part of the mighty current that exhibits itself in its richness but is not conscious of it. Everything is natural and easy. If the mystical life is creative, it is spontaneously so, if it is contemplative it is so unawares. It is released from the sense of self-consciousness, though it has not lost consciousness. The effort is displaced by harmony, for the prospect is all-embracing and finally transcendent. This advantage comes to the mystic because of his attitude to enjoy life in its fullness.

Chapter XX

Negative Path

Though the Upaniṣads have not forsaken the path of rational realization of the ultimate truth, still they have put emphasis upon life and its intuition. Reason and discrimination can be helpful to the understanding of the phenomenal as spiritually not comforting and consoling. Hence, the attempt has been always to get inspiration from life. The approach has been in two paths – *the path of contemplation* and *the path of negation.* The former is the life of *Dhyāna,* which gives us access into the finer secrets of life, which can never present themselves to the untrained soul. But the path of contemplation cannot help us to go beyond the concrete spiritual experiences and see the face of silence. In contemplation the attitude is receptive. But the heart of reality cannot be penetrated even with the persistence of the receptive attitude. The attitude of reception puts truth separate from us and keeps up the distinction between the *knower* and the *known*. It may give fine numinous experiences of the soul, but it cannot give the impress of the transcendent truth.

Realizing this shortcoming of an approach through contemplation generating the finest experiences of the spiritual harmony, the texts prescribe the path of negation "by which every predicate that can be stated in words becomes excluded from the Absolute, till finally God is designated as nothingness and nullity bearing in mind that these terms denote in truth the immeasurable penitude of being." The negative path takes us beyond all personal feelings in the spiritual life, beyond the sense of a personal and moral relationship with God. It takes us beyond the sense of the cosmic harmony and the cosmic being.

The Upaniṣads indicate Brahman in its Nirguṇa aspect by Neti, Neti. "It is not this. It is the other." But it is not Professor Otto's numinous reception of the "other." Spiritual experiences differ from other experiences in the presentation of the Numen, the "other." The "Numen" is the "other", because it is not what is presented to the senses and the mind. Professor Otto feels that the way to realize the "other" is not intellectual. It is numinous. The numinous in time perforce "begins to stir, to srart into life and consciousness." But this numinous feeling is another name for the subtle harmony of our being which awakens the sleeping beauties of the soul and makes us realize the moral holiness and the spiritual dignity.

The Upaniṣads have passages in them which exhibit the profound sense of the tremendous, the fierce, and the terrible. The mystical consciousness brings with it many attitudes, and sometimes contradictory attitudes; all contraries have their setting in the heart of reality; when the deeper harmony touches us it manifests the infinite riches of spiritual life—and, however seemingly receptive and over-coming some of them may appear, very soon the feeling of repulsion, fear, or terror is displaced by the finer and wider perception of their beauty in the setting.

The "other" reveals a new realm of existence with its inspiring message of eternal life and unique joy. This is the message of the immense. But there is still an "other" where the spiritual feelings and emotions are overweighed by the spiritual silence—where the sense of "the other" as distinguished from the sense of "this" equally vanishes. The numinous sense can grasp the other, the throbbing heart of being, but it cannot fathom its depth. It returns baffled. All the feelings and sentiments retire. The adept returns with the unique sense of freedom from the dream of life.

This silence is the quest. This silence is the rest. This silence is the mystery. It cannot be said to be even Anyadeva (the other) because this requires a discriminative reference. It is different from the known, different from the unknown. To call it known is to make it an object. To call it unknown is to deny its intimacy and immediateness. Nothing can indicate this. Hence, the Upaniṣads prescribe the negative path for the realization of the transcendent beatitude. Neti, Neti, therefore, denies positive thinking about it. It also negates negation. Thought posits or denies, but truth transcends the position or the negation of thought. Truth can neither be affirmed nor denied.

Indeed the height is terrifying, for it denies the very basis of our concrete being and knowledge. Only a few brave and adventurous souls can welcome and approach so dazzling a height of existence. Many will shudder at its apparent void. Many will take it to be death perpetual. Death it is not, void it is not. It transcends life and death. It transcends fullness and void. It is calm.

Neti, Neti asks us to give up the natural seeking of the vital and mental life and the values and meanings they set up. Nay, more, it seriously asks us to give up satisfactions in the concrete spiritual life. They are values also in the relative order and confine us by the expression of concrete spirituality. Whatever value and charm they carry with them, they cannot break the veil that hides truth, the silence that keeps us in the dance of life without being in the least touched and affected by it. Transcendence is sought, not because of its value – for it has no value to offer, but the value of freedom – as much for its truth. Nothing is higher than truth : the Upaniṣads appeal by this promise of truth and the freedom it brings from the contraries of life – from its alluring hopes and depressing failures, from the intoxication of the pleasant and from the constant thrill of life with its uncertainty, from the wanted course of constant seeking and adaptation, by opening the new vista. Everyone clings to life, including the gods and angels. The Upaniṣads show the path to freedom by pointing out that truth is the inmost of our being and urge us to seek it by putting aside all clingings to individual self and its vital and animal demands. "Neti, Neti" (not this, not this) therefore presents a check to the free flow of life and awakens the sharper and better understanding which can eventually find out the path for realization. It cries a halt to the habituated course of life and indicates a new method of search which rejects the surface coating of existence and apprehends the underlying entity.

This makes it sufficiently clear to us that the apprehension of truth implies a psychic *effortlessness,* but not a psychic inertia. This has in it neither the positive attitude of contemplation nor the attitude of denial. This is the attitude of the effortless intuition. But let us call it the way of silence. This introduces the next topic.

Chapter XXI

Self as Percipience

"Neti, Neti" is an attitude of shrinking. It is the spirit of rejection. Sākṣī is the perpetual witness, distinguished from the oscillations of life and mind. It does not wink. It is the unwinking vigilance of spirit-waking. It neither accepts nor rejects. Rejection or acceptance posit the quality of subject and object. It is a choice on the presentation of a datum to the subject. Life moves here in a groove, it has lost its flow. Consciousness works with a limitation set upon it – the limitation of working through selection. Sākṣī allows freedom from such limitations. The word means literally the detached percipience. It reflects everything, but it is never a logical subject. The subject works under the categories of knowledge and value, it cannot rise above the sectional impressions of life and experience received through the fixed concepts of intellect. Intellect is not, therefore, the proper instrument of apprehended truth. It can grasp the static relations and even the dynamic divergence or unity, but it cannot grasp truth that is neither statical nor dynamical. The subject works under a harassing limitation. The self is the subject not in its naked purity and simlicity but as a centre of reflection and desire. To understand truth the self must rise from the notion of itself as a subject, to the understanding of itself as the free creative principle and then finally as the percipience. The understanding of it as the subject limits its knowledge and activity to an object; it then cannot feel the free spontaneity of life. The rigidity of the logical construction based upon the conception of the self as subject cannot impress us with the spontaneity of the subject. The necessity arises, therefore, of understanding the self not only as a subject but as a creative agent. This is an important step on the path of realization. The structure which intellect builds up is made up of a constant reference and relation of the subject to the object, and hence, the subject cannot feel, so long as it works through concepts, its free nature and spontaneous creation. This spontaneity of the self has to be felt to make way for the final release, for it puts us beyond the world of rigid determination and makes us acquainted with the free creative activity of the self. In this sense the idea of spontaneous being has an appeal to the human mind, for this spontaneity puts us beyond the realm of law and determination to the reality of indeterminism and free expression which is the essence of spirit. The self as freely creative is an advance upon the self as constitutive.

Constitutiveness is implied in creation, but not creation in constitutiveness. This idea really helps us to free ourselves from the thought and imposition of alien elements, the object. But this is not the final vision of self or truth. The creative activity, though spontaneous, still implies a limitation. It establishes the dynamic conception of spirit and attracts by the elasticity of life, but truth is not revealed. The joy of perpetual creation and recurrence may be attractive, but creation may reveal power, and the delight of a free flow of life cannot be accepted as the final truth. It implies a limitation. At least it cannot be the self-contained Absolute. Truth is completeness. This completeness denies concentration and creativeness. They presuppose ideas of time, but time is an illusion. The complete truth in all its beauty and serenity denies change and becoming. It is complete in every moment of its existence and integral in every bit of expression. Nothing can be added to it, nothing can be taken away from it. It denies activity and passivism. But this kills integrity and completeness.

The conception of a free spirit as dynamism is further open

to the objection that it cannot be immediate. Truth must be immediate. The very knowledge of the dynamic or creative spirit implies a self-division in it. It implies a projection from the self to know itself and this knowledge implies limitation and checks or interferes with its freedom. The dynamic conception cannot be stricIty aconceptual, for its knowledge requires its turning back upon itself, which destroys its fluidity and immediacy.

Creative life may be a very attractive vision of spirit, but the creative life eternally complete in itself is hardly consistent. It may be freely and endlessly creative, but it cannot be immediately intuitive. If truth is dynamic, intuition cannot but be so, since truth and intuition must ultimately be one; but dynamic intuition is a process, and a process by itself is not complete.

At least it implies a turning back upon itself either in the particular or in the whole to know itself as truth. It must submit to a turning back to self to allow the vision of the whole and the complete. This changes its whole character. It ceases to be immediate. This is the difficulty that is felt in conceiving truth to be a dynamical reality which is complete in itself and which is intuitive alike. The dynamical reality cannot be at the same time intuitive, for in dynamism intuition is possible only when life turns upon itself, and not otherwise. Either dynamism ceases to be the last conception of truth, or it must not allow an intuition in itself of itself. Intuition of the dynamism cannot be dynamic. The notion of the dynamism of spirit confines our outlook and does not allow us to go deeper. The spontaneity of life is so absorbing a conception that it requires a very much finer life to feel and realize that the centre of dynamism is not dynamic. Life is an oscillation between movement and rest, between actuality and potentiality, but the spring of life transcends both. It is *reality*.

This introduces Sākṣī to us. Intuition is Sākṣī, but it is not dynamic. No conception of it as static or dynamic is possible. For both are conceptual. Sākṣī is, strictly, aconceptual. It is not life, it is not mind. It is not the psyche.

Knowledge is reception, reflection, and illumination. Sākṣī is illumination, but is neither reception nor reflection. Both reception and reflection imply a dynamic relation and a reference to self or something beside self. Both, therefore, imply an element of relation. Sākṣī is intuition without relation. It does not imply any relation to self or to object. It is non-relational percipience.

It indicates no bent of the soul and is eternally free from the relational contraries, and hence it is unique. And because it is unique it is in a sense complete. Its completeness does not lie in the fullness of its content but in the knowledge of all contents. The completeness is not realized through the contraries of life and knowledge, but through their transcendence. It cannot allow in it contraries of subject and object, the contraries of self and its expression. These contraries really reveal the self as the logical ego, but do not lay bare its transcendent nature.

It is a commonplace in the history of thought that the self is the architect, the creative, and the organizing force. The delight of creativeness is great. Creative impulse affords the joy of stirring, the delight of self-expression.

Creativeness may afford the delight of the realization of an idea or an ideal. It cannot fit in with completeness, which self is. The creative ideal is a fascination.

And the idea of the Primium Mobile appeals mostly to religious feelings. It shows its power, it exhibits intelligence and beningnity. The creative God appears as the living God. It inspires our whole being. Intellect is charmed with its superior wisdom, the heart with its beauty and poetry revealed in the creative order. The majesty, the beauty, and the sweetness of life are enough for most souls. They are absorbed in them.

Here even the best gifted souls of humanity cannot go beyond such joyous consciousness to apprehend the mystery of silence. They feel diffident before the mysterious awfulness of the supreme silence beyond the creative urges of life.

But the fit soul appraises life beyond creative efficiency and creative beauty in its silence. This silence is illumined silence. This silence is Sākṣī. This silence is the potent fact in life. There is a silence beyond the stars, there is a silence beyond the psychic oscillation. If the eternal regions above and the moral law within struck the imagination of Immanuel Kant, the Silence within and without struck the imagination of the Upaniṣadic seers. They find in it the face of truth.

This silence can be felt in the self, when the self stands detached from life.

The word "detached" indicates its transcendence and indifference, by implication to a previous attachment. But the self is neither.

This understanding is essential to liberation. Liberation is not a state to be realized. It is eternally realized. It is not the fruition of a dynamic spiritual culture. Every form of discipline implies some kind of fruition of our psychic being – it gives powers, it gives vision. But liberation is neither power nor vision. The former implies energism and activism, the latter passivism and receptivity. But liberation cannot be any one of them. It is freedom from both energism and quietism. Sākṣī is this freedom. It is not the fruition of activism. It is the freedom from the polarities of knowledge and the contrarities of will.

Sākṣī is dissociated from the active or passive psychism. This understanding of its singleness, its completeness, and uniqueness is the beginning of the Upaniṣadic wisdom. Normally this transcendence of Sākṣī is not felt, for the psychic being seems to be identified with it.

The freedom from psychic oscillation is truly the beginning

of wisdom. The normal bent of the mind is checked in this attitude of percipience and generally the difference is felt between the percipient and the psychic being. The psychic being, active or passive, is creative or recpetive. But Sākṣī is neither. This distinction is a positive help towards the realization of truth. It keeps us from the fine attractions, positive powers that follow from the purity and subtlety of psychic being. But the detachment of Sākṣī allows saving grace for the adept, and he cannot fall a prey to the immanental beauties and sublimities. Sākṣī has no touch with the fine pleasure of psychic life. The philosophy of activism would allow these delights as the successive fulfilments of the self. Every new experience, every new movement of life is welcomed as self-expression. Hence, the dance of life has a charm for most mystics. And sometimes the dance of life is followed by a respite in the silence of life. The mystics enjoy life through its silence and dance. Life alternates between these two. And this principle of alternation keeps up the equilibrium of our life and indicates the normality in psychic life. Any departure from it disturbs its normality. The mystic life is generally regarded as supernormal, not in the sense that it overcomes the law of alternation but in the sense that even here it enjoys the dance at its widest amplitude and the silence at its highest dignity. And this enjoyment is in all cases conscious.

But the Upaniṣadic bent is different. It emphasizes an indifference to the quiet or the dance of life and refers the principle of alteration to the psychic life. This detachment allows us to see more of the conscious life than is otherwise possible. It brings a new freedom from the alternation of the psychic life.

The attitude of Sākṣī is, therefore, superior to the attitudes of prayer and reception, joy and service. The latter do not allow freedom from psychic oscillation, the former does. Sākṣī in spiritual consciousness is, therefore, a great asset; it allows freedom from the psychic bent. Life is so much engrossed with psychism that none sees its freedom from it, none feels the freedom to be a value and an asset. But the attitude of a detached percipient soon establishes the calm which is free from the conflicts of psychism and the alternations of spiritual life.

The attitude of Sākṣī (Seeing) is different from the attitude of devotion. Devotion is a kind of psychism. It may give us the finest feelings and the richest experience. But it can never rise above offering and reception. The devotional attitude puts us in living touch with God. It fills us with love, joy, and strength. But Sākṣī in spiritual life puts us on a still higher ground. It frees us from the compelling sense of devotion and gradually recovers us from its joys and influences and allows us to see and appreciate the calm dignity of self, which is not disturbed by the finest devotional experiences. Religious consciousness has its joyousness. Sākṣī introduces us to a state which has no joyousness either intellectual or emotional.

Sākṣī cannot allow any kind of joyous consciousness. It frees us from all psychism. But it is not destitude of all feeling. It has no joy. It has *Peace*.

Exceptional calmness and freedom from psychism can give us the taste of the blessed peace of Sākṣī. Our being is in constant tension. Any form of mystical exaltation has a marvellous effect upon it. It allows it freedom from the tension of the waking consciousness. This absence of tension and the divine rhythm of being constitute an absorbing experience. It is not easy to overcome its influence. The sudden fall in the tension has its joy. The joy is felt all the more by contrast. And, therfore, it is not often possible to go beyond the joyous consciousness of the harmonious vibration of devotion and enjoy the peace in mystical life. Sākṣī makes way for it. Sākṣī is detached from tension of waking-consciousness and harmony of devotional consciousness. It is detached even from the cosmic vibrations. Devotional experiences bring satisfaction to the heart. Devayāna (the path of the gods) acquaints us with the fine planes of being connected with the cosmic life. Cosmic vibrations unfold for us the fine planes of existence. They make our psychic bodies fine, pure, and rich.

Sākṣī (the attitude of Seeing) leads on to *Sākṣī* (the state of being). The former in the beginning has tension—for the attitude of watching implies concentration; but this attitude soon allows us the understanding of the *nature of Sākṣī*. Here is constant percipience, but without the least tension in our psychic being, even without the tension of perception.

But it is not to be identified with psychical relaxation. Devotional joys are joys of relaxation of our psychical being. Scientific intuition is also a form of relaxation. These relaxations are not only the relaxation of the nerves, they are the relaxations of the active psychism. But with the relaxation of the active psychism the fine psychic being has its play. And this fine play is so absorbing by the light it sheds, and the blessedness it inspires, that the complete relaxation of psychic being is not possible in them. The psychic being is active, very gently and harmoniously so, but Sākṣī is completely free from tension and relaxation. Psychic life cannot touch it. Hence the experiences of psychical relaxation (so often identified with religious intuition) should not pass for Sākṣī. Sākṣī is free from the gentle tensions as well as from the easy relaxations of our psychical life. It is different from dynamic spirituality.

Never does it refuse nor accept any one of its forms of dynamic spirituality. A fine dynamism, on the other hand, is helpful to its realization, for it is conducive to fine understanding and receptivity. But Sākṣī is indifferent even to this. Life may unfold its fine possibilities—intellectual, aesthetic, moral, and devotional—and like the lotus may scatter its fragrance and beauty. But these fruitions and possibilities should not pass for high spirituality. They are values. They emerge as life grows fine. They are life's finest expression. They have their charms. The dynamic spirituality is a growth. But Sākṣī does not grow. When the idea of spirituality as something different from "growth" or "emergence" or "fruition" becomes clear in the possibility of fully grasping Sākṣī,then its value in life is appreciated.When life rises above the thoughts of enjoyment or of expression, when it has an effortless calm, then it can feel the transcendence of Sākṣī. Sākṣī gives the idea of transcendent spirutality as distinguished from dynamic spirituality. And, with the full grasp of Sākṣī, a new idea of spiritual life dawns upon us. Spiritual life is so often identified with dynamism that it requires a fine culture, a refined psychism, to feel the dignity of transcendent spirituality.

It appears for the moment that this attitude detaches us from the actualities of life. It does. But the true vision is not possible unless one is set free from these actualities. In the silent percipient the affective and the active attitudes are temporarily lost and a new feeling of relief, of ease, is the incredible consequence. The Upaniṣads enjoin upon us to rise above the psychic life and its absorbing delights. They admonish us to rise above life's thrill and to reach life's calm. Prayer and Samādhi give the calm in psychic being, but not the calm of Sākṣī; they wake up the fine being with psychic possibilities, but they cannot go beyond the life of alternation.

It is this that the Upaniṣads admonish us to do. The joy of life is the usual promise in mysticism. The freedom of life is the promise of the Upaniṣads. In Sākṣī and in its constant detached wakefulness the secret of this freedom lies, and whoever has been able to appraise this wakefulness his release is near.

Time, Psyche, and Sākṣī

The understanding of Sākṣī, the transcendent in our normal life, requires a clear discrimination of it from psyche and time.

Psyche is associated with time, Sākṣī is not. Psyche has its history of evolution in time, Sākṣī has no history. The history of the psyche or the mental life is continuous. Its changes follow in quick succession. Psyche is dependent upon time for its expression. Self-consciousness has no meaning apart from time. It is not a timeless perception. Our conscious life has its play in time. The psychic life leaves its footprints on the canvas of time. If the time sense is lost, life loses its meaning. The dynamic aspect of our being is so closely associated with time that we can hardly think of the mental life save and except as a process unrolling itself in time. Time in its discreteness or in its continuity is so closely associated with mental events or mental history that it has been a commonplace among psychologists to explain the psychological sense of time by the events of succession, before or after, by the sense of frustrated or unfulfilled desire.

Those who are influenced by the creativeness of spirit naturally think that time is a form of spirit. They go so far as to identify time with the creative spirit to which they give the name of duration. Whether time is the creative urge or whether it is a form of expression, it is in both cases associated with the spiritual or creative life. Spirit creates through time and endures through time. And this double delight of creativeness and duration through time has been the chief attraction for most people, who have not the still wider vision of truth. Naturally, they cannot think of spirit in any other but dynamic form. They cannot rise above time sense. Psychic life is associated with it, but to relate spirit to time and creativeness is entirely to misread it. In our ordinary psychic life it is very difficult to grasp the idea of a free being unrestricted by time. The spiritual life generally has great charm, for it enlightens us as to the nature of spirit as independent of and creative through time. This exhibits the free nature of spirit.

But activism is not the essence of our spirit. Activism is

the perpetual effort or strain, but spirit can have no strain in itself. Absolute activism is an impossibility, inasmuch as we understand activism only in opposition and restraint. At least, the idea so becomes clear to us. A free flow of activism is a metaphor. Activism and passivism, energism and quietism are opposites, and spirit transcends all opposites. Activism attracts us by its free creativeness, but creativeness is a limitation. It implies concentration and purpose. The fluidity of spontaneous creative life may be inherent in spirit. But is not spirit, for spirit transcends creativity.

Sākṣī is different from élan vital. Its freedom is not the freedom of unrestrained activity, it is not the ease of free creation and free inception. It is not the freedom of spontaneous dance and expression of life. It is awake to the oscillations of life. It is the freedom of the present as compared to the determinism of the past and the future. It is the ever-transcendent now. It is not the ever-creative now. The ever-creative now transcends the past and the future in time, but it cannot transcend the time sense altogether. It is in a way the essence of time, though detached from the sense of past and future. Indeed the ever-creative now is a free act.The transcendent now is not a free act, it is a free intuition. It is free being. Both are immediate. The one is the immediacy of activity. The other is the immediacy of intuition. But the immediacy of activity is not in itself known. It requires the light of intuition to know itself. Its knowledge at once makes it mediate, for in the act of knowing itself it must veer round itself. The ever-creative now, therefore, cannot be the immediacy of intuition. There is much truth in the assertion of Gentile : "The activity realizes itself in the other, or rather it is realized in itself as other." (Gentile : *The Theory of Mind as Pure Act,* p. 256.) It is, therefore, a relation with itself. But such is not the case with Sākṣī, which is intuition, but not an act. This reference to itself as other is involved in the ever-creative now to rise to knowledge or intuition. This is intuition as an act. Intuition when it transcends time and activity is what the Upaniṣads call the Sākṣī. It is the Ātman, the soul. In our spiritual life Sākṣī, the detached percipient, has great value.

The very attitude of Sākṣī releases us from mental reserve and limitation, which have become natural to us owing to false spiritual teaching, and exhibits the elasticity, magnitude, and springhtliness of our psychic being. It brings into relief the creative nature of the soul : and some who are seekers after spiritual life sometimes become so much absorbed in one or more of these suprasensuous activities of the soul that they soon begin to construct partial theories out of the deeps of the soul. This can explain why reason, love, or will is accepted as the ultimate reality of the universe. But the deeper insight of a mystic does help us to see that they are functions of the soul through which it builds auniverse of its own. The attitude of detachent enables us to appraise the psychical aspects of our being rightly and to evaluate their forces correctly. It refuses identification of our being with them, and in doing this it frees the soul from their limitations and attractions.

This is great gain, and indeed a supreme help. The great promise of mystic life is to see the self in its purity and in itself, and this is possible when the beauties and dignities, charms, and attractions of the psychic life do not distract our attention. They confine the self to the pleasure-ground. But wise men do not tarry on the pleasure-ground. The psychic sights and scenes screen truth. The psychic being exhibits its powers and potentialities to the seeker. It is indeed difficult to cross them. Many bright souls have fallen a prey to them. Detachment is to be kept up, even in the finest expression of life. This detachment does not come at once. It follows understanding or realization. Although the seeker is constantly advised to be detached, to allow of the entrnace of the higher and the finer life in him, still he cannot follow it and see its beauty in life unless he cultivates in himself the love of truth.

Sākṣī reveals the natural transcendence of the soul and its distinctness from its faculties and functions, from its manifestations in the psychic or physical planes. It reveals all the forces that are within us, the power of love, the majesty of will, the dignity of wisdom, and the joy of life.

It gives a detachment not only from the vital or the mental being, it allows a detachment from the world and realm of ideals. There lies the dignity of Sākṣī, because nothing can give this release but Sākṣī.

Before it stands revealed the creative spontaneity of the soul, the luminous expression of Buddhi with its archetypal ideas, the illuminated understanding, and the intuitive reason, but it never loses its speciality, the sense of detachment which refuses to be identified with any one of these. Sākṣī, therefore, is unique in its existence and transcendence.

If the detached attitude is to be evenly kept up, then our mental being should be luminous and free from the constant urges of the lower nature. Unless the soul is emptied it cannot be fulfilled. Nature abhors a vacuum. If the impulsive urges are quietened down, the fine urges fill our being, and the power of functioning on the higher and supramental planes becomes possible. The lower emotions, the common religious sentiments, the prudential thoughts—all ebb away. In their place the higher intuitions, feelings, and ideas in their perfect harmony and balance become active. Even in this chastened being and almost divinized self the Sākṣī remains untouched, for it is beyond both the gross or the finer psychism. But with the fine psychic nature its character and detachment become self-evident to us; and the more it is clearly apprehended, the more we are released from the psychic bent of being, even from the divine inspiration which shapes itself through the cosmic life and purpose. The dynamism of our nature is reinforced, transformed, and reshaped by the inflow of the divine dynamism, and the man becomes the superman, but even then the transcendence of

Sākṣī cannot be spoiled. It is by nature transparent, pure, and detached. The divine inspiration can touch our psychic being, but not Sākṣī.

The attitude of Sākṣī removes grossness and makes every part of our being consciously receptive. The whole being becomes transparent. Sākṣī reflects as a mirror the thoughts, the desires, the impulses, and the emotions. Nay, it reflects even the sleeping dynamic forces which in rare souls become active. It reveals the potential divinity in man. The calm of detachment releases the powers that usually find no expression in us either of the mental or of the higher mental life.

Every part of our being has its intuitive indications. Our instinctive and vital urges are immediately felt, the desires and the oscillations of the mental being are also immediately apprehended. But the mystical penetration exhibits the play of the still higher forces of Buddhi, its creative forms and ideals—which no longer remain a matter of inference. The intuitions of the buddhic body of the soul which inspire all creative thought exhibit themselves before Sākṣī. But this wealth of intuitions and experiences cannot in the least attract the soul because of the luminous transcendence of the Sākṣī. Nature's forces and psychic powers are best enjoyed in the attitude of detachment. Nature stands naked before the soul that is detached. It draws the veil where there is the least attachment. The attitude of the detached observer can see what is passing more fully than the attitude of active attachment and conscious seeking. Conscious seeking narrows the field of observation. Even the superasensuous and supramental receptions have their limitations. Sākṣī has no limitation. Because of its transcendence it has no limitation of space or time. It can reflect the oscillations of the psychic as well as of the cosmic life. Its fields enlarge with the growth of receptiveness of our being : Sākṣī, which reflects the individual psychism and life, can also reflect the infusion of the cosmic life into the individual life. If there is the perception of the immense, it is felt in our psychic being, but not in Sākṣī : for Sākṣī has no magnitude.

This reflection of the cosmic life becomes occasional in the life of the seeker, for there is a correspondence between the individual soul and the cosmic soul, and when the being becomes chastened and transparent the display of the cosmic life in us becomes possible and sometimes evident.

But Sākṣī, either in the individual or in the cosmic life, has the same character of detachment and transcendence : Life has changes, mutations, and contents, but Sākṣī has none. Intuition, when it does not reflect either the individual or the cosmic life, is exhibited in its true transcendence, aloofness, and non-relatedness. The reflector and the creator in our being stand apart. And Sākṣī gives us self-dissociation in place of self-integration.

It may sound strange that in the Upaniṣads self dissociation becomes the final stage in realization. True, but this dissociation helps self-realization. Unless the self is dissociated, in knowledge as it is in being, from the principles of becoming, activity, thought, mentation, the self-knowledge remains an illusion. In fact this dissociation reveals its truer and profounder nature. Sākṣī gives the delight of transcendence in place of the delight of creative expression. Anyhow the sense of percipience reveals a phase in our being – a phase which reveals its freedom and its uniqueness. Life is so often attracted to its urges with their fruitions that it becomes very difficult to stand quite as a detached observer. Hence, it is a common tendency amongst the mystics to emphasize more the intensive joy of life than the quiet blessedness of the soul. We have a parable in the Kaṭha Upaniṣad. In the tree of life two birds sit on its branches, the one enjoys its fruits, the other watches the enjoyer. This wonderfully expresses the deep truth of mystic life. There is in life the constant tendency to enjoyment. To live is to enjoy. But there is also the percipient which sees, but not enjoys. The enjoyment is of the psyche, the seeing of the soul. Man is divided in himself as the enjoyer and the seer : the former is his humanity, the latter is his transcendence.

Few souls can see this difference. Fewer still can feel the double nature of being. Life moves in detached silence. Light is always seen in the shadow, in its refractions, but not in itself. Its brilliance dazzles the untrained sight. The delight of the flux, the joy of living ever fresh in the ever-changing, has drawn the veil over truth. It indeed requires the highest powers to forgo the flow and the joy of life for the light of truth. But must it not be supposed that truth is not life? Truth is the essence of life, it is the spring of life.

And what value can life possess if it is divorced from truth? Truth is the fullness of life and the summit of existence, and before our intellect can measure it we lose ourselves in it. The attitude of detachment is different from the detached percipient, though the former helps the realization of the latter. It keeps down the disturbing instincts and psychic forces and secures that poise in mental being which can reflect truth. Sākṣī does not imply a reference to self or another. It frees us from the deeprooted natural conviction of the ego and from attachment to its creative power. A new sense, a new meaning of the self, dawns upon it – its loneliness and its transcendence. It is indeed difficult to rise above the conception of self as a creative entity, for the joy of creation and self-expression is so deep in us that it cannot be easily shaken off. And unless the sense of restriction and effort in the creation is felt acutely man refuses to leave it aside. Happily the joy of creation cannot long persist. The delight of creation is not unalloyed, since creation involves conflict and opposition and implies a mastery and momentary resolution of the conflict. Self-expression is the most silent but the highest possible self-assertion. And self-assertion is self limitation. It has in it always the sense of effort; and, however free it is, it has in it a sense of constraint and victory. It has a double experience of the feeling of a conflict and the pleasurable feeling of a conflict overcome. Hence, the being must be experiencing tension in creation, though the tension is subsequently replaced by harmony. Free creation has not restraint, since it has no conflict from without. It has the fluid joy of free life and free expression.

But if free creation does not meet with any external conflict, and expresses life in its spontaneity, still it cannot overcome the limitation inherent in creation. Creation is definite shaping and formation. It gives shape to the shapeless, form to the formless. Even if it is free, it cannot overcome this limitation, otherwise it loses its significance. A creation may be consistently purposeless, but a creation cannot be truly shapeless. And therefore, a free creative activity and urge is really the tendency to give forms to the formless, or mould the formless into forms. Creativeness necessarily implies a self-projection, a self-expression, and a self-concentration.

Between the delight of free creation and the delight of Sākṣī there is a difference. Delight in the former is the delight of unrestricted movement. It is the delight of free life. Delight in the latter is the delight of freedom from the contrarities of life. Life has its contrarities, Sākṣī has none. Hence, its freedom is also unique. It is not the freedom of unrestricted expression. Life attracts us, charms us. Sākṣī frees us. The free activity of life and detached dignity of Sākṣī may allow us redemption from the sense of personality and give the blessed freedom from the restricted view of life; but the freedom allowed by Sākṣī is in a sense higher than the freedom of creativeness. Creativeness is finer when it is spontaneous, and it is spontaneous when it is detached. The more we are detached, the better we can create.

We combine in us a free movement and a complete detachment. He who has understood the detachment of self has seen the best of it when he understands it as creative.

Chapter XXII

Psychism and Knowledge

The Upaniṣads (especially Kaṭha, Nādabindu, Haṁsa, etc.) lay down a discipline for psychic culture. Psychism requires purification before it can be a fruitful source of knowledge. The psychic culture is Yoga. Yoga essentially encourages fine forms of concentration. Its purpose is to reveal the secrets lying deep in our psychic being. The finest method of Yoga is Samādhi. Samādhi presupposes the psychical and vital fitness and fineness, and Yoga, therefore, in its complete course teaches the art of posture and breathing.

Before the fine psychic forces can be active in us, the vital and the physical bodies must be pure, so that they may be able to bear the strain of the higher mental and spiritual activity. Spiritual life requires a rhythm not only in the higher mental life, but also in the lower vital and physical self, otherwise the desired result is not possible. The spiritual harmony builds up the body accordingly.

Samādhi is an attitude of high mental tension and concentration. It makes us intuitive. But its intuitions mostly reveal the nature of the psychic forces. Psychic intuition has an effort of concentration, transcendent intuition has none.

Psychic intuition can reflect the truths of the psychic being—the mental-vital complex. A fine psychic discipline is, therefore, a preliminary course for the initiate, for it can give him a better understanding. But the apprehension of truth requires the transcendence of all psychism, fine or gross.

Intuition as a psychic process is not intuition as truth or reality. As a psychological process it can reflect all the shades of our being, it cannot reflect truth. It can reflect the finest impress of the cosmic consciousness upon our psychic being. It can divine the cosmic secrets hidden in the cosmic soul; but it cannot divine the transcendent truth. Psychism, however fine and chastened, can have no play there. It can give us the glimpse of transcendence. But it is only a glimpse. The fine psychism casts the light of truth, just as the dawn scatters the light of the sun. It heralds the appearance of the dazzling light of transcendence. Samādhi is the highest effort and finest tension of our psychic being. Samādhi is the psychic attitude of perception. Transcendence is not reception. It is being.

Hence, it is clear that the fine psychic receptivity which originates in Samādhi is a preliminary discipline for the life of knowledge. The Upaniṣads lay emphasis upon it. But the psychism that these texts prescribe is not the psychism that develops powers.

Power is the natural sequence of psychic development, but powers are not the desired ends, and are not sought. Powers draw the soul earthward and bind it to the earth, but do not allow that quiet and detachment which make the final illumination possible. Power makes our being eager for refined satisfactions and delights, but cannot give that peace which passeth understanding. This peace is the promise of transcendent wisdom, and one who aspires after peace should be wise and bold enough to part with powers. Truth is the greatest conqueror. Psychism gives us the conquest of powers. Transcendence gives the conquest of truth. Truth conquers powers. Though in the Upaniṣads there is mention of psychic powers for progressive souls still the powers are not sought. Even if they came, they should be completely ignored. They come unawares and take possession of the soul. The seeking soul should be sure of peace and truth that he may not fall victim to the subleties and powers of the fine psychism. The deep sense and eagerness for truth can alone save the seeker from the allurement of powers. Brave are the souls which do not feel drawn to the delights and prospects of powers and can keep up the spirit of seeking truth. The path is sharp as the edge of a razor. Very few gifted souls can walk safely in this path.

In some Upaniṣads (e.g. Haṁsa, Nādabindu, Dhyānabindu) the method of approach has been chiefly through Yoga and Samādhi. There is a dynamism at the base of the spinal cord. This dynamism is not active in ordinary men. It is made active in the seeker. The seeking soul stands covered with a new appearance and clothed with a new joy.

It brings in its train the delightful music of Nāda, which enraptures and absorbs the soul by its delightful and voiceless cadences.

The favourite practice amongst the Indian mystics has been to liberate the coiled-up psychic energy which soon saturates our whole being and opens the wider spiritual vistas and gazes.

Such expansive feeling is accepted by the theists (e.g. Raṅga Rāmānuja) as a phase of synthetic intuition which, according to them, is the secret teaching of the Upaniṣads.

Śaṅkara regards it as the heightening of our mental consciousness in Upāsanā, and as a desirable and agreeable feeling. These shades of joyous feeling are effects of finer psychism, but they should not pass for truth.

Samādhi breaks the polarization of the psychic forces. The neutral equilibrium of our being cannot be established if there is a constant outward tension. It is necessary to go within and to effect a neutralization of the forces and enjoy the calm. This neutralization is the highest effect of Samādhi, for it produces the greatest calm in our psychic being. Yoga is the prelude to a life seeking wisdom. It may generate understanding and give freedom.

Chapter XXIII

Life Through Four Stages

The Upaniṣads find the highest truth in the free and emancipated life. They find the greatest art in the right regulation of life. Philosophy defines truth, mysticism gives its realization, the art of life gives the regulation, which can mould life in a way that can make realization possible and easy. In the full code of life the three go together – understanding, setting, and realization.

Life is plastic. The finest understanding and realization can be properly assisted when the plasticity of life is regulated in a definite way. The fullest flowering goes with the most delicate handling and living. And this is especially true where the end is not merely an intellectual satisfaction. Truth is the highest promise of *living*. Life is inspired by understanding.

This art of living cannot be the same with every individual. But where the art of life has an influence towards better understanding and realization, the art generally must have a uniform nature and character. The final realization is consequent on the finest opening of our being and the opening must follow a method and a course. Life has infinite intuitions, definite forms will require distinct settings of life. The realization of the Upaniṣadic truth requires, therefore, a distinct art which may not be serviceable in other spheres of life. This is true in the case of the few adepts who make realization their direct objective in life. Their interest lies there. Their life takes, therefore, a peculiar setting. Other callings have no demands upon them. They are free in life. The art of life they follow cannot fit others walking in different paths. Hence, a distinction is natural between those who are naturally fit and those who have to acquire fitness. And this fitness is not generally intellectual fitness, but fitness of life. Intellectual fitness gives the right understanding; the fitness of life puts us on the right path of developing intuition and achieving realization. Those that have fine understanding often cannot live and practice the truth; they are surely misfit in the height of life. The chords of life should be rightly strung in order that the truth discovered by philosophy may be the truth of life. Philosophy and life should continue to know truth and to make truth living in us.

The truth that the Upaniṣads teach – the truth of the commonality and transcendence of spirit – demands complete renunciation of the other calls of life.

They rise from the partial perspectives of life. Truth cannot be realized where life runs after its dubious calls and when it cannot rise to the height of welcoming the fullness hidden in the inmost being. We find what we seek. Truth is hidden from us, because we are after shadows and appearances.

The call does not reach both spiritually fit and unfit alike. Even amongst the fit souls there are degrees of fitness. Some are Galahads among them, some are Percivals. The misfit cannot hear it. Some take time to prepare themselves. They occasionally hear the call. A realistic sense binds them to their duties at hand. But they do not lose sight of the goal, and reach it in due time.

Considering this, life has been divided into four stages, corresponding to the fitness of life and eagerness of the soul. There are souls who are fit from birth. They are of the finest type. They do not suffer from the earthly touch; they have their illumination with their nativity and birth. A case in point is Vāmadeva, who did not require instruction and preparation, being already the light incarnate. Such souls cannot be included in any of the four stages of life. They are a category by themselves. They are eternally perfect. They have the vivid presentation of the living truth in themselves.

Leaving aside this type, transparent in being, installed in truth, we can divide the rest into two broad categories : (1) The seekers after truth who are not in touch with the affairs of the world; (2) The seekers after truth who are in touch with life and life's affairs. Both these types require a preparation and pass through the first period of discipline. This stage is common to all. This is the period of instruction. This is the period of intellectual fellowship. The first type hears the call and passes immediately into the life of contemplation and silence. The second type hears the call from a distance. It takes time before he can be in every way fit for realization. Naturally the art of life in the two cases will be different. This difference discriminates the different stages of life. The active callings – on the path of duty – must be distinct from the wise passiveness in the life of insight and meditation. The common life is the path of the householder awakened to the values of life and responsive to every one of its calls.

The householder may combine in himself the higher stretches of imagination and vision, but he cannot renounce the duties at hand. He is true to the kindred points of heaven and home. He passes through darkness and light, and is moulded by life through the actualities of life. The glimpse of transcendence may occasionally attract him, but cannot constantly possess him. He may bid for it, but he may not live the life of renunciation. The text prescribes renunciation after gratification in most cases, complete renunciation in few cases. Renunciation is natural when life stands unmasked.

But the door of wisdom is shut to none, though close concentration and devotion to the ideal is not possible unless freedom is attained from the urges of life. When the silence is to be fully faced, the text prescribes immediate renunciation.

The setting of the householder's life is different from the setting of the wanderer's life. But in every stage of life the call has been to feel and realize the sacredness of life and the holiness of relations. The Taittirīya Upaniṣad gives us the noble picture of moralizing and idealizing the forces and the social and family relations of life. Life is to grow fine, to give us the finest blessings. Even the vital urges are to be refined, to allow of finer satisfaction to life. This appears true when life is seen in its complete setting. This notion of the entire life as a sacrifice takes away the sting from gratification and lends a holy touch to it.

The dignity of the race attracts us. Its possibilities inspire us, its hoariness overpowers us. We feel it sacred, we want to preserve it. Race preservation is not looked upon as the crude impelling of nature. It is thought of as the original move of self-expression. It becomes a divine act.

The Chāndogya in the Parjaṅka Vidyā has drawn our attention to it. Life moves in spirit. The movement may be centric or eccentric; the centric movements of life are to be spiritualized; they are actually spiritualized if we can see and appraise them from the philosophic height whence every move of life appears fine and beautiful. Creation is not disparaged, it is only idealized, for creation is the impress of spirit upon matter.

The cosmo-centric insight changes the meaning and value of impulses in life. This cosmic impulsion reads sacrifice in gratification, adds a redeeming touch to the instinctive impellings, and becomes the sure index of movemen tin higher mentality and spirituality.

To awaken the finer possibilities it is necessary to evaluate properly the instinctive demands, not with a view to kill or stifle them, but with a higher intuition to regularize and transform them. The nature of man is divided unto itself, and this division cannot be set aside so long as there is not harmony between the benevolent and the malevolent forces, between the forces of light and darkness in man. Matter instead of obstructing spirit becomes a helpmate to her.

When the opposition between spirit and matter, between reason and instinct, is removed, the higher formations of life begin to reveal themselves and the life instead of being a plaintive becomes a delightful strain. Struggles arise when the forces are seen in their isolation, but in the full setting there is harmony and not conflict.

Matter was the bar, matter becomes the helper. This art of life fits the householder. The householder is to enjoy life in expression; and, if the original sense of opposition is not removed, life's expression and spirit's revelation through nature cannot be rightly appriased.

But a new chapter of life begins in the third stage and culminates in the fourth stage. These are the stages of centralization in self; and, instead of transforming nature, the attempt is now made completely to transcend it. The least touch of nature is discarded, for the silence of life is sought to be installed in place of music. The art of life then must be different, for here the effort is to lose oneself in the centre of being.

The householder cannot completely give himself up to the inward urge of the divine life. He sees the play, he enjoys the game—but it is not possible to see and enjoy the whole drama of life when we play an active part in it. The full acting can be seen when we stand apart from active life.

And this is provided for in the third and the fourth stages of life. The contemplative life in the third stage prepares us for the final realization in the last.

The adaptation is different. Though at times the householder can attain the serene detachment and can deliver himself completely to the spiritual urge, still he cannot be free from clinging to nature.

The beauty of the contemplative life is that it concentrates on the attainment of wisdom, but it is wrong to suppose that it is dead to human feelings and joys.

It is, on the contrary, so finely attuned in being that it radiates love to all, because it realizes that the self is all. Divine imagination helps it to realize the identify of self, and divine inspiration fills it with love that resides in the heart of reality. Unless the illusion of the self breaks down completely, the divine love cannot stream into the heart and move us to embrace all humanity in the light of the exalted self.

The wanderer's life is a great art. It is life of adventure with spirit, for the real test of the awakened spirit lies in the dissolution of the cords that bind us more or less to flesh and the revelation of the wider and better unity in spirit. The wanderer is free from the instinctive urges. He is anxious to enjoy the freedom and the commonality of spirit. He sacrifices the aesthetic impressionism in order that he may enjoy the intellectual beauty,for the finest form of expression of life is his delight; and the finest is reached in the life of dignity and freedom of spirit.

And in this height of intellectual life, the order of relative values cannot have any play. Life has its finest and greatest play where it does not show the least division—and its gradeur is realized in calm detachment. Life has its finest secrets for those who are not deceived by illusion. It is not true that the wanderer does not enjoy life. He enjoys the finest phase of it. The greatest art of life is to be artless. The wanderer is the unconscious artist, for he opens his whole being and reserves nothing to himself. He practises no concealment. He need practise none, for he is fixed in the height of being which is self-revealed.

The wanderer enjoys the delight of freedom from the creative responsibilities; for, where life is deep, creativeness has no play. But this does not mean that he is lost to life. He is living vigorously, although there is no ripple on the surface.

Carrying the most kindly feeling for all, regarding every self as his own self, unconcerned with the sweetness or bitterness of life, the wanderer moves as the figures of wisdom and love harmoniously set to each other – wisdom saves the self, love saves others.

There is not the slightest stiffness of being, not the least contradiction. The forces are evenly set in the harmony of life.

Civilization finds its highest expression in him. The wanderer moves in the soul's peace, making the whole humanity, the whole living creation the radius of his activity in love and knowledge. He enjoys perfect harmony and transcendence. His life is a living poem; conflicts melt away before the touch of love and wisdom. Such a soul gives an intimation of the supramundane existence and establishes peace on earth. He lives in divine peace. He carries the aroma of divine life with him.

But the wanderer in the fourth stage of life is centred in the mystery of silence. He is awakened to the fullness of life and joy and has not the sense of the least difference between life and truth. He enjoys the dignity of life more in its silence than in its play.

This is natural. When spiritual development reaches its culmination it sees the presence of spirit everywhere. And it feels that the self is spirit. When the time-sense fades, realization becomes different. The soul enjoys peace.

This aspect of spiritual life appears to be unique; for man's outlook by habit and adaptation is confined to dynamic spirituality. It is difficult to rise above the finer urges of life to realize the silence in the heart of being.

Many cannot see the truth of silence and few can realize it. And naturally they shudder at the thought of its impenetrable depth. Hence, they mistake life's fullness for barrenness. But the Upaniṣadic seers set the premium upon silence and naturally its realization demands the fullest and the closest attention.

Chapter XXIV

The Wise Man

The wise man is the ideal of the Upaniṣads. He is the Jīvan Mukta. He enjoys the unique privilege of liberation in life. He is emancipated. He is installed in peace.

The wise man, instead of passing into the quiet of retirement, can live an active life. This is merely a matter of habit. This is a question of activism or passivism in ethical life. Activity and passivity do not affect the emancipated soul. He is neither active nor passive. Activism and passivism are adaptations. The forces may be active in the enlightened soul, but it is quite indifferent to them. Life in its finest beauty has no fascination for it. The free soul is above all attraction of life. It has an even attitude in life's distraction and attraction. It is perfectly installed in truth. Quietism and activism are attitudes of life, but not wisdom.

The wise man does not necessarily seek retirement. In cases where the mind canot with ease settle down and where the psychic being is not transparent enough to reflect truth always, retirement is thought necessary even after illumination. But, where the psychic being has a transparent fitness to reflect light, life can never deflect from it.

These two types are rperesented in the Upaniṣads in Janaka and Yājñavalkya. Janaka is the king. Yājñavalkya is the sage and the teacher in the court of Janaka. Both were wise. But the teacher took up the life of renunciation. Janaka continued to be the king.

Plato makes philosophers (wise men) the guardians of the state. He sees "in this calm life of the philosopher, in the contemplation of what is essential and eternal, a far more glorious and attractive end".[1] He does not believe in the absolute and unconditional value of public life. Yet he believes in public life. It affords an opportunity for the active exercise of knowledge and virtue. The wise men are the best guardians, because they are above interest and passion. They are the finest specimens of humanity, they are the natural guardians of society. The emphasis on the contemplative life makes Plato's philosopher resemble the wanderer in the Upaniṣad.

The wanderer is the contemplative type amongst the Jīvan Muktas.[2] But there is the active type among them – which meets the kindred points of heaven and home. This type compares favourably with Plato's philosopher. Plato's philosopher is ruled by the dictates of duty. The Jīvan Mukta is free from such dictates. He has no compelling sense of duty, nor has he the need of contemplation. He is beyond the oscillation of the psychic being, and is far from the psychic bent of either contemplation or action. He has a poise of being which can immediately pass into contemplation or action. But he is aware all the time that he transcends them both.

The contemplative soul is led by cosmic impelling. His expansive vision and transcendence put him on a superior plane and his ethics cannot be on the same level with the ethics as usually understood and as commonly practised. The rigidity of the latter is displaced by the elasticity of the former, but this elasticity dispenses with the conflicts of the practical life and places the adept beyond the categories of common morality. The realization of truth endows the adept with vision and power. He naturally cannot be bound down by the ethics of personality. He is often a mystery to the mean intelligence, for he is not governed by the human ethical code. He stands beyond virtue and vice, good and evil, right and wrong; he is above the rigidity of moral life, for the ethics of preparation cannot be the ethics of consummation. In such lives the forces begin to move cosmically, and therefore, they become the source of uncommon powers, possessors of unheard-of wisdom, and promulgators of great movements. The condition of unhindered power is not therefore a condemnation but rather a commendation, since it demonstrates unmistakably that the emancipated consciousness is beyond the restrictions of common life.

The ideal appears not strictly moral to the superficial observer because the ethics of personality has such a charm for us, that not seldom the ethics of preparation is thought to be the highest moral ideal, and from a distance it is not possible to judge the elasticity and freedom of a free life. The Jīvan Mukta is freed from the sense of compulsion, from the sense of responsibility, and when he moves, he moves on by cosmic urges.

But this elasticity of life following realization is no elasticity of the vital being with its desires and impulses, with its sense of increased life and activity, with its pleasures, joys, and gratifications. This elasticity is, in fact, the truly spiritual expansion of our being freed from the sense of conflict or from the sense of hedonistio relaxation and impulsion of being. This elasticity has an effect upno the texture of our being. It produces harmony in all the parts of our being. And in this elasticity lies freedom. Karma has lost its hold upon the liberated soul because he is above the conceit of agency.

The conceit of agency creates the sense of moral obligation and responsibility. The liberated soul has no conceit of agency. He has seen no responsibility. The liberated soul becomes the wielder of powers, though all along he knows he is far above and beyond them. Nature has in its gifts these privileges for the soul who is bold enough not to seek them. Detachment is the secret of rare powers, and, whether one wills or wills not, the soul seeking and practising transcendence becomes the possessor of uncommon powers. He may or may not exercise them. These uncommon powers are looked upon with no concern.

Professor A.B. Keith thinks that emancipation is merely a condition of unhindered power, the ideal of a despot. (*Philosophy of the Upaniṣads,* p. 587.)

This shows a lack of sympathetic insight into the ideals of the Upaniṣads. Spiritual insight is not purely an intellectual understanding, nor merely an occasional insight. True spirituality is the unceasing consciousness of the unity wherein the vital mental complex stands revealed and completely exposed. Emancipation isnot merely a logical concept,it is a psychological revelation, and implies a psychological upbuilding. But the psychological revelation has tremendous moulding effect upon the entire nature of the adept, and its influence penetrates into every part of our being, and transforms in its light the mental and the vital being.

The philosopher walks with his intellectual apprehensions leaving the rest of his being to adapt itself according to the conditons of normal ethics. The adept lives the truth. The spiritual insight into truth has its effect on all parts of our complex being. Intellect becomes intuitive, feeling rises into fine shades of blessedness. The man is completely reborn.

Spirituality is not an expression in emotion, nor an indulgence in sentimentality. Spirituality is something superior to religion as ordinarily understood. It is the life of vision and a life of complete transformation. The spiritual insight does not leave the lower nature cold. It effects a complete change in our being. Its influence permeates the vital and the mental being, so that the supramental truth can be effective on the vital-physical planes.

Whenever there has been such a call there has been an unhesitating abandonment of the wonted course of life, for this call comes from the deep of being. The call may come in any stage of life, before or after illumination; but, whenever it comes, it comes with irresistible force. The call for illumination is to be distinguished from the call for realization. The former is a call for preparation and training, the latter for unbroken illumination. Both require fitness, but the fitness for illumination is to be distinguished from the fitness for its continuity. In both cases vital and mental beign are to be purified and sharpened, but in the latter they should be made so transparent that the spiritual life can have the medium completely fit for its expression. The Jīvan Muktas may not differ among themselves in their illumination, and they make no difference in the logical sense. But psychologically a diference exists between the Jīvan Muktas, and this difference is indicated in the texts (Muṇḍaka) in the conception of Brahmavit, Brahmavitvara, Brahmavit-variṣṭha. Logically they are in the same category, for they have crossed ignorance; but life is greater than logic, and, with the fitness of our psychic being, a difference in the power and illumination of the psychic being is the natural result. Transcendence is the same everywhere, but the fitness of psychic being, and vision is not the same. With a fine psychic being, illumination can be long sustained; this psychic being is reared up by discipline, it is the evolution of the finest mentality. The finer the mentality, the greater the illumination. The forces of our being become wonderfully balanced as the supramental light is focussed through the psychic being.

The different stages in Jīvan Mukta are, therefore, a psychological possibility based upon the uprearing of the mental and vital life in a way which can reflect the light of the soul in uninterrupted perpetuity. The oscillation of the mental dynamism cannot stop unless the forces are completely exhausted; and, therefore, with the visitation from the living soul, the desired consummation, the forsaking of the mental-vital-physical sheaths, does not at once take place.

Nor can the vision of the truth leave the mental being blank with its native forces moving in it. The Jīvan Mukta's psychic being becomes finer and finer, and therefore his mental dynamism works in a different way from the rest. It is finer, therefore can be wielded in any way for surer and finer activity.

But with the finer vitality and mentality, with the quicker and subtler dance of life, with greater dominion over the flesh, the emancipated souls sometimes becomes centres of uncommon power – what Keith calls unhindered powers. The great illumination gives them a transcendence and a physical being with fine respectivity to catch and comm and the subtle forces. They stand to their call, the vision gives Jīvan Mukta the freedom of being. It also endows him with powers. Powers follow illumination, the psychic change is the secret of powers.

The powers that work in him are cosmic; and therefore his conduct more often baffles our moral estimates by its over-poweringness and incalculability. The Chāndogya gives a description of the complete autonomy of will of the liberated souls.[3] Their will is unfailingly effective, not only on the physical but also on the finer planes o fexistence. Their wills are immediately creative; and in this respect their will has a supernatural bent, inasmuch as they do not require the intervention of any other thing to give it proper shape and effective expression. Though this autonomy of will is a source of uncommon power, liberated souls do not disturb the cosmic harmony.They will not. Because the world-harmony reflects the greatest wisdom and the highest power of Īśvara. The autonomy of will and power, however high and great, cannot interfere with cosmic will and power. And there is no necessity for interference since the cosmic order seems to their privileged knowledge to be perfectly regulated. And from the nature of the case they cannot interfere. The identity of being is a fact in transcendence, but the identity of being cannot give the identity of powers, for powers are the possessions of the divided souls.

The Upaniṣads emphasize the identity of being, but not the identity of powers. Personalities have hierarchies according to their psychic fitness and possibilities.

But power is not the ideal to be sought; it comes unawares, with purity and elasticity of being. The greater knowledge gives better facilities. The loss of individuality is replaced by the awakened self, and the sleeping powers soon begin to stir in the wise, but the ideal of power has never been great in the Upaniṣads, for the wise soul is beyond all that can be wrought by engrafting of psychic powers. He is always awake in transcendence.

The Jīvan Mukta is the long run becomes anxious to be more and more transcendent, not only in wisdom, but also in adaptation; for the finer is the vision of transcendence the greater is the freedom from psychic powers. The silence is the ideal, and, in the complete fruition of individual life, the adept leaves aside the psychical and the physical complexes and passes into the calm.

Keith thinks that the Jīvan Mukta is the ideal of a despot. But Keith is wrong. A despot is conscious of his powrs, a Jīvan Mukta is not. He is not supposed to be a product of a long evolution through which he has acquired powers. Powers he does not seek, they seek him. And, therefore, no virtue can be attributed to him. He is free from the impelling of life, individual or cosmic.

There is, therefore, a difference between the person moved by a cosmic impelling and the Jīvan Mukta serving a cosmic end. The former is conscious as an agent, the latter is not. The former is conscious of a purpose, the latter is not. The former may be attuned with the cosmic life, the latter transcends it; and hence, if the latter moves for a cosmic end of humanity, he is not, strictly speaking, so conscious. He is conscious of completeness, of the timeless eternal, and therefore what is realized in time has no meaning for him. This detachment, absolute detachment to both the denials and assertions of life, is what makes a Jīvan Mukta different from the spiritual personalities who are conscious of their ends and their powers. The dynamic ideals of values are prominent in them. They are divine agents, sentifically they can be regarded as spiritual emergents representing a superior type of humanity. In logical language they are "descents" into the arena of human society. But a Jīvan Mukta is neither an emergent nor a descent. The language of evolution or emanation cannot be applied to him. A Jīvan Mukta is not a product of evolution. He is not even a product of culture. Though a fine evolution in culture and spirit is a necessary requirement, it is a unique blessedness. It supposes something which neither evolution nor culture can give. Where the native intuition is finest, the realization is most natural and spontaneous. Truth visits us often unawares. Such a soul is by nature endowed with spiritual fitness. He has an intuitive being. He does not require culture. He reads from the book of life. He has attained the ideal development of human nature. It is his native blessing or birthright. With others it requries a long process of evolution.

It is perfectly true in his case that the finest intuitions go along with the most refined culture and formed habits. Intuition is not opposed to intellect. Intellect finds its finest blossoming in intuition. It is not prior to our independent of reasoning. The opposition between intellect and intuition probably originates because of the over-emphasis laid upon comceptual thinking. In the anxiety for system-building, the aspiration fot the living touch with truth is naturally neglected. Intellect does not rise to intuition. Spinoza is perfectly right in placing Ratio before *scientia intuitiva*. The seer of the Upaniṣad has done the same. He has recorded the successive stages of knowledge as instruction, ratiocination, contemplation, and intuition.

The Jīvan Mukta, therefore, is not active in the usual sense.

He merely exhausts his residual Karma, of which he is not strictly conscious, for he is no longer a person. Karma shapes itself through personality; when the sense of personality is lost, the Jīvan Mukta cannot be held to be working out an end. The idea of an end or a direction marching towards something which implies the reality of time and progress has no meaning for the Jīvan Mukta. He lives in the eternal present, for he sees the complete. The time sense has no value for him. Evolution or progress has, therefore, no meaning for him. He sees the truth eternal. He feels he is the truth transcendental. The adept can live under any form of life, since his realization of truth puts him on a vantage ground of complete freedom. This freedom is fostered in detachment to active seeking or passive withdrawal. The autonomy of the Jīvan Mukta enjoys, is not the restricted autonomy of will or freedom of a person in a community of persons. It is the autonomy of knowledge. It is freedom from the illusions of knowledge. It is freedom from the illusions of personality, Karma, and stirring, which endows the adept with peace attending the fullness of life and light.

References

1. Zeller : *Plato and the Older Academy*.
2. Jīvan Muktas are those who have attained the highest enlightenment and realized the greatest truth of the Upaniṣads in life, viz. the identity of being in Man and God.
3. Chap. VIII, 1, 2, 3, 4, 7.

Chapter XXV

Ways of Exit

The Upaniṣads speak of the *path of the gods* and the *path of Pitṛs*. These are the ways of exit. All souls cannot enjoy the privilege of emancipation, since they are not endowed with the final wisdom of Ātman. They still suffer from the native tendencies of the soul. Such souls cannot pass into light when they forsake their physical sheaths at death.

Two paths are conceived. The finer souls disciplined in the various Upāsanās pursue the path of the Devas after death. This is the path of light. The finer souls can follow this path. It carries them on to the finer planes of existence.

The path of Pitṛs is the path of life, and not of light. The souls disciplined in Karma follow this path. They have no inner light to reflect the guiding light, remain satisfied with the promise of earthly life, and do not aspire to a higher and finer existence. The Chāndogya says that the souls pursuing the former path do not return to their earthly abode. The Bṛhadāraṇyaka says that by Karma we make a conquest of the Pitṛs, by Vidyā we make a conquest of the Devaloka.

The two paths correspond to the life of instincts and the life of knowledge. In the former, intincts have the better of knowledge; in the latter, knowledge has the better of instincts. The instincts confine us to an existence where we can catch the radiance of spirit. They confine us to the joy of vital life. The path of the Pitṛs cannot carry us beyond the vital planes of existence, and the souls naturally are drawn again to earth, for they are not free from vital tendencies.

The path of the Devas is the path of finer light. It is the upward path, not confined to the vital planes. The souls are freed from vital desires. They go onward. From life they are elevated to light. They have no attraction to the vital urges and demands. They feel free. They become radiant with light. They may not yet have been installed in silence. But they catch the glimpses of the hidden light. They can have no fall. Life in them is one with light.

The Upaniṣads speak of the exist of the advanced souls through the path of light. The path extends from the heart-centre and passes through the brain to the region of the invisible light. The Yogis, adepts in Upāsanā, pass out of the body through this path. A subtle connection is felt and conceived through the path between the individual self and the cosmic self. Where the path is open the adept can freely go out of the body and freely can re-enter it. At death he can pass by this path to the realm of light perpetually shining. Blessed indeed are the souls who are free from earthly desires. To them alone the path becomes open. The effulgence of the world of light is reflected at times upon us through this path.

But the soul bathed in silence has no need to find a way out of the body. Such souls become free from all tendencies, dark or bright, instinctive or supramental. They are conscious of the limitation of existence in the finer realms of light. They do not set any value upon them. Life and light vanish before silence.

In Christian mysticism life, spirit, and light are used as indicating the phases of supreme existence. And confusion should not be made between life understood in the sense of *Prāṇa* enfolding instincts and life associated with the finest vibration of light. Prāṇa has finer and grosser aspects, the latter being active in the path of Pitṛs. The former is active in the path of Devas, but it is not active in the realm of silence. Those who are adept in the regulation of Prāṇa finally pass into the cosmic Prāṇa and enjoy the finer life and transparent light.

Chapter XXVI

Release

The greatest attraction of spiritual life lies in its promise. Spiritual life embraces and yet transcends moral and aesthetic life; it exhibits life in its fullness. Moral enthusiasm and aestheticism are of the fine fabric of our being, but spiritual experience has in it something which is unique, and which is its own. Holiness and æsthetic joyousness are invaluable possessions that should find place in spiritual life, but to identity such life with them is to miss its significance. Spiritual life has in it something which is not probed by fine aesthetic feelings or dignified moral virility. Spiritual life presupposes all these, since it is the fullest unfolding of life; and, where it has its finest expressions, there the chords of life sound in finest harmony. It touches the very core of our being and therefore transcends all else. Its essence lies in numinous experience. It is neither intellectual nor emotional. It includes these qualities, but it transcends them.

The discovery of this "something" is the unique privilege of mysticism. This "something" is so near and intimate to us that it escapes our observation. The wealth of life hides its essence; and the intellectual, the moral, and the aesthetic aspects of life become sometimes so dominant and overpowering that, unless the seeker can resist them, the visit from the living soul does not take place.

Mokṣa, or release, has been the catchword of Indian mysticism to indicate the promise of the mystical life. Generally a certain amount of indifference to life and its achievements is associated with Mokṣa; and Indian systems, especially the one accepting the avowed ideal of Mokṣa, have been accused of denying life, its struggles, its defeats, its successes. In short, they are accused of insisting upon fleeing from life and evading its responsibilities.

This torturing of life is no part of the teaching of the Upaniṣads. And, rightly understood, it has not been the ideal among the Upaniṣadic seers. The ideals of the detachment from and a renunciation of the claims of life have been used not to deny and avoid all life but to invite a better and a fuller life. The delicate touch of spirit is felt in the fine repose of being and not in the "madding crowd." And the seeking of silence is uniform among the mystics, for the psychic being must recover itself from the claims of life before it can feel the rapturous music of life and the calm dignity of the soul.

The mystic is a solitary being, because solitariness gives him the most and the best of life. The mystic is anxious to enjoy the finest urge in life. He passes by, therefore, ordinary claims and duties. He moves in an atmosphere or complete freedom and serene silence.

This is his divine privilege. He is brave enough to forgo partial delights to enjoy the fullness of life.

The fullness of life dawns suddenly upon receptive souls. It can come to him alone who has the proper attitude; and this attitude is nothing but a silent watch of the soul. Constant watchfulness helps the soul to be receptive to the finest expression of life. This watchful silence unties the knots of our psychic being, and makes it responsive to the soul. It also makes it responsive to the currents of life, revealing its divine orientation. The seeker is reborn. This is the great claim of mysticism.

Few indeed are the souls who prove fine enough to be fit

recipients of the direct currents from the source of life. Fewer still are those who give themselves up completely to such a life of reception, transformation, transfiguration, and continuous living in the divine. Mystical experience is vividly joyous, finely intellectual, and fully divine. In it the soul is touched from within by the silent hand of spirit.

But even now the meaning of Mokṣa has not become clear. It may be claimed, and it has been claimed by some, that such contemplation of and impress from the divine life upon us is not only the positive enjoyment of the aroma of divine life but also has a negative aspect of forsaking the wonted course of life which seeks joy in flesh and blood. This forsaking is natural, for the real touch of spirit redeems the soul from flesh and blood. The adept is transferred from death to life. Even if he carries a tabernacle of flesh he does not feel its weight. The flesh can no longer torment the spirit.

But even such a life has its play (līlā), and that divine play has also its stings. Spiritual drama cannot be free from the stings of life, otherwise it cannot be played. Even divine love has its stings, and the saintly lives bear witness to it. The plan of life in manifestation is based on contraries and the spiritual life is not free from them. The spirit in essential being must be something different. It must transcend all contradictions. It enjoys its undivided nature—its impartibleness. The Upaniṣads hold out this promise as the summation of spiritual life. What is it?—The ideal of Moksa. That state is not a paradise regained, for the soul realizes that it never was lost.

When knowledge breaks all the spells of life the evershining reality of self becomes evident to us. The great asset that wisdom gives it the love of self or truth, and not the love of shadows of self or expressions of truth.

To this love at its highest, wisdom, which even the gods envy and mortals fear, is at once vouchsafed. "The wise becomes free from forms and names and attains the effulgent, the supreme being – the being of beings." The Muṇḍaka has it : "Behind the veil exists the ineffable Brahman without parts. It is transparently shining. It is the light of lights, the self-knower only knows it."

But Mokṣa should not pass for a state in which the whole existence is reflected and stands revealed. Such a state is, indeed, a blessed existence which allows of the finest realization of our being and the finest cosmic intuition. It is an ideal development of the human mind, which is then free from contraries and conflicts. It has vivid feeling and knowledge of the totality, and peace and tranquillity of the soul. Such a consummation approaches Spinoza's ideal of the free man. The free man realizes his place in the scheme of things and his whole being is interpenetrated with the love of God which arises from the clear knowledge of himself and all things. Spinoza's *scientia intuitiva* is a kind of cosmic intuition which presents the vision of God and his immanence. The love of God fills his being, which rises to the highest point of seeing God in all things and all things in God. Spinoza's intuition has in it an exquisite feeling, the feeling and the blessedness which follow the removal of the limitations in knowledge and being. But the Upaniṣads soar beyond. They are an immanent vision of the divine.

The Upaniṣads are not satisfied with pantheistic exaltation which still keeps us confined to God, nature, and man. The barrier is for the moment overshadowed. The immanent God becomes prominent before our vision. This vision is cosmic, but not acosmic. The Upaniṣads emphasize the acosmic intuition, and where Spinoza has laid emphasis upon it no difference exists between his acosmic intuition and the transcendent intuition of the seers.

Spirituality is high knowledge and not only fine feeling. In the last stage it dispenses with all relativities of ethics, knowledge, and experience. It gives us the blessed freedom in the transcendent. Knowledge is here intuitive, delight supernal, and life free from subconscious, conscious, and superconscious ways. It is not the freedom associated with the silence of our being. This silence is the accomplished fact. It is not the silence of the urges. It is not even the silence of sleep. The former is artificial, the latter is natural. But this freedom is neither artificial nor natural. It is the silence permanently residing in the heart of being.

The human soul can feel itself identified with this silence when it is freed from the psychic urges with their possibilities of fascination. Life is best enjoyed when there is a fall in the psychic dynamism, for it allows us to see and feel the dignity of silence. The constant agitation in our psychic being hides the truth from us, and the greatest sacrifice is called for to realize the highest truth. And this sacrifice is the sacrifice of life – for who can ever dream of the conquest of truth with the claims of the little ego set prominently before him? The finest realizations of mystical exaltation are still in play upon the fine psyche, but truth transcends all psychic possibilities and delights. The supreme sacrifice gives the supreme peace. Happily, truth is more powerful than error, and if once the supreme truth has been realized in the heart of being it never leaves us. "The conquest of truth is slow and laborious, but, once the victory is, it can never be wrested back again." (Schopenhauer).

Mokṣa, therefore, is the state of being which is beyond all real or ideal creative projections, and represents being in its independence of creative relativity. The human mind is so much engrossed with the actualities of life that it cannot habitually rise to this height and go beyond the delights of creativeness to welcome the delight supernal of silence. Mokṣa implies release from the sense of relativity in all its forms, ethical, spiritual, or creative. It is, therefore, indicated by the negative term of release from bondage; but it is the presentation of the Absolute in its uniqueness, in its independence of all kinds of relativity.

Bibliography

Original Sources :

Aitareya Āraṇyaka with the com. of Sāyaṇa ed. by R. Mitra, Bibliotheca Indica, Calcutta, 1876.

Aitareyabhrāhmaṇa with the com. of Sāyaṇācārya, Anandashrama Press, Poona, 1896.

Āpastamba Paribhāṣā com. by Dhūtraswāmi & Tr. by Bhattacharya, S.S., Calcutta, 1932.

Aṣṭāṅgahṛdaya of Vāgbhatta ed. by H.M. Patel, Sastu Sahitya Vardhaka Karyalaya, Bombay, 1966.

Atharvaveda com. by Sāyaṇa ed. by Viśvabandhu, Vishveshvarananda Vedic Research Institute, Hoshiarpur, 1960.

Atharvaveda Pariśiṣṭa pub. by Chaukhamba Orientalia, Varanasi, 1976.

Baudhāyana Dharmasūtra, com. by Govindaswāmī, ed. by Shri Nivāsācārya Government Branch Press, Mysore, 1907.

Bhāgavadgītā, Sastu Sahitya Vardhaka Karyalaya, Bombay, 1939.

Bhāgavata Purāṇa ed. by Shastri G.M., Sastu Sahitya Vardhaka Karyalaya, Princess Street, Bombay, 1937.

Brahmāṇḍa Purāṇa ed. by Phanasikar Vasudeva, Nirnaya Sagara Press, Bombay, 1914.

Brahmasiddhānta by Oza Madhusudan, Benaras Hindu University, 1961.

Brahmasūtrabhāṣya of Madhva Tr. by Rangacarya B.R., Poona, 1848.

Brahmasūtrabhāṣya of Nimbārka ed. by Pandit Shri Dhundhiraj Shastri, Chawkhamba Sanskrit Series Office, Benaras, 1932.

Brahmasūtrabhāṣya of Rāmānuja Tr. by R.D. Karmarkar, University of Poona, 1934.

Brahmasūtra Śāṅkarabhāṣya, Nirnaya Sagar Press, Bombay, 1948.

Brahmasūtrāṇubhāṣya by Śrī Vallabhācārya, Nirnaya Sagar Press, Bombay, 1924.

Bṛhadāraṇyaka Upaniṣad com. by Śaṅkara, Gita Press, Gorakhpur, 1942.

Bṛhad-Devatā ed. by Mitra Rajendralala, The Asiatic Society of Bengal, 1892.

Caraṇavyūhapariśiṣṭasūtram by Śaunakamuni, Chaukhamba Sanskrit Series, Varanasi, Samvat, 1959.

Chāndogya Upaniṣad, Gita Press, Gorakhpur, IInd edn. 1945.

Gautamasūtras with the com. of Vātsyāyana ed. by V.G. Apte Anandashrama Sanskrit Series, Poona, 1922.

Gopatha Brāhmaṇa, ed. by Dieuke Gaastra, Leiden, 1919.

Halāyudhakośa ed. by Joshi Jayashankar, pub. by Prakashana Bureau, Suchana Vibhaga, Lucknow, U.P., 1826.

Jaiminīya Upaniṣad com. by Upaniṣad Brahmayogin, Adyar Library, Madras, 1969.

Jaimini Gṛhyasūtra, Tr. by Caland W., Motilal Benarasidass, Delhi, 1922.

Kaṭhopaniṣad with the com. of Śaṅkara, ed. by Apte V.G., Anandashrama Printing Press, Poona, 1849.

Kauśikasūtra com. by Dharila, Tilaka Vidyapitha, Poona, 1972.

Kenopaniṣad, pub. by Gita Press, Gorakhpur, 1946.

Kūrmapurāṇa ed. by Bhattacharya R.S., Indological Book House, Varanasi, 1969.

Kuvalayānanda of Appaya Dīkṣita, ed. by Phanashikar, V.S., Bombay, 1937.

Mahābhārata, Tr. by Shastri, S.P., Sastu Sahitya Vardhaka Karyalaya, Princess Street, Bombay, 1956.

Manusmṛti, Tr. by Shastri G.M., Sastu Sahitya Vardhaka Karyalaya, Princess Street, Bombay, 1952.

Muktikā Upaniṣad, ed. by Pandit Jibananda Vidyasagara, Sanskrit College of Calcutta, 1872.

Muṇḍaka Upaniṣad, Gita Press, Gorakhpur, 1947.

Māṇḍūkya Upaniṣad, Gita Press, Gorakhpur, 1949.

Nirukta of Yāska, Anandashrma Press, Poona, 1926.

Patañjali Vyākaraṇa Mahābhāṣya, ed. by Shastri Guruprasad, Rajasthan Sanskrit College Granthamala no. 30, Benaras, 1938.

Praśna Upaniṣad, Gita Press, Gorakhpur, 1945

Ṛgveda with the com. of Sāyaṇa, Vedic Research Institute, Poona, 1946.

Ṛgvedādibhāṣyabhūmikā, by Swami Dayananda S., Pub. by Vaidika Yantralaya, Ajamera, V.S. 1960.

Ṛktantram, A Prātiśākhya of the SV, ed. by Shastri Suryakanta, Meharchanda Lachhamandas Sanskrit Book Depot, Lahore, 1933.

Sāhityadarpaṇa of Viśvanatha, Chaukhamba Sanskrit Series, 1947.

Satapathabhāhmaṇa, Tr. by Pandita Gangaprasad Upadhyaya, pub. by The Research Institute of Ancient Scientific Studies, New Delhi, 1967.

Śvetāśvatara Upaniṣad, Gita Press, Gorakhpur, 1950.

Taittirīya Āraṇyaka, Commented by Bhatta Bhashkar Mishra, Pub. by Govt. Press, Mysore, 1902.

Taittirīya Āraṇyaka, com. by Sāyaṇa, Ananda Ashram Press, Poona, 1897.

Taittirīya Brāhmaṇa, com. by Bhaṭṭa Bhāskara, ed. by Shastri R.S., The Govt. Branch Press, Mysore, 1921.

Taittirīyasaṁhitā, with the coms. of Bhaṭṭa Bhāskara Miśra and Sāyaṇācārya, ed. by N.S. Sontakke & T.N. Dharmadhikari, Pb. by Vaidika Samsodhana Mandala, Poona, 1970.

Taittirīya Upaniṣad, with the com. of Śaṅkara, Ananda Ashrama Press, Poona, 1889.

Taittirīyopaniṣadbhāṣyavārtikam, by Sureśvarācārya, Anandasram Printing Press, 1883.

Tarkasaṁgraha of Annaṁbhaṭṭa, ed. by Athalye, Y.S., Bhandarkar Oriental Research Institute, Poona, 1974.

Vācaspatyam Bṛhat Saṁskṛtābhidhānam, Chaukhamba Sanskrit Series, Varanasi.

Vaikhānasa Gṛhyasūtras, ed. by S. Shastri, Baroda, 1921.

Vaiyākaraṇa Siddhāntakaumudī, ed. by Pandit Gopalashastri Nene, Chowkhamba Sanskrit Series Office, Varanasi, 1966.

Vāyupurāṇa, ed. by Mitra Rajendralal, The Asiatic Society of Bengal, Calcutta, 1888.

Viṣṇupurāṇa, Gita Press, Gorakhpur, 1934.

General References :

Abhedananda : 'The Upaniṣadic Doctrine of the Self', Oriental Publishers and Distributors, 1488, Pataudi House, Darya Ganj, New Delhi-110 002.

Allen, W.S. : 'Phonetic in Ancient India', Oxford University Press, Oxford, England, 1958.

Allen, W.S. : 'Sandhi', Oxford University Press. Oxford, England, 1967.

Altekar, A.S. : 'The Āśrama System' Ghurye Felicitation Volume, ed. by K.M. Kapadia, Popular Books Depot, Bombay-400 007, 1954.

Altekar, A.S. : 'Education in Ancient India', Nanda Kishore and Bros., Benaras, 1944 (2nd edn.).

Apte, V.M. : 'The Practical Sanskrit English Dictionary', Prasad Prakashana, Poona, 1958.

Aufretch, Theodor : 'Catalogus Catalogorum,' Wiesbaden Vol. I-II, 1962, Leipzing, Vol. III, 1903.

Bal Gangadhar, Tilak : 'The Orien or Research into the Antiquity of the Vedas' Pub. by Tilak Bros., Lokamanya Tilak Road, 568, Narayana Peth, Poona-100 002, 1955.

Balasubramanian, R. : 'Taittiriyopaniṣad Bhāṣyavārtika of Sureśvara', Centre for Advanced Study in Philosophy, University of Madras, 1974.

Belvalkar, S.K. and Ranade, R.D. : 'History of Indian Philosophy', Vol. II, Creative Period, Bilvakunja Publishing House, Poona, 1927.

Bhatta, Vishnuprasad : On the meaning of the title 'Bṛhadāraṇyaka Upaniṣad, Journal of the Oriental Institute, Vol. 23, Nos. 1-2, Baroda, 1973.

Bhattacarya, Debika : 'Comparative study of the Atharva-vedic and Indo-European Occult Practices', Pubd. in Journal of the Oriental Institute, Baroda, Vol. 26, No. 4.

Blair, C.J. : 'Heat in the Ṛgveda and Atharva-veda', American Oriental Society, 1961.

Bokil, V.P. : 'The History of Education in India', Oriental Book Agency, Poona, 1925.

Burrow, T. : 'The Sanskrit Language', Feber and Feber, 24 Russell Square, London.

Cassells, Ger : 'German English Dictionary', Cassell and Co. Ltd., London, 1957.

Chatterjee, Chinmoy : 'Vedantic Education' Gauranga Cultural Research Institute, Lucknow, 1957.

Chhattopadhyaya Sudhakar : 'Traditional Values in Indian Life', India International Centre, Delhi, 1961.

Cooley, C.H. : 'Social Organisation A Study of the Larger Mind', Scribner's New York, 1929.

Das, Bhagavan : 'Praṇavavāda of Gārgāyana', Benaras Hindu University, 1910.

Dasgupta, S.N. : 'A History of Indian Philosophy',

Vols. I, (1922), II (1940), Cambridge University Press, London.

Dave, T.N. : 'Taittirīya Upaniṣad', A Mine of Cultural and philosophical informations, Sharadapitha Pradeep, Vol. 5, No. 2, Dwarka, 1965.

David M. Knipe : 'In the Image of Fire', Motilal Benarasidass, Delhi, 1975.

Deussen Paul : 'Āśrama', ERE Vol. II, 1951.

Deussen Paul : 'Philosophy of Upaniṣads', Dover Publications Inc., New York, 1966.

Dwivedi, R.C. : 'Selections from Brahmanas and Upaniṣads' Motilal Banarasidass, Delhi-7, 1965.

Dhavan, K.K. : 'Poetic Elements in the Upaniṣads', Vishveshvarananda Research Institute, Hoshiarpur, 1976.

Fatasingh : 'The Vedic Etymology' National Publishing House, Delhi-6.

Firth, Raymond : 'Elements of Social Organisation', Watts and Co., London, 1951.

Gaden, A.S. : 'Ascetism (Hindu) Encyclopaedia of Religion and Ethics, Vol. II', T & T Clark, New York, 1953 (3rd edn.).

Gairola, Vacaspati : 'Sanskrit Sāhitya Kā Itihāsa', Chowkhamba Vidyabhavana, Varanasi, 1960.

Ghurye, G.S. : 'Caste and Class in India', Philosophical Library, New York, 1952.

Ginsberg, M. : 'Sociology', Oxford University Press, London, 1950.

Gispert Sanch, S.J. : 'Bliss in the Upaniṣads', Oriental Publishers and Distributors, New Delhi, 110 002.

Hobhouse, L.T. : ERE, Vol. I, end. III, 1955.

Hume, R.E. : 'The Thirteen Principal Upaniṣads', Oxford University Press, London, 1951 (Reprinted).

Jacobi, H.J. : 'Cosmology, Cosmogony, Encyclopaedia of Religion and Ethics', Vol. III, T & T Clark, New York, 1953 (3rd edn.).

Kane, P.V. : 'History of Dharmaśāstra', Vol. II, Part I, Government Oriental Series, Class B, No.6, BORI, 1941.

Kantawala, S.G. : 'Cultural History from the Matsyapurāṇa', M.S. University of Baroda, Baroda, 1964.

Kapadia, K.M. : 'Hindu Kinship', The Popular Book Depot, Bombay-400 007, 1947.

Karve, Irawati : 'Hindu Society - An Interpretation', Deccan College, Poona, 1961.

Keay, F.E. : 'Indian Education in Ancient of Latter times', Oxford University Press, Oxford, 1938.

Kaith, A.B. : The Veda of the Black Yajus School, entitled Taittirīya Samhitā', Part I, HOS, Vol. 18, Cambridge, Massachusetts, 1914.

Keith, A.B. : HOS Vol. No. 31, 'Religion and Philosophy of the Veda and Upaniṣads', The Harward University Press, Combridge.

Kunhanaraja, C. : 'Education in Ancient India', The Adyar Library, 1950.

Kunjunni Raja, K. : 'New Catalogus Catalogorum', University of Madras, Vol. I revised edn. 1959; Vol. II, 1966, Vol. III 1967; Vol. IV 1968; Vol. V 1969; Vol. VI 1971; Vol. VII 1973; Vol. VIII 1974.

Kuppuswami, A. : 'Śrī Bhagavadpāda Śaṅkarācārya', Chowkhamba Sanskrit Series Office, Varanasi, 1972.

Macdonell, A.A. : 'A Vedic Reader', Geoffrey Camberlege Oup, 1954.

Macdonell, A.A. : 'Sanskrit English Dictionary', Longmans Green and Co. Ltd., London, 1893.

Macdonell, A.A. : 'Vaidic Devatasastra', Benaras Hindu University, 1961.

Macdonell, A.A. and Keith A.B. : 'Vedic Index Names and Subjects', Vols. I, II, Motilal Banarasidass, Varanasi, 1958.

Maciver, R.M. : 'The Elements of Social Science'. 7th edn., Methuen and Company Ltd., London, 1949.

Maclver, R.M. and Page C.M. : 'Society : An Introductory Analysis', Macmillan & Co. Ltd., London, 1950.

Mahadevan, T.M.P. : 'Upaniṣads' Arnold Heinemann Publishers, New Delhi-16, 1975.

Mayrhofer, M. : 'A Conscise Etymological Sanskrit Dictionary' Carl Winter, Heidelberg, 1953.

Max Muller : 'The Upaniṣads', SBE, Vol. I, 1926 (2nd edn.), Clarendon Press, Oxford, 1883.

Max Muller : SBE, Vol. 23, 'The Zend Avesta' Part I SBE, Vol. 31, 'The Zend Avesta' Part II, Glarendon Press, Oxford, 1883, 1887.

Modi, P.M. : 'Development of the System of Āśramas', Proc. and Trac. of the 7th AIOC, Baroda, Dec., 1933.

Mookerji, R.K. : 'Ancient Indian Education', Macmillan & Co. Ltd., London, 1947.

Muir, J. : 'Original Sanskrit Texts', tra. by Ram Kumar Rai, Chowkhamba Vidyabhavan Varanasi, 1965.

Narahari, H.G. : 'Ātmā in Pre-Upaniṣadic Vedic Literature', Adya Library, Madras, 1944.

Nath, R. : 'On the authenticity of the Allopaniṣad' Journal of the Oriental Institute, Baroda, Vol. 26, No. 3, Baroda, 1977.

Palsule, G.B. and Bedakara, V.M. : 'Sixty Upaniṣads of the Vedas', Motilal Banarasidass, Delhi, 1980.

Pandita, Bhagavad Datta : 'Vaidika Vaṅmaya kā Itihāsa', Vol. I, Shree Ramalal Kapoor Trut, Amrtasara.

Prabhu, P.M. : 'Hindu Social Organization', Popular Prakashan, Bombay, 1963, 4th edn.

Radhakrishnan, S. : 'Indian Philosophy' The Macmillan Co., New York, 1956, 7th edn.

Radhakrishnan, S. : 'Philosophy of the Upaniṣads', Georg Allen and Unwin Ltd., London, 1924.

Radhakrishnan, S. : 'The Principal Upaniṣads', George Allen and Unwin Ltd., London, 1953.

Raghavan, V. : 'Sāmaveda and Music', Journal of Music Academy, Vol. 33, pp. 127-133, Madras, 1951.

Rai, Ganga Sagar : 1. Śākhās of the Ṛgveda, 'Purāṇa', Vol. VI.

2. Śākhās of the Yajurveda, 'Purāṇa', Vol. VII.

3. Śākhās of the Sāmaveda, 'Purāṇa', Vol. VIII.

4. Śākhās of the Atharvaveda, 'Purāṇa', Vol. IV, 1964, 1965, 1966, 1972 respy.

Ranade, R.D. : 'A Constructive Suvey of Upaniṣadic Philosophy', Oriental Book Agency, Pona, 1926.

Sharma, Jogeswar : 'The Philosophy of Education in the Upaniṣads', Oriental Publishers and Distributors, New Delhi-110 002, 1978.

Shah, J.G. : 'Śrī Vallabhācārya - His Philosophy and Religion', Puṣṭimārga Pustakālaya, Nadiad, 1969.

Sharma, B.N.K. : 'Philosophy of Śrī Madhva', Bharatiya Vidya Bhavan, Bombay, 1962.

Sharma, Baldeva Raj : 'The Concept of Ātman in the Principal Upaniṣads', Dinesh Publications, New Delhi-110 015, 1972.

Shastry, Alladi M. : 'The Taittirīya Upaniṣad', Samata Books, Madras, 1980.

Swami, Atmananda : 'Śaṅkara's teachings in his own words', Bharatiya Vidya Bhavan, Bombay, 1958.

Swami, Chinmayananda : 'Discourses on the Taittirīya Upaniṣad' Madras.

Swami, Madhavananda : 'A Bird's Eye view of the Upaniṣads' Cultural Heritage of India, Vol. I, The Ramakrishna Mission, Calcutta, 1958.

Swami, Nikhilnanda : 'The Upaniṣads', Phoenix House, London, or Munshiram Manoharlal, Oriental and Foreign, Booksellers, Delhi-110 006.

Swami, Nikhilananda : 'Vedānta-sāra or essence of Vedānta of Sadānanda Yogīndra', Advaita Āśrama, Mayavati, Almora, Himalayas, 1949, 3rd edn.

Swami, Sharvananda : 'Taittirīyopaniṣad', Sri Ramkrishna Math, Mylapore, Madras, 1949.

Swami, Vivekananda : 'Complete Works of Vivekananda', Vol. II 1921; Vol. IV 1923; Vol. V, 1924, Advaita Ashrama, Almora.

Thite, G.U. : 'Sacrifices in the Brāhmaṇa Texts', University of Poona, 1957.

Upadhyaya, Baldeva : 'Śrī Ācārya Sāyana aur Mādhava', Hindi Sahitya Press, Prayag, 1947.

Upadhyaya, Baldeva : 'Śrī Śaṅkarācārya', Hindustani Academy, Allahabad, 1963, IInd edn.

Van. J.M. Boetzelaer : 'Sureśvara's Taittirīyopaniṣad Bhāṣyavārtikam' Leiden, Brill, 1971.

Varma, Siddheshwar : 'The Etymologies of Yāska', Vishveshvaranand Institute Publications, Hoshiarpur, 1953.

Velankar, H.D : 'Ṛgveda Maṇḍala VII', Bharatiya Vidya Bhavan, Bombay-400 007, 1963.

Venkatachalam : 'A Convincing case of Interpolation in the TU', SP a AIOC (26), Ujjain, 1975.

Venkataraman Iyer : 'Sṛṣṭi Vākyās in the Upaniṣads', Vedānta Kesarī, Vol. 53 (11), 1967.

Weber, Albrecht : 'The History of Indian Literature', Kegan Paul, Trench, Trubner & Co. Ltd., Broadway House, 68-74, Carter Lane, E.C. London, Fourth edn. 1904.

Webster : 'New World Dictionary' 2nd edn. American Publishing Co. Pvt. Ltd., New Delhi.

Winternitz, M. : 'A History of Indian Literature' Vol. I, University of Calcutta, Calcutta, 1927.

Index

K

L

M

N

O

P

R